The Knights of Labor in the South

Melton Alonza McLaurin

Contributions in Labor History, Number 4

Greenwood Press

WESTPORT, CONNECTICUT • LONDON, ENGLAND

Library of Congress Cataloging in Publication Data

McLaurin, Melton Alonza.
  The Knights of Labor in the South.

  (Contributions in labor history.; no. 4 ISSN
0146-3608)
    Bibliography: p.
    Includes index.
    1. Knights of Labor. 2. Trade-unions—Southern
States. I. Title. II. Series.
HD8055.K7M24   331.88'33'0975   77-87916
ISBN 0-313-20033-5

Library of Congress Catalog Card Number: 77-87916
ISBN: 0-313-20033-5
ISSN: 0146-3608

First published in 1978

Greenwood Press, Inc.
51 Riverside Avenue, Westport, Connecticut 06880

Printed in the United States of America

10 9 8 7 6 5 4 3 2 1

To My Daughters
Natasha and Nicole

Contents

Tables

Acknowledgments

NO WORK of history is the author's alone; rather, it results from the efforts of many people. I owe a special debt to Dr. Gustavus G. Williamson, Jr., Virginia Polytechnic Institute, who suggested this study. His encouragement, constructive suggestions, and aid in the necessary research made this work possible. Dr. Tom E. Terrill, University of South Carolina, also contributed criticism which proved extremely helpful, as did Dr. Betty Brandon, University of South Alabama. Support from the University of South Alabama Research Institute made possible much of the research on the Knights and is gratefully acknowledged. Without the able assistance of Anita Bayles, interlibrary loan librarian at South Alabama, the work would still be uncompleted. A number of student assistants at the University of South Alabama helped type the manuscript. Among these were Gwen Pelman, William Brantley, and Sandra Killion. Finally, sincere appreciation is extended to Doris Watt, secretary of the Department of History at the University of South Alabama, for her helpfulness in any number of tasks necessary to ready the manuscript for publication.

The Knights of Labor in the South

Introduction

FOR decades, labor historians virtually ignored the South. While the organizational efforts of northern workers were chronicled in detail, it was assumed that the South, an agrarian society, had no class struggle to relate, no industrial labor force to examine. Historians of the region did little to rectify that judgment. In probing the South's past, they concentrated on the peculiarity of its politics and its fascination with the race question. Indeed, slavery has perhaps become the most studied institution in American history. Few labor systems have been examined by so many professional historians, with such disparate results.[1]

Recently, however, historians have begun to examine the history of urban, industrial southern labor. This interest was sparked by bitter, often violent strikes in the coal and textile industries during the Depression and New Deal. But all too frequently historians have focused on the twentieth century, usually on the years since World War I, and have thus tacitly supported the concept that prior to that date the South had no industrial work force worthy of examination. This approach is illustrated in George and Broadus Mitchell's *Industrial Revolution in the South* (1930). The Mitchells perceived the southern laborer as docile until the textile strikes of the late 1920s. Prior to that time, "his [the Southern laborer's] own large numbers yet unindustrialized and his dire necessity made him tractable under labor conditions outgrown in the rest of America."[2] Ray Marshall's *Labor in the South*, the only major survey of organized labor in the region, devotes but 18 of 351 pages to union activity before 1928. Of these 18, fewer than half deal with the nineteenth century.[3] Even in an account of labor unrest in Alabama's coal field prior to 1900, two respected historians see that unrest as atypical, accepting George Mitchell's contention that "unionization was in general unimportant in the South before World War I."[4]

Just as early southern labor history generally has been ignored, so, too, has the role of southerners in specific unions, especially those of the nineteenth century. Historians of the Knights of Labor provide excellent examples of this omission. Although no study dealing specifically with the Knights exists, two major works chronicle the rise, activities, and decline of the order. The earliest, Norman T. Ware's *Labor Movement in the United States, 1860-1905* (1929), contains but four sentences on the order in the South. It completely ignores major strikes, political activity, and cooperative efforts engaged in by the order within the region.[5] In his brilliant study of American labor union ideology, *Workers and Utopia*, Gerald Grob pays a bit more attention to the Knights in the South but limits his account almost exclusively to the racial issue.[6] Marshall devotes but three pages to the Knights, most of which also deals with the question of race.[7]

Partly because the history of organized labor in the South prior to the New Deal is so seldom examined, two myths about southern laborers continue to exist. The first is that southern laborers are docile and tractable, eager to perform their best for minimum compensation. The second is that southern laborers, because of the region's heritage of individualism, have little interest in organized labor. And when they do join unions, they maintain "constructive" and "reasonable" positions toward management. Both myths were created by promoters of southern industrialization, especially of cotton mills, in the 1870s and 1880s. They proved so successsful that chambers of commerce, town councils, and even state governments used them to lure northern industries as late as the second half of the twentieth century.[8] Indeed, the fervor with which many southern politicians support present right to work laws as bulwarks of the employee's individual liberties suggests that the myths and the promise of cheap labor that they imply have not yet been abandoned as a means of attracting industry to the region. And as late as 1962, a historian could write of southern lumber millhands and loggers, "Physically, the people of the [lumber] camp were usually well cared for. They had enough to eat and wear, and were *content* [italics mine], knowing nothing better than life in little two- and three-room shacks."[9]

Despite the success obtained by promoters of industrialization through the promise of docile, cheap labor, the history of the region's labor force does not support the image of the laborer created by the industrial promoter. Since the 1880s, southern laborers have responded to organized labor despite great odds against their doing so. Although labor unions experienced difficulty in establishing permanent footholds in the region, it does not mean that they failed because of the docility or lack of interest shown by southern laborers. Rather, they failed because of unyielding managerial opposition, the racial issue, the relative ignorance of southern laborers about an industrial economy, and, to a lesser extent, the weaknesses of the unions involved. Southern laborers, including those of the nineteenth century, did not merely respond to union organizational efforts. They actively sought to use the unions to improve their economic and social status through a variety of activities.

The Knights of Labor provide an excellent case study of the response of nineteenth-century southern laborers to the concept of organization. The Knights, who reached their peak strength in 1886, at the height of the New South industrialization campaign, were the nation's largest and most powerful labor organization of the time. The South had experienced rapid development in cotton textiles manufacturing, tobacco manufacturing, furniture making, iron and steel producing, coal mining, lumbering, and several lesser industries. With few exceptions, the labor force utilized by each of these industries was composed of native southerners—whites in the textile, furniture, and tobacco industries; whites and blacks in the iron, coal mining, and lumbering industries. With the exception of the iron industry, the labor force came from the rural population and was little versed in the intricacies of an industrial economy. If the new southern industrial work force had been docile or uninterested in organization, the Knights would have fared poorly in the South.

Such was not the case, however. The Knights established strong footholds in every southern state under study, with the exception of South Carolina. In every case, the order was first established among urban and industrial workers and then spread to more rural areas. Three southern states formed state assemblies as large as those of many states in the North and Midwest. Southern Knights founded newspapers to proclaim the order's programs, at least three of which

achieved statewide circulation. They experimented with both producers' and consumers' cooperatives, with some limited success.
More significantly, they engaged in bitter, protracted strikes involving laborers in all the region's major industries as well as many minor
ones. Finally, they entered the political arena, successfully electing
municipal and legislative candidates and members of Congress and
obtaining the passage of major reform legislation. Such activities are
hardly those of a docile labor force uninterested in organization.

This study focuses on the Knights of Labor in seven southern
states—Virginia, North and South Carolina, Georgia, Florida, Mississippi, and Alabama. Specific activities of the order in Tennessee
and Louisiana also received some attention. The first seven states
represent every aspect of the region's industrial development during
the New South era and provide an opportunity to examine the order's
activity in each of the South's major industries. In every state, the
Knights challenged the economic and political power of the new
southern industrial aristocracy. In each, they were defeated. Their
efforts and ultimate failure and the reasons for them comprise an important part of the New South's history, one which presents the industrial laborer of that era in a totally different perspective.

1 The New South: An Economic Survey

DURING the 1880s the industrial revolution reached the South. The region experienced rapid industrial expansion and fundamental economic changes which resulted from several factors. Rather than representing a new departure for the region, however, these changes had their roots in the economic development of the previous decade. Among the changes wrought by the industrial revolution were the creation of a southern industrial work force and a significant increase in the region's urban population. These two developments made possible a third, the introduction of organized labor. Although some trade unions had existed previously among the more skilled urban workers of the South, it was the Knights of Labor who first introduced the concept of unionization to large numbers of southern laborers. Their appearance and success in the South represented labor's first response to the economic changes sweeping the region.

The industrial revolution in the South was the product of a new economic aristocracy which came to power after the Civil War. The war had broken the nearly total control of the economy by the planter class. The new arbiters of the South's economic destiny, though primarily of southern birth, frequently came from mercantile, banking, and industrial backgrounds. A few were carpetbaggers; others sprang from the old planter families but managed to make the transition to an industrial economy. These men were dedicated to transforming the South into an economic, if not social, carbon copy of the conquering North.[1]

A study of 186 Alabama businessmen prominent during the period from 1865 to 1900 revealed that only 27 percent had fathers who engaged in agriculture, while over 50 percent came from business or professional backgrounds. Forty-three percent were native Alabamians; 35 percent were natives of other southern states. Only 7.5 percent came from states outside the South, while a higher percentage, 14, were of foreign birth. Over 88 percent had upper- and middle-income backgrounds, and over 37 percent had attended college. The survey, which included leaders in banking, commerce, iron manufacturing, transportation, textiles, and iron and coal mining, indicates that the economic leadership of the New South closely resembled that of the North.[2]

Surveys of the leadership in three major southern industries—tobacco, iron and coal mining, and textiles—reveal the same patterns. Washington Duke, founder of the Duke Tobacco Company, was a farmer before the Civil War and a tobacco peddler afterward until he began to manufacture smoking tobacco. R. J. Reynolds, a partner of the Dukes and later the founder of his own company, also began his career as a peddler of plug tobacco. James B. Duke, Washington's son, grew up in the tobacco industry; and his business acumen transformed his father's firm into the huge American Tobacco Corporation.[3]

One of the founders of Birmingham's coal and iron industries was Henry DeBardeleben, a native Alabamian. The ward and son-in-law of Daniel Pratt, a prominent antebellum cotton gin and textile manufacturer and a transplanted Yankee, DeBardeleben brought one of the state's largest personal fortunes into the iron and coal industries in 1877. Truman Aldrich, Birmingham's first coal baron, emigrated from New York to Alabama in 1872. After a year in the banking industry, he organized the Montevallo coal mines. In 1878, he formed the Pratt Coal and Coke Company with DeBardeleben and James Sloss. Sloss, a prewar merchant and speculator, entered the coal and iron industries through postwar ventures in railroading. Another early industrialist in the Birmingham area who fit the New South leadership pattern was Enoch Ensley, a Tennessee capitalist who arrived in Alabama in the early 1880s.[4]

Firmly established in the antebellum era, the textile industry provided many postwar industrial leaders. Companies established by three antebellum manufacturers grew to corporate status in the postwar era, guided by managements whose economic abilities were at least as good as those of their northern counterparts. George P. Swift, a Boston dry goods merchant, moved to Georgia in 1832 and established a small cotton mill in Wymanville. He, his sons, and his son-in-law built a textile fortune after the war, beginning in 1869 with the founding of Muscogee Mills in Columbus. The sons of Edwin M. Holt expanded their father's antebellum North Carolina mill into one of the nation's leading textile firms in the postwar era. In South Carolina, William Gregg's pioneering efforts at Graniteville Manufacturing Company expanded during the postwar era under the guidance of H. H. Hickman, Gregg's company treasurer.[5]

Another factor in the region's sudden industrial growth was the utilization of recent technological developments. Prior to the Civil War, southern industries, including textiles, had been relatively crude in comparison to northern standards. But the war destroyed part of the region's industrial machinery, leaving the South free to employ the latest technological advances in its postwar industrial expansion. In textiles, for example, southerners extensively employed the double spinning ring spindle, humidifiers and temperature regulators, and the automatic loom in mills constructed during the postwar years.[6] In the tobacco industry, James Duke pioneered in the use of the Bonsack cigarette-rolling machine and developed machinery to manufacture cigarette cases.[7] The iron and coal barons of Alabama converted their furnaces from charcoal to coke in the late 1870s, installing some of the most modern coke furnaces. And during the 1880s, they constructed some of the nation's most modern and efficient blast furnaces.[8]

Like the rest of the nation, the South also experienced a rapid expansion of its rail system during the 1880s. The South surpassed New England, the Middle Atlantic states, and the Old Northwest in the amount of track laid. Only in the states west of the Mississippi did track mileage increase more rapidly than in the South. The development of a modern rail system, including the adoption of the standard gauge in 1886, opened northern markets to southern products and for the first time truly integrated the industries of the South into the national economy. The consolidation of numerous small lines into larger regional and interregional lines during the decade aided in this merger. By 1890, three rail systems alone—the Louisville and Nashville, the Richmond and Danville, and the East Tennessee, Virginia and Georgia railroads—each with access to northern markets, controlled more than ten thousand miles of track, or over one-third of the South's total.[9]

The availability of northern capital also spurned southern industrial development, although southerners financed much of their own progress, especially in the textile industry. Railroads, because of their capital intensive nature, relied heavily upon northern capital. By 1890, as a result of that reliance, northerners accounted for 269 of the 571 directors of the fifty-eight major southern railroads. Northerners comprised 66 percent of the directorships of the ten southern roads with over five hundred miles of track that were chartered before 1880, and they accounted for over 78 percent of the directors of similar lines chartered after 1880. The shorter lines appeared to be controlled locally but, because of complicated financial arrangements, were actually controlled by northern capitalists. By the late 1880s, only fifteen of the fifty-eight major ones were controlled by southern capital. [10]

Northern capital also invaded Alabama's iron and coal region during the decade, partially because development of the mineral region was linked to the Louisville and Nashville Railroad, which was financed by northern capital. By 1883, Thomas Fortune Ryan, Jay Gould, and Russel Sage sat as directors; and in 1884, New York and British interests acquired the road. [11] Between 1884 and 1908, the L and N invested over $30 million in the Birmingham area. Northerners invested heavily in the Sloss Iron and Steel Company in the mid 1880s, and the arrival of the Tennessee Coal and Iron Company in the area in 1886 brought still more northern capital. [12] Northerners also invested heavily in southern timber, especially along the Gulf Coast. By the end of the 1880s, "Northerners controlled the best stands of Southern yellow pine and cypress." [13]

In the upper South, however, the tobacco and textile industries relied primarily upon native capital. In both industries, the high profits derived from the manufacture of a consumer product through the use of cheap labor and advanced technology provided capital for expansion. In 1880, experienced southern textile manufacturers expected well-managed mills to average a 15 to 20 percent return on invested capital, and many did. Between 1882 and 1901, Dan River Mills of Danville, Virginia, expanded from one factory of 6,000 spindles and 260 looms to seven factories of 67,650 spindles and 2,772 looms. Had one investor purchased 100 shares in the company in 1882, by 1901 his original investment would have grown to 278 shares of preferred and 55 shares of common stock. If sold at par in 1901, the stock would have returned 36.7 percent annually to the investor.[14] Expansion in the tobacco industry was as rapid. In 1881, the Duke firm began production of cigarettes, with but two local markets. By 1884, the firm had captured Atlanta markets and had established a branch factory in New York; and in 1887, it was producing sixty million cigarettes a month. Two years later James B. Duke formed the American Tobacco Company, a trust that merged the five leading cigarette companies in the country.[15]

All of the southern industries that developed in the postwar years processed readily available raw materials which, in every case, had existed prior to the war. The textile factory was often literally constructed in the cotton fields of the Piedmont South. This location allowed farmers to ship their cotton by rail to such mill towns as Danville, Spartanburg, and Augusta, thus bypassing the traditional southern cotton ports which had previously exported the fiber to the mills of Great Britain and New England. The tobacco industry, centered in Richmond, Durham, and Winston-Salem, purchased tobacco from the farmers of southern Virginia and eastern and central North Carolina. The vast pine barrens of the coastal plain, sweeping southward into Florida and westward along the Gulf of Mexico, contained billions of board feet of virgin timber. One expert estimated that in 1887, Alabama alone possessed fifteen billion board feet of lumber in its yellow pine forests.[16] Coal deposits in Virginia, Tennessee, and Alabama were rapidly developed after the war. In the Birmingham region, limestone and iron ore deposits at places such as Red Mountain made the development of an iron and steel industry inevitable.

With new economic leadership, improved transportation systems, the latest technological advances, and adequate sources of both capital and raw materials, the South possessed all the ingredients necessary for an industrial revolution, provided it could obtain the necessary labor. Fortunately, the region also possessed a more than abundant work force. Or, more accurately, it contained large numbers of agrarian workers, both black and white, who yearned for an escape from the drudgery, isolation, and poverty that were the realities of life in the rural South. Historians have thoroughly and frequently explored the plight of the southern farmers in the late nineteenth century, and their problems need no further detailed study in this work.[17] Increasingly, black and white southern farmers found themselves caught in the crop lien system which developed after the war. Lacking capital, they received supplies and provisions from country merchants, pledging their crops as collateral. Merchants insisted that farmers plant cash crops, leading to overproduction and declining prices. As a result, thousand of landholders lost their farms to merchants and became tenants on land they had previously owned. Tenants worked throughout the year to produce a crop that could not pay the debts they had incurred in raising it.

To such people, the factory or mill provided hope, a chance to escape the economic treadmill of tenancy. For some whites, the hope was a reality; and thousands flocked to the cotton mills, tobacco and furniture factories, and iron and steel mills. Racial prejudice banned blacks from all but the most menial positions in cotton mills, furniture plants, and the smoking tobacco industry, although blacks had comprised the majority of the labor force in the plug chewing tobacco industry. However, blacks were employed in positions requiring heavy labor, especially in the coal and iron mines, unskilled foundry jobs, and the logging woods. By 1887, for example, 46 percent of Alabama's mining force was black, 35 percent native white, and approximately 19 percent foreign born (primarily British).[18] Most of the South's new industrial work force came straight from the farm. Unskilled, frequently uneducated, and ignorant of factory methods, they adjusted with amazing rapidity to the work regime of an industrial economy. Within little more than a decade, southern workers were challenging New England's supremacy in textiles, manufacturing iron products competitive with those of Pennsylvania, and producing the finest bright leaf tobacco products in the world.

Given the region's antebellum preoccupation with agriculture, the South's industrial expansion during the 1880s is phenomenal. While the 1870s had seen gradual advances in the South's industrial productivity, they were small compared to the advances of the next decade. This expansion in industrial productivity was achieved despite the relative inexperience of both the labor force and management in an industrial economy. Census data reveal that the concept of the New South represented considerably more than the rhetorical and editorial abilities of such proponents of industrialization as Henry Grady, Francis Dawson, or Edmond H. Edmunds. Table 1 illustrates the rapid growth of the manufacturing economy in the seven states upon which this study focuses.[19]

TABLE 1
Indices of Southern Industrial Growth, 1870-1890

ITEM	*1870*	*1880*	*1890*
Number of manu-facturing establish-ments	9,573	9,158	21,729
Capital invested in manufacturing establishments	$57,822,092	$89,499,221	$254,530,394
Average number of wage earners	83,546	120,346	220,958
Total wages	$21,646,307	$23,232,494	$63,377,901
Value added	$124,321,520	$151,685,239	$317,738,304

Statistics on individual states prove to be just as significant and, to a certain extent, reflect the growth of individual industries. In South Carolina, where industrial development was heavily concentrated in the textile industry, capital invested rose from $5,400,418 in 1870 to $11,205,894 in 1880 and to $29,276,261 in 1890. The respective figures for the dollar value added were $9,858 in 1870, $16,738,000 in 1880, and $31,926,681 in 1890. Total wages increased from $1,543,715 to $2,836,289 to $5,474,739, while the number of wage earners in manufacturing increased from 8,141 to 15,828 to 22,748. In Alabama, the iron and coal industries were primarily responsible for the increases in industrial activity. Total wages paid in that state rose from $2,227,968 to $2,500,504 and then jumped to $10,799,747 in 1890. Capital investments for the three decades were $5,714,032, $9,688,008, and an incredible $46,122,571 by 1890. Value added stood at $13,040,644 in 1870 but had not reached $14,000,000 by 1880. By 1890, however, it had increased to $51,226,605. Data from Virginia, which had the most diversified economy of the states under consideration, told the same story. Capital invested in manufacturing increased from $18,455,400 to $26,968,990 to $63,456,799 by 1890. Wages paid grew from over $5,000,000 in 1870 to nearly $7,500,000 in 1880, expanding to $15,816,930 in 1890. From 1870 to 1890, the industrial labor force doubled; and the value added to manufactured products grew by approximately $50,000,000, with an increase of over $36,000,000 between 1880 and 1890. [20]

Predictably, industrial development spurred urbanization. Iron and coal created Birmingham and other Alabama towns. Tobacco boosted the growth of Richmond, Lynchburg, Durham, and Winston-Salem. Textiles brought workers to Danville, Charlotte, Augusta, Columbus, and Atlanta. While the lumber industry was located in rural areas, increased lumber exports helped to expand such Gulf ports as Pensacola and Mobile. Cities such as Charlotte, Atlanta, Birmingham, and Richmond became regional transportation and financial centers. Census data reflect this trend toward urbanization. Of the seven states considered in this study, only Virginia had more than 10 percent of its population living in urban areas in 1880. During that same year, 96.9 percent of the population in Mississippi was rural, 90.6 percent in Georgia, 96.1 percent in North Carolina, 92.5 percent in South Carolina, and 94.6 percent in Alabama. By 1890, only North Carolina and Mississippi remained more than 90 percent rural, with 92.8 percent and 94.6 percent respectively. [21]

Like those which preceded it, the industrial revolution in the South was built upon the exploitation of labor. That such exploitation resulted from several economic factors and was, perhaps, inevitable under any economic system neither alters the experience endured by the individual workers nor changes the fact that cheap labor was the wellspring of capital accumulation. Southern industrialists employed any tactic to insure that labor would remain a commodity that could be purchased on a surplus market and controlled once purchased. Among the devices used were the company village, scrip wages, company stores, child labor, the "family wage" concept, and convict labor. The threat of employing the South's black agrarian labor force and an entire battery of psychological control factors supplemented the more standard measures of control. Industrialists appealed to a common southern heritage, stressed their role as benefactors of the region's poverty stricken masses, and "protected" the worker from the efforts of either the state or the unions to strip him of his right to work long hours for low wages.

Used extensively in the textile and lumber industries, the company village was also employed by iron- and coal-mining firms. The company village gave management almost complete control over labor. Management dictated social, religious, and moral aspects of village life, as well as the economic. Persons considered disreputable—including prostitutes, gamblers, and union organizers—were banned from the village. Housing conditions and the available social services varied widely from village to village, much as they had on the plantations of the antebellum South; and in many ways the company village was an extension of the slave quarters system. Dwellings ranged from well-constructed cottages to the weatherboard shacks of logging villages. Some firms provided educational, medical, and recreational facilities; others hardly assured an adequate water supply. In the best of the company villages, especially in the textile industry, the physical environment and services available surpassed the average tenant's fondest hopes. Most, however, merely allowed the farmer to exchange one dreary existence for another. [22]

Company stores and scrip wages combined to save management operating capital and prevent laborers from obtaining cash, a situation too familiar to those workers recently off the farm. The cotton, mining, and lumber industries all relied heavily upon scrip, which could be redeemed only at the company store. Few textile firms did not use scrip at some time during the 1880s. In 1887, for example, the vast majority of North Carolina's mills used the system. Frequently, even scrip wages were issued at long intervals, sometimes a month or more. Since it could be cashed only at the company store, scrip enabled management to recover much of what was paid in wages. Some firms would redeem scrip in cash, but only at a considerable discount. Other firms paid cash but were so geographically isolated that workers were forced to use the company store. Scrip wages and "pluck me" stores aroused the southern workers' wrath more than any other issue except wages. [23]

Child labor posed special problems in the textile and cigarette industries, both of which also employed large numbers of women. Technological developments encouraged the employment of women and children in both industries, with the result that the percentage of women and children in the total labor force rose as the industries became more sophisticated. By 1880, for example, children comprised 25 percent of the labor force in Virginia's tobacco industry and 30 percent of that industry's North Carolina laborers. In the adult work force, however, men still outnumbered women. In the textile industry, women and children comprised approximately two-thirds of the labor force throughout the 1880s. [24] New machines could be operated by adolescents and women; male labor was more expensive and, according to some industrialists, more difficult to control. The use of women and children also allowed manufacturers to employ the "family wage" concept. A family with a wife and two or three children employed in a textile or cigarette factory, even if the father was unemployed, could earn a family income that seemed astounding to the tenant farm family. Since children labored on the farm, the old southern agrarian labor system was again moved to the factory. In the factory, however, neither children nor adults could work at their own pace, as they could on the farm. Once in the factory, machinery set their work pace; and the machine was an unrelenting taskmaster.

The convict lease system represented the most flagrant exploitation of the southern worker. It degraded and brutalized the convict while posing a constant economic threat to the free laborer. Most southern states adopted the system during Reconstruction, and by 1880 it was a thriving institution. Convicts worked on railroads, in turpentine forests, and on construction projects; but most were employed in the mining industry, especially in Tennessee, Georgia, and Alabama. While the system provided an integrated work force, Negroes also comprised the majority of convict laborers. Southern industrialists "rented" convicts from the state at less than eight cents a day, in addition to providing food, shelter, and clothing. In 1888, for example, the Tennessee Coal and Iron Company contracted with the state of Alabama to lease its entire penitentiary population for ten years. The same firm also leased convicts from Alabama county jails, as did other firms. By 1894, nearly fourteen hundred convicts labored in Alabama's mines. Although such "contracts" called for adequate care of prisoners, the states made no effort to enforce them. As a result, convicts were worked relentlessly, beaten, starved, and in general forced to endure conditions scholars have compared to those in the prison camps of Nazi Germany. [25]

The South of the 1880s presented a nearly perfect example of a laissez-faire economy. Industrialists were completely unfettered by state regulations concerning wages, hours, or working conditions. The laborer sold his labor for whatever he could obtain, accepting responsibility for any injury he might sustain on the job. In most southern industries, laborers received wages considerably below those paid their northern counterparts. Most noticeable was the wage differential in the South's cotton textile industry, which relied heavily on cheap labor for an advantage over the mills of New England. Wages varied from year to year and from state to state, but they were always low and were always the first cost factor management attempted to reduce when the industry encountered financial difficulty. Spinners received from 30 to 60 cents a day. Weavers, paid by the "cut" of cloth, received 24 to 40 cents per "cut" and earned from 75 cents to $1.25 a day. Female spinners in New England frequently earned two or three times more than southern spinners. Weavers in the South received more equitable treatment, receiving approximately 20 percent less than those in the North. In 1887, for example, female spinners averaged 46 cents a day in Georgia, 60 cents in South Carolina, $1.42 in Massachusetts, and $1.47 in New York. [26] Table 2 illustrates hourly wage differentials for spinners, loom fixers, and weavers in 1890. [27]

Wage differentials also existed in the lumber industry. In 1880, the average southern mill laborer received a daily wage of approximately a dollar. Unskilled loggers received less. By 1889, common laborers averaged $20 monthly, but some unskilled hands received as little as 50 cents daily. Federal census data reveal that in 1890, lumber mill workers averaged $1.54 in the South Central states and only 87 cents

TABLE 2
Hourly Wages of Cotton Textile Workers, 1890

STATE	Male Loom Fixers	Female Spinners	Male Spinners	Female Weavers
S.C.	13.28	3.03	6.85	6.15
N.C.	11.36	4.46	9.92	8.03
Ga.	13.38	5.23	6.99	6.96
Mass.	18.39	9.11	13.53	11.87

SOURCE: U.S. Commissioner of Labor, *1904 Report*, 480.
NOTE: All data in cents per hour.

in the South Atlantic, compared to the $1.54 daily wage in the North
Atlantic and $1.51 in the North Central states. In the same year, log-
gers in the South Central region received $1.35 a day compared to
$1.89 and $1.50 paid to loggers in the North Atlantic and North Central regions respectively. Historians of southern industry believe
census figures exaggerated the wages of loggers and mill workers,
since firms frequently compensated employees with commodities or
paid scrip wages. For example, Mississippi firms procured surplus
labor supplies by providing meat at meals for their workers, and lumber hands in Georgia in 1887 received 85 cents a day in scrip wages
that were worth no more than 90 percent of their face value. [28]

Statistics on the tobacco industry are less conclusive than those for
the textile and lumber industries, but those available reveal similar
wage discrepancies. The tobacco industry operated primarily on a
piece goods system. Cigar makers received payment by the thousand,
as did cigarette rollers in the bright leaf tobacco industry of Virginia
and North Carolina. Data from the Bureau of Labor Statistics reveal
that Florida cigar makers received as much or more per thousand as
their northern colleagues. Centered in Key West and of Cuban de-
scent, they were the exception. In 1890, cigar makers in the South
Atlantic region averaged 26.7 cents an hour, compared to an average
of 28.6 cents in the North Atlantic states and 27.1 cents in the North
Central region. Data on the cigarette industry in this period is scarce
because the tobacco industry was just converting to the manufacture
of cigarettes. Tilley reports, however, that female cigarette rollers in
1883 earned from $4.50 to $9.00 a week. Stemmers, those who strip-
ped the leaf from its stem, received $1.00 to $1.25 a day in 1887. In the
plug or chewing tobacco industry, laborers received a flat daily wage
that varied from 75 cents to $1.25. In a Riedsville, North Carolina,
factory in 1887, plug makers received 50 cents per day, while stemmers received 25 cents. The introduction of the cigarette-rolling and
-cutting machines in the mid-1880s allowed day labor wages to be
paid in that industry. [29]

In the mining industries, southern wages appear competitive; but
they do not reflect the use of convict labor. Again, both wages and
methods of payment varied greatly. Some miners received a daily
wage; others were paid by the amount of coal they mined. Payment for
each carload of coal varied from region to region and from year to

year. [30] Federal data for 1890 show Alabama coal miners averaging
$2.00 per day, compared to the $1.68 paid in Pennsylvania. In 1889,
Alabama miners received $2.19 daily; those of Pennsylvania received
$2.15 two years later. Per ton payments were also similar in the two
states. Alabama mine operators paid between 45 and 50 cents per ton
in the mid-1880s; those of Pennsylvania paid from 45 to 59 cents from
1889 to 1890. In 1890, Alabama iron miners averaged $2.05 daily,
while Pennsylvania miners received $1.29, and Tennessee miners
earned an average of $1.20. [31] Reports from miners, however, indi-
cated they received much lower wages. Virginia coal miners complained of payment in scrip of a dollar a day as late as 1887; and in
the same year, Alabama miners reported wages of $1.50 a day. While
some mine operators paid standard prices per carload of up to a dollar
per ton, miners employed by other firms complained that the company often "claimed" coal they dug, thus robbing them of their pay.
Common laborers in the mines often received as little as 85 cents a
day. [32]

The iron industry around Birmingham paid competitive wages,
with some exceptions in unskilled positions. Blast furnace fillers in
Alabama received $1.23 and $1.10 in 1889 and 1890 respectively,
compared to $1.48 and $1.67 in Pennsylvania. Puddlers in Alabama
received $3.60 in 1889; their Pennsylvania counterparts averaged
$3.19. Rollers in bar mills in Alabama averaged $7.04 daily in 1889,
nearly $2.00 more than the recorded wages paid in Pennsylvania. [33]

Wages paid to skilled laborers and artisans in the urban South
varied so much from city to city that any computation of averages is
practically impossible. Like industrial laborers, craftsmen operated
in a commodity market. If a town experienced a boom, increased demand led to increased wages. Periodic economic slumps resulted in
depressed wages. Such port cities as Mobile or Savannah, which relied
on the export of agricultural products, experienced wage fluctuations
associated with seasonal shipping activity. Wages also fluctuated
wildly in such boom towns as Birmingham and Bessemer, Alabama.
For the unskilled urban laborer, wages remained at subsistence levels,
because the South's agricultural hinterland furnished urban areas
with an inexhaustible labor supply. Reports from Knights in various
southern towns provide significant data on the wide spectrum of
wages paid to urban labor, skilled and unskilled. Birmingham

Knights reported that carpenters averaged $2.00 a day, or about $44 a month; but a Durham Knight reported carpenters making only 75 cents a day, while a Florida Knight indicated carpenters received anywhere from a dollar to $2.00 a day. [34] In Bessemer, Alabama, carpenters received from $1.50 to $3.00 a day, masons $4.00, painters $2.00 to $2.75, and common laborers from $1.00 to $1.50. A Norfolk member reported that masons received $4.00 and hodders $2.00 daily. [35] In smaller towns, wages were often lower. Masons in Statesville, North Carolina, received $1.50 to $2.00 a day, painters $1.00 to $1.25, and day laborers 60 to 75 cents. In Scranton, Mississippi, day laborers received $1.00 to $1.25, while mechanics earned from $1.50 to $3.00. [36]

Data from the Bureau of Labor Statistics indicate that southern skilled laborers received lower wages than those in the North. In 1888, bricklayers received $1.35 daily in South Carolina, $1.86 in North Carolina, and $2.00 in Georgia. The corresponding wages in Massachusetts, Pennsylvania, and New York respectively were $3.30, $3.84, and $3.78. In the same year, carpenters and joiners in Georgia averaged $1.73 daily, while those in South Carolina received $1.13. Laborers in the same trade averaged $2.06 in Massachusetts, $2.66 in Pennsylvania, and $2.68 in New York. [37]

Domestics and rural day laborers, who were primarily blacks, occupied the bottom rung of the South's economic ladder. They scrounged for jobs, frequently working for several different employers each week. Lacking both skills and education in a surplus labor market, they lived in a state of resignation, their energies devoted to the task of survival. Again, reports from Knights in the rural South provided an excellent picture of their economic status. Farmhands in North Carolina received $5 to $7 a month, when they could find work. Georgia day laborers got 50 cents a day, from $6 to $8 a month; and Florida laborers received approximately the same wages. One North Carolina Knight reported day wages for field hands as low as 35 cents and noted that work was available only during the harvest season, approximately three months per year. Domestics fared as poorly. From rural South Carolina came reports of payments of 15 cents a day for field laborers and 10 to 30 cents for washerwomen. Housemaids in Riedsville, North Carolina, received $2 a month, plus room and board. [38] Census data on wages paid to farm laborers in North Carolina, Alabama, and Georgia during the 1880s reveal that northern and western laborers received wages two and three times higher. In 1889, for example, North Carolina farm laborers averaged 50 cents daily, compared to an average of $1.50 in New York and $1.15 in Minnesota. [39]

While more uniform than wages, the hours of southern laborers also varied considerably. Those required to work the fewest hours still put in a long day, for rarely did any southern laborer work less than ten hours. In the textile industry, eleven hours was considered "normal"; but mills frequently ran twelve hours or more. Mills on a ten-hour, six-day system often forced their operatives to work additional hours for the same pay if market conditions demanded increased production. [40] The eleven- or twelve-hour day was common in the tobacco industry. In the cigarette factories, hand rollers worked eleven hours a day. The installation of rolling machines did not shorten the industry's workweek. [41] In the lumber industry, a fourteen-hour day was common, the twelve-hour day a goal to be achieved. [42] Miners worked an eleven- to twelve-hour day, as did many iron and steel workers, although most iron companies in the Birmingham area operated on a ten-hour day. Federal reports of an average sixty-hour workweek for Alabama miners in 1885 and fifty-five hours in 1889 simply do not reflect the situation encountered by Alabama miners. [43] Construction workers labored from sixty to seventy-two hours a week, depending upon the trade and location. Masons generally worked a ten-hour day; carpenters and painters worked eleven or twelve hours. [44] Employers of farm laborers observed the traditional agricultural work day of from dawn to dusk, or from can see to can't see.

Working conditions ranged from deplorable to barely endurable. In the textile industry, the clatter of machinery obliterated other sounds; cotton lint, moistened by humidifiers installed to prevent the thread from breaking as it spun, clogged the air. Workers breathed the lint and dust of the factory twelve to fourteen hours a day. The lint irritated their eyes and clung to their hair and clothing, giving rise to such epithets for mill workers as "lint heads" and "cotton tail." [45] Workers in tobacco factories constantly inhaled particles of tobacco dust. One manufacturer found "the tobacco dust very debilitating to me. It keeps me constantly coughing—day and night." But, he added, "I don't think it unhealthy to most people." [46] Mines were inadequately ventilated and shored, and dampness was pervasive. An Alabama miner complained that falling rocks and bad air made every trip down a possible final one. [47] Lumbering was a particularly hazardous industry. In the woods, falling trees could kill or maim. In the mills, workers moved among unguarded saws six to eight feet in diameter. Despite such unpleasant and dangerous conditions, protests were infrequent. Rather, southern laborers voiced their dissatisfaction with the more directly economic problems of low wages, scrip wages, company stores, and child and convict labor. [48]

To the industrialists of the New South, however, the working conditions endured by the laborers and the economic status they occupied seemed a natural product of what they saw as *progress*, a sign that the South had finally joined the national economic mainstream. To justify their exploitation of labor, industrialists constructed an elaborate philosophy in which they became heroes, not villains; the laborer's champion, not his adversary. Their vision of the New South was expounded everywhere—in the press, the pulpit, at educational institutions, and at industrial exhibitions. A mixture of laissez-faire capitalism, social Darwinism, southern racial concepts, and paternalism, this vision not only rationalized the state of the southern laborer but also required that he accept his position with gratitude.

The bedrock upon which southern industrialists founded their vision of a new economic order was a curious combination of Reconstruction mythology and the Lost Cause mentality. Proponents of industrialization who sought to remodel the southern economy after a northern pattern were partially motivated by the desire to see the South independent of the North. Indeed, while proposing industrialization, New South proponents created an idealized vision of the Old. Industrialization would create an independent South, a prosperous South, a South respected and admired by its recent conquerors. It would prove the South could compete in the "modern" world of "progress." Yet this industrialized South would retain the graciousness and the essentially humane, nonmaterialistic values that had been credited to antebellum society. [49]

Reconstruction, according to New South spokesmen, reduced all southerners to absolute poverty. From this state of equality, a new, natural leadership class had emerged. After first ridding the South of a corrupt carpetbagger and Negro regime which threatened to destroy the values of southern civilization, these leaders turned to the task of rebuilding the economy. Profits were of secondary importance. Their primary task was to lead the South out of the economic wilderness, to provide an escape from the grinding agrarian poverty that ensnared most southerners. [50] In the cotton and tobacco industries, owners coupled their economic generosity with motives of racial solidarity. Jobs in these industries were reserved for whites, as long as they accepted them without question. Thus the manufacturer furnished the poor white with an escape from degrading competition with the black tenant. Just as political Reconstruction had saved whites from Negro rule, so would economic Reconstruction save whites from black competition. Management convinced itself that its motivation was concern for the worker, a concept New South spokesmen projected backward into the antebellum era with their portraits of kindly masters and happy slaves. Like the plantation master, the industrialist became a benefactor, not an employer or master. He bestowed upon his workers housing, schools, churches, and medical facilities. In short, he "looked after his people."

The southern industrialist saw himself as more than the laborer's benefactor. He was also his friend and protector. Within such a paternalistic relationship, the industrialists could pose as labor's champion and maintain a rigid control over their work force. And management was genuinely motivated by both of these concerns, although not so much by the former as to advocate meaningful changes in wages, hours, or working conditions. As protectors, industrialists guarded the morals of their charges. Textile mill owners forbade alcohol and frowned upon smoking in company towns. Applicants for positions at tobacco factories underwent "a most thorough examination as to character and habits, and none are admitted who, after careful examination, are discovered wanting in good moral character." Lumbermen "exercised the power of law enforcement and soon got rid of most of the undesirables"—drifters, gamblers, and whiskey dealers— in the mill towns of the Deep South. As the laborers' friend, owners listened to their problems, even those of a personal nature. Industrialists, especially those in the textile industry, often knew their employees by name and insisted that they would be happy to discuss any grievance a laborer might have, as long as the discussion remained on an individual level. [51]

The men who built the mills and factories of the New South were rugged individualists, convinced that with a little luck and no governmental interference, they could duplicate the feats of the Rockefellers and the Carnegies of the North. Enoch Ensley, who invaded the Birmingham mineral region from Tennessee, built a new town for his enterprises, which he characteristically named Ensley. DeBardeleben, who founded Bessemer, Alabama, described his entrepreneurial exploits in these terms: "I was an eagle and I wanted to eat all the crawfish I could, swallow up all the little fellows and I did." [52] Julian S. Carr, advertising genius of the Blackwell Tobacco Company, summed up the industry's competitive nature into the motto "Let buffalo gore buffalo, and the pasture go to the strongest." [53] Daniel Thompkins, prominent textile manufacturer of the Carolinas, saw more significance in a northbound train loaded with southern goods than in the identity of a man killed beneath the train's wheels. [54] The southern industrialist held to a social Darwinism even more fiercely competitive, if possible, than that of his northern colleagues. [55] In his view, he had reached the top in an economic struggle made more difficult by the economic devastation of the Civil War and Reconstruction. He was the fittest, and being the fittest had its privileges.

Such men saw their mills and factories not just as private property but as their personal property, as much under their direct control as the plantation had been under the planter's. The labor force was merely a part of the industrial plantation, also under their personal control. While the industrialists saw that control as benevolent, they never questioned their right to it or their use of it. Nor were they unaware that control over the labor force gave them a tremendous advantage in economic competition. To such men, the concept of organized labor was anathema. It violated southern individualism and the principles of laissez-faire economics. It threatened a cornerstone of their expanding industrial empire, the cheap labor of the South, black and white.

But perhaps more importantly, the specter of organized labor challenged their view of themselves. For if laborers organized to seek better wages, shorter hours, and improved working conditions, it would mean that the image of the industrialists as the benefactors, protectors, and friends of labor was false. It would mean that labor was unhappy on the industrial plantation, that the interests of management and labor were not one and the same; and these concepts held grave implications for the region in terms of both the past and the future. So management insisted that all was well, that laborers "are contented and happy," that "perfect harmony" existed. "Perfect unity of feeling between employees and employer. They are contented and have no other desire seemingly but to see business prosper," wrote a North Carolina iron manufacturer. "I have a good lot of men in my employ," wrote another North Carolina manufacturer, "and I think they are satisfied with their wages and treatment." A textile manufacturer noted that "the relations existing here between the employees and employers are quite favorable indeed."[56]

Thus at the height of the New South campaign of Henry Grady and other proponents of the industrial gospel, the Knights of Labor presented the new economic aristocracy with a serious problem, both economic and ideological. The Knights attempted to give voice to the dissatisfaction of the laborers, to achieve for them a modicum of economic justice. But if the Knights' complaints were valid, the industrialists' role as benefactors and protectors was invalid. And the Knights' demands carried a price tag, one that would have to be met from profits and dividend payments. Therefore, southern industrialists summoned all the power at their disposal to crush the Knights, not just because they were an economic threat, but also because they suggested that all was not well in the New South Eden. Management had to be right, the Knights wrong. "The most refractory element of our employees are the K. of L.," wrote a North Carolina businessman. "They exact prices that are out of proportion to the services rendered."[57] For the southern industrialist to admit any other possibility was to think the unthinkable.

2 The Southern Labor Force

ANY assessment of the Knights' efforts to organize southern laborers must consider not only the conditions encountered by workers but also the composition and basic characteristics of the work force. In some respects, the southern work force differed substantially from that of the North, thus presenting the Knights with complex, difficult issues. In several other ways, however, the southern work force was remarkably similar to that of the North, especially since before 1890, the urban North had yet to experience the full impact of the New Immigration. The composition and characteristics of the southern labor force, both its unique features and those it shared with its northern counterpart, influenced the workers' initial response to organized labor and contributed to the ultimate failure of the Knights.

Above all else, the southern work force was a native work force. Whether white or black, rural or urban, the average worker was born in the state in which he labored. And if he was not a native of the state in which he was employed, in all probability he was a native of a neighboring state. The lumber industry recruited whites and blacks from the farms of the pine barrens above the Gulf Coast of Florida, Alabama, and Mississippi. Laborers employed by the coal and iron mines, coke ovens, and foundries of the Birmingham area also came from the immediate vicinity. Textile workers, too, came from farms surrounding the mill towns and villages that stretched along the Piedmont from Virginia to eastern Alabama. One prominent Alabama industrialist boasted in 1883 that enough whites could be found within a fifty-mile radius of the Tennessee River Valley town of Florence to operate as many factories as existed in Lowell, Massachusetts, without disturbing the area's supply of agricultural labor. As late as 1900, 97.7 percent of all southern textile workers were native born of native parents. Native labor also comprised the bulk of the urban work force as well as the workers employed in tobacco manufacturing and such minor industries as brick making and paper manufacturing.[1]

Skilled workers and supervisory personnel proved the only exception to the employment of native labor. In most industries, a lack of experienced natives often compelled employers to recruit outside the South to fill positions that required skilled labor. Prior to 1883, Birmingham iron foundries needed skilled labor so desperately that they offered wages 10 percent higher than those paid in Pittsburgh to molders, puddlers, and other skilled workers. The increased wages attracted skilled ironworkers from Pennsylvania, Ohio, and other northern states; and they were retracted once a pool of skilled employees was established. In the tobacco industry, the Dukes imported cigarette rollers from New York before the installation of cigarette-rolling machines during the period from 1884 to 1886. A manufacturer of newsprint in South Carolina employed an all-native labor force except for his superintendent, a Scot, and his machinist, an Englishman. Textile manufacturers also employed skilled laborers, especially machinists and supervisors, from the older mills of New England.[2]

Within the textile industry, however, only four or five such positions might exist in a mill that employed several hundred people. Even in the iron industry, which required more skilled personnel than any other southern industry, unskilled laborers comprised a large majority of the work force. According to James H. Sloss, who in 1883 employed over 269 persons at the Sloss furnace outside Birmingham, less than 10 percent of his work force were skilled laborers. The mining industry of the Alabama mineral belt probably employed a higher percentage of foreign born laborers than did any other southern industry. Approximately a fifth of Alabama's miners were foreign born in 1887; most of these were British. Like the nonnative ironworkers, many of the foreign miners worked in skilled positions, such as handling explosives, or in supervisory positions.[3]

The southern labor force was most different from its counterpart in the North, and in other industrialized nations, in its racial composition. The emphasis placed by historians on the development of the southern textile industry, however, has contributed to a generally held misconception about the role of black labor. The popular concept is that the region's urban and industrial work force was essentially white. Blacks held only the most menial industrial positions, if any, and were employed primarily as agrarian labor. Such a view of the labor force is essentially correct for the cotton textile industry and, to some extent, for the cigarette-manufacturing industry. However, it does not hold true for either the urban work force or the work force of other industries. In actuality, outside the textile industry, the non-agrarian economy relied heavily on Negro labor; and some industries preferred to employ blacks.

Although slaves had been used within the antebellum cotton textile industry, a pronounced shift to the employment of whites began even before the Civil War. This trend was especially true in the more highly mechanized mills of the Carolina Piedmont, including the Graniteville mills, established in that South Carolina town by William Gregg, and the mills of Alamance County, North Carolina, established by Edwin M. Holt. After the war, however, blacks were practically excluded from the mills. In 1900, only 1.4 percent of the South's textile workers were black, and most of them were employed in menial positions outside the mills.[4] Mill owners chose to employ white labor because it was plentiful, because they believed whites had better work habits than the freedmen and were thus more capable of adapting to the regular workday and routine dictated by the machine, and because whites could be intimidated by the threat of employing blacks. The use of whites had the added advantage of leaving the supply of black agrarian laborers untouched but available if needed. Thus while mill officials frequently voiced the opinion that blacks were unsuited for cotton mill employment for such ludicrous reasons as "their fingers are too stiff," mill owners experimented with Negro labor throughout the 1880s and were convinced that black labor could be employed in the mills if white workers became too demanding.[5]

The number of blacks employed in the South's mineral belt contrasted sharply with figures for the textile industry. In some industries, blacks comprised nearly half the work force. In 1887, for example, 46 percent of Alabama's miners were black, a figure slightly higher than the percentage of blacks in the state population.[6] Nor was the work force segregated, as was the case with the few blacks employed in the textile industry. Blacks and whites worked together in the mines without trouble. Above ground, however, they lived in segregated housing. John Lopsley, president of the Shelby Iron Works, preferred to use black labor to quarry limestone and mine iron ore for his furnaces. Blacks also worked at the South's blast furnaces. James H. Sloss, president of the Sloss Furnace Company of Birmingham, employed 269 laborers, almost all of whom were black. The exceptions were those who held skilled positions. Sloss, too, preferred to use blacks for the hot, back-breaking manual labor at the furnaces, explaining his preference by noting that "the negro likes a warm place." Lopsley was more honest in revealing that he hired blacks because they were less expensive and less likely to strike. Blacks, he believed, naturally submitted to authority and did not desire land or homes "bad enough to rebel for it." Indeed, Lopsley felt that as long as southern manufacturers had black labor to rely upon, "there will be no war between capital and labor." In addition to manning the South's mines and furnaces, blacks also worked in the region's iron foundries. While most were employed as unskilled laborers, some worked as skilled laborers. Here again, most skilled positions in the foundries, as in the mines and at the furnaces, were held by whites. [7]

The antebellum tobacco industry had relied heavily upon black labor, both slave and free; and blacks continued to comprise a large segment of the work force employed by plug tobacco factories during the postwar era. Such factories were usually small, lacked any major industrial machinery, frequently were barely beyond the handicraft stage of production, and often relied upon black labor as much as had their antebellum predecessors. A North Carolina manufacturer of plug chewing tobacco, for example, reported in 1887 that 80 percent of his work force was black. In the bright leaf smoking tobacco and cigarette-manufacturing industry, however, the labor force, as in textiles, was overwhelmingly white. [8] The movement within the tobacco industry to white labor with the increased utilization of machine production followed a pattern already established by the textile industry; blacks did heavy or manual labor, while whites ran machines. This pattern, although to a lesser degree, also applied to the role of black labor in the region's mining, metal, and less mechanized industries.

Black manual labor was also employed extensively in other industries, although whites supplied the majority of the work force. Blacks labored in the region's quarries, cutting granite, limestone, and other stones. Brickyards in urban communities throughout the South employed a predominantly black labor force. A Columbus, Georgia, brick manufacturer, for example, employed thirty-five hands in 1883, the majority of whom were black. During the same year, a South Carolina paper manufacturer employed a racially mixed force of twenty-eight white males, nine white females, and nineteen black males. Millers regularly used both black and white laborers, although whites obtained the more skilled positions because owners believed, as one miller expressed it, that "colored can't handle jobs of authority." Manufacturers of wood products, including sashes, doors, carriages, and other items, employed blacks who worked side by side with whites. Again, blacks usually held inferior positions. These firms, like those manufacturing plug tobacco, frequently were small, employed fewer than thirty to fifty workers, were barely beyond the handicraft stage of production, and sold almost exclusively on the local market.[9]

In the lumber industry, blacks supplied most of the manpower for firms working the eastern and Gulf Coast pine and cypress forests. But white loggers were also employed and worked the woods with the blacks. Housing in the lumber camps, however, was segregated. Whites also filled the positions requiring skilled labor within the mills and worked as supervisors both in the mills and in the woods. A Mobile, Alabama, lumberman, for instance, preferred to employ black labor; and blacks comprised the majority of his four hundred-man labor force, with whites employed only in skilled positions. However, the absence of a large black population in the upper Piedmont regions of the South dictated the employment of whites. And in the hardwood forests of that area, whites performed the manual labor. A Gadsden, Alabama, lumberman used whites exclusively as loggers and haulers. Whites also held all the skilled positions in the mills, where a few blacks were employed in menial positions. Lumbermen in western North Carolina also relied heavily upon white labor, both in the woods and in the mills.[10]

Blacks also comprised a large segment of the urban labor force. They were especially well represented as construction workers, as draymen, and as stevedores. The participation of blacks, both slave and free, in the urban work force had been significant during the antebellum period and simply continued into the postwar era.[11] Again, urban blacks primarily furnished "muscle power" while whites supervised; but a surprising number were skilled laborers, some working as independent contractors, especially in the construction trades. In Birmingham and Montgomery, for example, blacks worked as plasterers, carpenters, and masons; and black carpenters and masons contracted their work, employing up to eight or ten hands. Alfred Jackson, a black plasterer, testified in 1883 that over half the plasterers and mechanics of Birmingham were black and that throughout the region, blacks worked in carpentry, bricklaying and several other trades.[12]

While some blacks and whites professed that blacks made excellent wages if they were "willing to work," others indicated that competition for jobs between black and white laborers kept wages depressed, with blacks usually receiving the lowest pay. A black Birmingham carpenter believed that black laborers received from fifty cents to a dollar a day less than their white fellow workers, even for superior performance. Another black construction worker, while expressing the view that blacks frequently would not work or save, nevertheless called for the employment of more blacks in southern factories. A white North Carolina building contractor, surveying the labor scene in 1888, flatly stated that "the colored man competes with the white man, and on all common buildings he is largely employed, tending to keep wages down."[13]

The competition for urban jobs resulted as young men, black and white, drifted into towns and cities from the outlying rural areas. This population shift reflected the depressed state of the region's agrarian economy and would have occurred with no encouragement from outside sources. But urban newspapers, anxious to see their towns "progress" and to insure a surplus labor pool, accelerated the movement of rural labor into the city by "booming" the towns in which they were published.[14] Skilled mechanics and craftsmen resented such tactics and the lack of any regulation of tradesmen, which contributed to their success. Since no formal apprenticeship system existed, any individual, black or white, with a rudimentary knowledge of a trade could strike out on his own to seek employment in the city. As one craftsman summarized the situation, "The trouble about wages in this county is, as soon as a man can daub on a coat of paint, shoe a horse or stick a house together, he sets himself up as a workman and takes jobs or hires for half price of a master workman. We have but

few men in the county who are masters of their trades." [15] While this
situation infuriated master craftsmen, especially whites, it provided
both white and black unskilled rural laborers with an opportunity for
economic advancement in urban areas. However, it also led to
increased competition between blacks and whites for positions in the
nonindustrial urban work force. Whites increasingly demanded more
rigid standards to determine occupational status and to attempt to
force blacks out of or prevent them from entering jobs requiring
skill. [16] The competition between the races for the limited number of
such jobs provided one of the most serious challenges to the Knights'
efforts to organize the South.

The southern industrial work force also differed from its northern
counterpart in that it was located in rural areas to a much greater extent. The iron and coal mines of Alabama were located miles from
Birmingham, as would be expected. The production of other
materials in such states as Georgia, North Carolina, and Virginia also
occurred in rural areas. Lumber camps and mills were situated in
rural, often practically uninhabited areas. Even in cotton textiles, the
industry tending to have the most modern factories, mills were often
located in rural areas, frequently in former cotton fields. Of all major
southern postwar industries, only the tobacco and iron industries
were concentrated almost exclusively in urban areas, although much
of the textile industry was located in such towns as Augusta, Columbus, Charlotte, and Atlanta. Thus a large number of southern industrial workers continued to live and work in an essentially rural environment; and the labor force was divided into agrarian, rural industrial, urban industrial, and urban nonindustrial elements.

The rural location of much of the South's industry combined with
the rural origins of the region's work force to perpetuate an agrarian
mind set among laborers. During the 1880s, the overwhelming majority of the industrial and urban work force, black and white, was recruited from rural areas. Coming from the farm, where many had
been tenants, the new workers brought their rural, pre-industrial culture with them into the region's cities, towns, and mill villages. In this
respect, the labor force resembled that of New England in the 1850s
and the new immigrants who supplied labor for the industrial North
after 1890. Predictably, southerners reacted to the new industrial
order in much the same manner as did the other groups. [17]

On the farm, both blacks and whites had been accustomed to rigorous manual labor which often required long hours. But except for the planting and harvest seasons, farm work could be performed at a pace set by the farmer. Time for relaxation—hunting, fishing, and other outdoor activities—could be incorporated into the rural work culture without disturbing the farmer's free time on Sunday. The machines of industry and the pace of urban life, however, dictated a more regular and constant work pace; and whites and blacks resented the iron discipline of the machine. In adjusting to this discipline, southerners, especially blacks who were just two decades removed from slavery, frequently reverted to the customs of the old order. Management frequently complained that their new laborers thought nothing of "taking off" days to fish, hunt, or otherwise relax when the work schedule became too monotonous. Management cited this trait of southern labor in order to justify the need for surplus labor pools and often "employed" more laborers than necessary, although "employees" were paid only when they worked. Textile firms regularly maintained a labor pool 20 percent larger than the work force required on a given day. The same practice existed in other industries. James Sloss revealed that in 1883, he maintained a payroll of 569 men to ensure the work force of 269 required to keep his furnaces fired. The average hand worked only fourteen and one-third days a month. This astounding rate of absenteeism left Sloss unperturbed, for, as he noted, "I have got another set [of laborers] down town that I can drum up whenever those who are at work leave."[18]

The southern laborers' rural background also influenced their view of management. Since many had been tenants, they were accustomed to the paternalism and power of an employer. In several industries—especially textiles, mining and lumber—the mill owner replaced the landowner, the company store the country store, the company house the tenant house, and so on. The mill or mining village system gave the employer tremendous power over the economic, social, and even to some extent political lives of his employees. This power was reinforced by the tendency of some workers to be so grateful for employment that they ignored the difficulties of their new situation. Too, once a farmer deserted the land, he was often viewed with scorn by his former neighbors, who held to their belief in the virtues of the agrarian way of life in spite of, and perhaps also to some extent because of, the depressed state of the agrarian economy.[19] Finally, in leaving the land, the farmer admitted defeat, an admission that undoubtedly carried with it some loss of self-esteem.

In some instances, the workers' rural background aided their transition into an industrial economy, especially when management tailored its policies to fit the preindustrial culture of the labor force. For example, management in the textile, tobacco, furniture, and other industries encouraged the "family wage" concept, employing entire families, especially women and older children. Since the family had worked as a unit on the farm, this practice did not seem unusual to many laborers. But factory employment, unlike farm life, frequently denigrated the position of the adult male from provider and head of the household to that of an economically superfluous member of the family. Nevertheless, to many rural families even scrip wages seemed an improvement over the crop lien system, which often resulted in a year's labor without any monetary reward.

Management justified the family wage as a means of keeping families united and improving their economic status. One paternalistic North Carolina carpet manufacturer noted that "many who came here poorly clad, now have comfortable, decent dress, and but one family has left us in two years and they now want to come back."[20] Even those industries that employed only adult male labor encouraged their workers to think of the family as an income-producing unit. A Birmingham coal mine operator noted that his miners could obtain a decent livelihood: "if his wife were industrious, she could support herself by washing and other work. Many of them do that."[21]

Southern laborers carried other preindustrial cultural patterns and concepts into the factories, mines, and towns of the New South. In this respect, recent historical scholarship suggests that they differed little from their northern counterparts.[22] Deeply religious, they maintained their fervent evangelical protestantism and were convinced that "Heaven and hell were localities as real and material in their make-up as Georgia and Florida." For the laborer, religion meant sin and the salvation of souls, not the social gospel. Their religion stressed the rewards of the future life while helping them endure their present situation with the belief that "unearned and inherited wealth bring no blessing."[23] Thus the Knights and other labor organizations encountered difficulty in their efforts to identify their cause with Christianity. [24] And southern management encouraged a religious fundamentalism which emphasized the condition of the soul, while often ignoring the maintenance of the man.

The unyielding individualism of the South's agrarian past remained within the work force of the immediate postwar era. Most of the "poor whites" who entered the industrial work force were poor in economic terms only. They had not given up; they retained their sense of dignity. "Poor, but proud," a common phrase in the region, better described the laborer than did "poor white trash." Blacks, too, despite the burden of slavery, struggled for a sense of individual worth. The Reconstruction era had just ended; legal segregation and disenfranchisement was yet to come. Blacks still had faith in an improved future; and whites expressed concern over this "new Negro," unfettered by the restraints of slavery. The individualism of the southern laborer, however, caused him to be somewhat suspicious of all organizations, including labor unions. Management frequently encouraged this characteristic by dealing with employees on an individual, if paternalistic, basis. In fact, the individual laborer with a complaint was often listened to by management, although little was usually done to redress grievances.

Like the laborers in the early factories of the North and the "new immigrants" of rural European background who entered America's factories and mills after 1890, the southern laborer clung to the belief that he would return to the land. He often saw his acceptance of an industrial position as temporary, a step necessitated by the economics of farming. Many never abandoned the agrarian cultural ideal, the belief that life on the land, provided one could obtain a livelihood, was the best possible of all economic endeavors. And so they labored looking backward, hoping to save enough to someday return to a farm they would own. [25]

Finally, the laborers carried yet another legacy of the antebellum South's preindustrial culture into their new positions, ignorance. The region's general poverty, the reluctance of Bourbon Democrats to spend funds for public education, and the rural nature of the society combined to deny educational opportunities to at least two generations of southerners born after the Civil War. As a result, the southern labor force was much less educated than that of the North. As late as 1905, North Carolina employers revealed that over half of their adult work force was illiterate. Although this figure was unusually high, literacy figures of 60 to 70 percent were standard in many industries; and lower figures were not uncommon during the 1880s. [26] This appalling lack of formal education, coupled with the new laborer's total lack of knowledge of an industrial society or any concept of organized labor, presented a formidable obstacle to efforts to organize the South.

Although southern laborers shared preindustrial cultural patterns with their northern counterparts to a much greater extent than is generally believed, in another significant area, the southern labor force differed substantially from that of the North. The South's industrial and urban work force represented a much smaller percentage of that region's total population than did that of the Northeast. As noted earlier, despite rapid industrialization beginning in the late 1870s, the South remained an overwhelmingly rural, agrarian region throughout the nineteenth and well into the twentieth century. In 1890, approximately three years after the Knights had reached their peak strength, the rural population of Alabama and South Carolina stood at 89.9 percent, 86 percent for Georgia, 94.6 percent for Mississippi, 92.8 percent for North Carolina, and 82.9 percent for Virginia. These figures revealed a glaring difference in the relative strength of the southern and northern work forces, even when compared to corresponding data for the southern Mid-Atlantic states. For example, corresponding figures for Maryland and Delaware were 52.4 percent and 57.8 percent. The number of wage earners in each state even more graphically illustrates that the labor force represented a small minority of the South's population. In 1890, Virginia, the least rural southern state, had only 53,566 wage earners in a total population of 1,655,980. The same statistics for Alabama and Mississippi, respectively, were 31,137 of 1,513,401 and 14,465 of 1,289,600. In contrast, 97,808 of Maryland's total 1890 population of 1,042,390 were wage earners. Thus Maryland, with a smaller population than Alabama, Mississippi, or Virginia, had nearly seven times as many wage earners as did Mississippi, over three times as many as Alabama, and nearly twice as many as Virginia. [27] Such data plainly indicated that unless labor could forge an alliance with agrarian groups, its chances of effecting change within the existing economic structure, no matter how consolidated its forces or how concerted its efforts, were dim indeed.

In the early 1880s when the Knights of Labor began a serious bid to organize southern laborers, the very nature of the work force presented the order with serious difficulties. Unlike its northern counterpart, which was only beginning to experience the new wave of immigrants, the southern work force was badly divided by race. It was less educated and comprised only a fraction of the regional population. In some industries, it was geographically isolated and remained essentially a part of a rural environment. The southern workers also shared some of the handicaps of their northern brethren before 1890, the most significant being a preindustrial mind set which increased the difficulty of their adjustment to both urbanization and industrialization and heightened their willingness to acquiesce to managerial paternalism. Also, a surplus labor force created competition for jobs, strengthening the economic power of the employer.

Under such conditions, the prospects for success for any organization attempting to organize southern laborers were bleak, at best. Yet by 1886, the Knights of Labor had penetrated every southern industry, created strong state and regional organizations, and in some areas pulled together a powerful political coalition of reform forces. That they did so proved that while southern laborers were uneducated and lacked an understanding of industrial society, they were neither naive nor unquestioning in their acceptance of managerial policies. Many of them realized the inequities in their lives and, despite the odds, attempted to improve conditions. One Birmingham ironworker's answer to a querry by a member of the 1883 Senate Committee on Capital and Labor revealed both the laborer's desire for a better life and the struggles labor as a whole would encounter as a result of their efforts to achieve it:

Q. And you think you ought to have a share in that advantage which [capital in] Birmingham has. A. I think so . . . . I called the attention of the president of our company to that matter. I told him that we labored under disadvantage here and pointed out to him that the company had advantages. He wanted to know wherein. I told him on account of the material necessary to produce iron, coal and everything being cheaper. He told me that was none of my business. [28]

3 Organization of the Southern Knights

IN DECEMBER 1869, nine Philadelphia tailors founded the Noble Order of the Knights of Labor. All nine had belonged to the recently disbanded local Garment Cutters Association, and all hoped to establish a secret fraternal order of workers which would elevate the economic and social status of the American laborer. From its inception, Uriah S. Stephens provided leadership, becoming the local's Grand Master Workman when it adopted a formal structure in January 1870. Stephens held the position until 1879. Under his leadership, the order's one local grew slowly until 1872 when a second assembly was organized. The following year saw the order expand to eighty locals, all in the Philadelphia area. In 1874, the order spread into New York, New Jersey, Delaware, Massachusetts, and western Pennsylvania. By 1875, district assemblies existed in Philadelphia, Camden, and Pittsburgh; and the order continued its rapid growth, especially in western Pennsylvania.

Expansion forced the order to formulate plans for a national structure, but feuds between the Philadelphia and Pittsburgh districts prevented their implementation for over two years. Continued depression and the shock waves produced by the violent eastern railroad strikes of 1877 caused the feuding districts to close ranks; and the Knights held their first General Assembly at Reading, Pennsylvania, in January 1878. The General Assembly (G.A.) performed the usual tasks associated with creating a national organization. It created an organizational structure governed ultimately by an annual G.A. comprised of delegates from district assemblies and from locals where no districts existed. The G.A. adopted a constitution which placed executive power in the hands of the Grand Master Workman and a General Executive Board (G.E.B.), both elected by the G.A. Delegates also established a strike fund, adopted a dues structure, and decided to remain a secret society. Despite frequent modifications, the structure created by the first G.A. served the order until its demise. [1]

Although structured as a representative democracy, the order was controlled by a small group of men who determined its general ideology and direction. Among this group, Terence V. Powderly of Scranton, Pennsylvania, emerged as the most influential. Machinist, Greenback-Labor politician, businessman, and reformer, this controversial figure served as the Knights' Grand Master Workman (G.M.W.) from 1879 until 1893. His tenure spanned the order's rapid ascent to national prominence and its equally swift decline. [2]

Ideologically, the Knights represented a continuation of the antebellum reform tradition rather than an innovative response to the problems of industrial America. The order rejected the wage system and the separation of labor and capital. It sought to reunite capital and labor and to return the laborers to the proprietary status they had enjoyed before industrialization. Violence and radicalism, according to Powderly and other leaders, could never accomplish this goal. Instead, the order proposed a program of arbitration, education, and cooperation. Arbitration would settle disputes between labor and capital before the wage system was abolished. To abolish the system, the order had to educate the worker to the social, economic, and political "truths" that would allow him to take his rightful place in society. All other goals, including the achievement of higher wages, shorter hours, or better working conditions, were at best secondary and at worst a hindrance to the order's true mission. Thus the order regarded strikes and boycotts as hindrances to the development of its programs.

The Knights taught that cooperation would provide the means by which the laborer could regain his lost status. Owned and operated by workers, cooperative factories would produce goods to be distributed through consumer cooperatives. Since labor would own and manage the factories, conflict between capital and labor would cease. Unlike the more realistic Socialists, the Knights saw no reason for the state to own the means of production for "the people." Rather, they relied upon their own version of private enterprise. Laborers would save enough from their wages to purchase or establish cooperatives, which would produce profits to be reinvested. Such a naive view of capital accumulation could survive little practical application, and the national order spent far more time and effort discussing the theory than implementing it.[3]

One of the most complex, naive, and incongruous organizations in the history of American labor, the Knights nevertheless dominated the union movement from the late 1870s to the late 1880s. In reaching their dominant position, the order actively sought to build a southern membership. Despite obstacles to organized labor within the region, their efforts met with considerable success. Throughout the South, laborers, black and white, responded to the Knights' organizers. By the fall of 1886 when the Knights held their G.A. in the old Confederate capital of Richmond, the order appeared to be firmly established in most of the region's major urban areas and in many of its small towns.

Both the nature of the organization and the economic conditions in the region at the time contributed to the Knights' successful foray into the South. The ideology and structure of the order was more appealing to southerners than the "business unionism" of the trade unions which supplanted the Knights. The order's basic reform ideology struck a responsive chord among southerners of different classes, all of whom felt themselves victims of institutions controlled by the wealthy of the Northeast. The Knights provided a common forum for members of various occupations and trades who demanded more fair treatment for themselves and their region.

The timing of the Knights' bid to organize southerners also contributed to their success. Catapulated to national prominence by the 1885 strikes against the Jay Gould southwest rail system, the Knights took advantage of economic changes occurring in the South. Their national prominence coincided with the decade of rapid industrial development which created the New South. For the first time in its history, the South developed an industrial work force in addition to experiencing urban growth. Members of the urban and industrial work force, employed in a society with few indigenous institutions for their protection, gravitated to what seemed a powerful and friendly national organization.

As utopian reformers, the Knights appealed not just to the urban industrial worker but to a broad spectrum of southern society which included professionals and white-collar workers. Indeed, most southerners, with the exception of the industrialists and large planters, could agree with some part of the order's program. The Knights denounced trusts, railroads, foreign landowners, the national banking system, and other traditional enemies of the South. The order's rejection of the wage system conformed to southern concepts. The southern prejudice against capital, a prejudice shared by the majority of the new industrial work force, dated back to Jefferson, had been masterfully articulated by Calhoun, and still lived in the minds of most southerners, even though they derived the economic benefits of industrialization. Thus the order's lack of emphasis on the methods of a class struggle, including the strike and boycott, and its stress on total reform seemed appropriate and natural, even if its panacea, cooperation, did not.

The structure of the order also aided its efforts to establish a southern presence. On paper, the Knights had a highly centralized organizational structure. Beneath the G.A. were state, district, and local assemblies. In areas where few locals existed, assemblies affiliated directly with the G.A. The southern order followed this pattern. In North Carolina, Alabama, Florida, and Mississippi, the Knights organized state assemblies; and in Virginia and Georgia, large districts in Richmond and Atlanta functioned much as state assemblies. Although all units below the G.A. were theoretically governed by the G.A., the Grand Master Workman, and the G.E.B., in practice no higher body ever exercised full control over state, district, or even local assemblies. Units beneath the G.A., including locals, possessed tremendous autonomy, often defying even the G.A. with impunity. This practical autonomy appealed to southerners but caused both the regional and the national order considerable grief.[4]

Because they wished to unite all "producers" into a reform organization, the Knights welcomed members from all classes and occupations. The order excluded from membership only lawyers, bankers, gamblers, stockbrokers, and liquor dealers. As a result, the national order was heterogeneous beyond description and beyond control. Its membership included Socialists, trade unionists, ex-Greenbackers, farmers, social reformers, and politicians. In the South, this liberal membership policy contributed significantly to the order's success. It encouraged workers from different trades to attempt to organize by allowing them to join together. It also provided the southern order with leadership. The region lacked an experienced proletariat. As a result, the southern order recruited its leadership from the ranks of professionals, small businessmen, editors, and other nonlaborers. They provided the leadership essential to the success of the order in the region. A labor organization with more rigid membership requirements could not have produced, at that time, the necessary leadership to obtain a foothold in the region.

The ability of locals to affiliate directly with the G.A. also helped the order in the South. From 1880 until 1883, all southern locals affiliated with the G.A. because there were no functioning district or state assemblies in the region. The first district to be formed in the 1880s in the seven states under consideration was established in Richmond in 1885. No other districts were formed until 1886. But even after southern districts were created, many newly organized locals preferred to affiliate directly with the G.A., especially if they existed in areas distant from the nearest district within the state. Direct affiliation with the G.A. also provided locals with more autonomy, relieved them of dues payments to district and state assemblies, and ensured them of representation at the G.A. On the other hand, direct affiliation caused severe jurisdictional problems which bedeviled the order throughout its existence.

The lack of occupational divisions within the Knights' structure aided the order's southern efforts. Actually, the Knights were more a fraternal order of laborers than an industrial union or federation of unions. Members joined the order directly, not through membership in a trade or industrial organization. Nationally, there was opposition to this lack of occupational identity. A large faction within the order supported organization by trade but was kept at bay by Powderly and other leaders. In an effort to reach a compromise, the Knights created "trade districts" which were, of course, composed of "trade locals." The compromise failed. Few trade districts were formed, and the dispute over the place of the trade union within the order would play a major role in its decline.[5]

To accomplish their goal of uniting all "producers" into one organization, the Knights developed the "mixed" assembly, which took full advantage of the order's liberal membership policy. Anyone not prohibited from membership could join a mixed local, regardless of trade or occupation. Mixed locals frequently contained both members of various crafts within a single industry and members from several industries. Often they contained any number of professionals, clerks, salesmen, and other white-collar employees, in addition to manual laborers in fields such as construction. Such a flexible basic organizational unit encouraged the order's growth in the South because it allowed even a few laborers from each of several different trades or occupations in a given area to work together to establish an assembly. The mixed assembly also encouraged the new industrial worker, who lacked a craft union heritage, to unite with his fellow workers across occupational lines. By 1886, the majority of the order's locals were mixed assemblies. In the South, mixed assemblies far outnumbered all others. True industrial assemblies, especially in mining and textiles, ran a poor second; and craft locals existed only among Knights with previous organizational experience—telegraphers, typographers, cigar makers, and so forth. [6]

The Knights made no attempt to organize the South until after the formation of the General Assembly in 1878. The G.A. empowered the G.M.W. to appoint organizers, who were commissioned by the general secretary. The order required that each organizer commissioned be recommended by a local or district assembly. Acting under these instructions, Stephens appointed seventy-nine organizers in 1878. Among them were four southerners—E. W. Conner of Rome, Georgia; Peter Westgerand of Melrose, Florida; Edward S. Marshall of Montgomery, Alabama; and Michael Moran of Helena, Alabama, a town situated in the state's mineral belt. The Georgia and Florida organizers failed to establish the order in their states, although Conner managed to found a local which existed in Rome for approximately a year. [7] The Alabama organizers, however, formed several assemblies, permanently establishing the Knights in that state. By the time Marshall attended the second General Assembly in January 1879, he had organized locals in Mobile (700) and Montgomery (716). Moran had formed two assemblies in Helena (945 and 949). [8] The efforts of Moran and Marshall established an organizational pattern the Knights would follow in the region until 1886. First, they organized the urban laborers, especially the skilled. Second, they organized the laborers of the region's new industries, such as the miners in the Helena area. Alabama, with the major cities of Mobile, Montgomery, and Birmingham, and a large industry, became the center of the Knights' southern activity until 1883.

During 1879, the Knights commissioned six additional southern organizers—three from Montgomery, two from Mobile, and one from Raleigh, North Carolina. The order failed to gain a foothold outside Alabama; but in that state it progressed to the formation of district assemblies, which at that time could be comprised of as few as four locals. Reports by the general secretary-treasurer to the third G.A., held in September 1879, revealed the formation of D.A. 29 in Helena. This assembly was comprised of but two locals with a combined membership of 63. Two Mobile locals attached to the G.A. reported a combined membership of 159. Evidently the Montgomery local had lapsed, for it did not report.[9] At the 1880 G.A., Alabama remained the only southern state with active locals. District Assembly 29, comprised of miners and laborers in the mineral region, claimed six locals and 165 members as of October 1, 1880. In Mobile, the number of locals had grown to four, with a combined membership of over 100. The four locals formed Alabama's second D.A., number 31. Again, no Montgomery locals were reported; and the order had evidently ceased to function in that area of the state.[10]

The Knights maintained a precarious presence in Alabama during the early 1880s. By 1881, both Alabama district assemblies had lapsed, and only five locals with a combined membership of seventy-one reported to the G.A. that year. The following year only two locals, a revived number 716 in Montgomery and number 1382 at Pratt Mines, reported to the G.A. The Montgomery local had forty members; the Pratt Mines local had forty-nine. Mobile's locals had lapsed, and the order seemed on the verge of extinction in the state.[11]

By late 1883, however, the order had reversed its decline in Alabama and had begun to expand into other southern states. Organizers had established at least one local in each of the seven states considered in this study, and the new locals demonstrated a desire to actively participate in the deliberations of the national order. Delegates from locals in Atlanta and Newport News attended the 1883 G.A. held at Cincinnati in September. Alabama still maintained its position as a leader with five locals, but Virginia and Georgia had an equal number. Florida, Mississippi, South Carolina, and North Carolina claimed one local each. Most of the southern locals were small, a majority containing fewer than forty members; and the region still had no district assembly. With the exception of the locals in Alabama's mineral region, all of the assemblies were in the urban areas— Atlanta, Newport News, Charlotte, Charleston, and Jackson, Mississippi. [12] During the year, the order established sixteen new locals in the seven southern states being considered and in addition formed eleven locals in the urban centers of Tennessee and four locals in the New Orleans area. [13]

Locals organized in 1882 and 1883 followed the pattern of urban organization. Members of skilled trades joined first and then laborers in semiskilled occupations. The telegraphers, who joined the Knights in 1882 as the Telegraphers National District Assembly 45, comprised a large number of the southern locals, including ones in Montgomery, Brunswick, Atlanta, Birmingham, Charleston, Macon, Jacksonville, Lynchburg, Charlotte, and Wilmington. Disgusted by the defeat in August 1883 of their strike against Western Union, the telegraphers withdrew from the order, taking with them a large portion of the southern locals. But the southern order survived the telegraphers' defection. The majority of the remaining locals were mixed assemblies containing a large number of construction trades personnel. In the Birmingham area, miners and mine laborers continued to provide the majority of the membership. [14]

The order held its own in 1884, experiencing a slow but steady growth in the urban areas. Most of the assemblies formed during the previous year continued to function, and twelve new locals were organized. Richmond became a center of the Knights' activity, with eight locals formed in the area. The order also continued to expand in Atlanta and Birmingham, and it established locals in the Raleigh-Durham area of North Carolina. Most of the new locals were mixed assemblies; and the southern order remained exclusively white, except in the Atlanta area where at least one black local was formed. The order's increased southern activity was reflected at the 1884 General Assembly. General Secretary-Treasurer Frederick Turner reported many requests for information about the creation of locals from laborers in Alabama, Florida, and North Carolina; and he requested the G.A. to place a "good, live organizer" in the South. John Ray, who represented a Raleigh local at the G.A., requested that paid organizers be placed in every southern state. The G.A. failed to act on either request. Nevertheless, by the end of the year the order had functioning locals in every southern state, with the exception of South Carolina, and was especially strong in Alabama, Virginia, and Georgia. [15]

While both the ideology and the structure of the order facilitated its efforts in the South, its growth in urban areas in 1883 and 1884 resulted in large measure from the depression which began in 1882. In the South, as in the nation as a whole, urban laborers faced wage reductions and unemployment as management sought to cut losses by reducing labor costs. Some southern laborers, especially those hit hardest by the depression—including construction workers, mechanics, and unskilled day laborers—turned to the Knights in an effort to obtain some protection. They gravitated to the Knights for several reasons. During the winter of 1883-84, successful strikes in the North against wage reductions by the glassworkers, the Philadelphia shoemakers, and the Union Pacific Railroad shopmen, all Knights, lent the order an aura of strength. This appearance was the more striking since similar strikes by old-line trade unions had met defeat. The Knights were on the scene, having been introduced to many southern towns by the telegraphers in 1882. Finally, because of the mixed assembly, the Knights could organize threatened workers from several trades into a single unit. Thus the initial growth experienced by the Knights in the urban South after the disaffection of the telegraphers represented an essentially defensive reaction to hard times and paralleled developments within the labor force in other parts of the country. [16]

Fortunately for the Knights, for a number of reasons the impetus of organizational activities derived from the depression carried over into the mid-1880s. The depression of 1882 was not as severe as that of 1873. It was also short-lived, with recovery beginning in 1885. The depression of 1873 had continued nearly twice as long, and it was its length as well as its severity that resulted in the outbreaks of labor violence in 1877. The depression of 1882, on the other hand, was severe enough to frighten labor into seeking protection through organization; but it was brief enough that labors' frustrations never reached the bursting point encountered in 1877. The early recovery of the economy combined with the order's success in penetrating the region in 1883 and 1884 placed the Knights in a position to take advantage of events in 1885 which would transform the union overnight into a formidable national labor organization. Prior to 1885, the southern order had grown in a defensive pattern, its members recruited from laborers faced with immediate economic setbacks. But in 1885, the order began to recruit members because it offered a hope of increased economic returns.

A number of factors combined in 1885 to initiate a period of rapid growth for the order in both the South and the nation as a whole. First, the national leadership, impressed by the order's southern expansion, decided to place greater emphasis on the organization of the region. Prior to 1885, the order had not sent a national officer into the region and had relied exclusively on local organizers. But in January, Powderly began a month-long southern tour. Deporting from Washington, he traveled to New Orleans by a circuitous route that carried him through Richmond, Raleigh, Atlanta, Chattanooga, the coal country of Tennessee, Kentucky, and Alabama, Birmingham, Pensacola, and Mobile. At every stop, Powderly preached the need for organization while observing firsthand the difficulties encountered by the region's labor force.[17]

Powderly's visit caught the attention of southern laborers at a propitious moment. From April to September of 1885, the Knights of the Southwest had engaged the Jay Gould rail system in a bitter strike initiated by a lockout of members of the order. Begun and directed by local workers and only reluctantly authorized by the national leadership, the strike was nevertheless successful. The Gould system agreed to reemploy the locked out Knights without discrimination. The Knights appeared as giant killers, an organization capable of defeating the mighty Jay Gould. At the same time, the economy began to show signs of recovery. Workers who had suffered wage reductions during the depression now anticipated their restoration. Caught in a spirit of optimism invoked by the Knights' success and the general economic upturn, thousands rushed to join the order in the South, as in the rest of the nation. The number of assemblies organized in the seven states considered in this study jumped from twelve in 1884 to ninety-two in 1885. While half of this growth occurred in Virginia, the order registered increases in every state except South Carolina. And while its growth remained concentrated in urban areas, for the first time the order began to invade the towns and villages of the region. [18]

Prior to 1885, a few men, many of them transplanted Yankees previously affiliated with the order, maintained the Knights' southern organizational efforts. In North Carolina, John Ray, originally from Massachusetts, struggled to organize locals in the Raleigh-Durham area. He was aided by W. H. Roberts, also a newcomer to the region. A New Yorker, William Oree, brought the order to the Richmond area. He was ably assisted by a native, William Mullen, a printer and member of the typographical union, who early in 1885 organized Richmond's sixteen locals into the South's first district assembly, number 84, since the demise of the two pioneer Alabama districts in 1880. In Mississippi, John Power, who moved to that state from Connecticut in 1884, organized the Knights' first locals. [19]

The sudden popularity of the order altered its basic organizational pattern. In the latter half of 1885 and into 1886, as new locals were formed, members swamped Powderly with requests for organizers' commissions. While most requests for commissions came from urban members, reform-minded individuals in small towns and villages sought to obtain information about forming assemblies. Applications for commissions ranged from the pompous to the pathetic. "I will undertake the responsible duties [of organizer] with a deep sense of feeling of the anomalous position in which I will be placed," wrote a Mississippi man. A group of blacks in the Tampa area wrote Powderly that "we have just heard of your noble order and write to ask if colored men can become members and if so please send us your constitution and by laws." [20] Responding to the increased southern interest in the order, Powderly commissioned new organizers, many of whom were themselves recent recruits. As a result. The southern organizational activity became increasingly dominated by men of questionable ability.

Older organizers, too, became more active. John Ray of North Carolina traveled southward to organize South Carolina, the last holdout. He established an assembly in Columbia and placed E. A. Hatch in South Carolina to continue organizational work. In the Richmond area, Mullen continued to organize, branching out into the black community. And in Key West, Florida, C. B. Pendleton established seven locals, comprised primarily of cigar makers, by May 1886. [21]

As in the rest of the nation, the Knights' southern organizational activity crested in 1886. That spring, Richard F. Trevelick, the Knights' national organizer and a veteran labor reformer, toured the upper South, generating increased interest in the order. [22] Powderly continued to receive requests for organizers' commissions. Most such requests from members of established locals were honored without question. Since organizers were paid by retaining a portion of the initiation fees of charter members, organizers crisscrossed the South seeking converts to the order. Some, in direct defiance of the order's regulations, advertised their services in the newspapers. Their efforts were rewarded. In February, twenty-six locals were formed in the South and over five hundred nationally. The previous month, the Knights had established seventeen southern locals. [23]

In its rapid expansion, the order outgrew its ability to assimilate new members. In March, as an attempt to control the order's growth and consolidate its gains, the G.E.B. suspended all organizers' commissions for thirty days. This action proved ineffective. In May, the *Journal* reported 41 southern locals organized during the previous month; in June, it reported 36 new locals. [24] At a special G.A. held at Cleveland in May, the Knights took drastic measures to control their growth. The delegates authorized Powderly to revoke all commissions and placed more strict regulations, including examinations by special officers to be appointed in each state, on the issuance of commissions in the future. Still, the order continued to grow, with over 800 new locals organized nationally from July to November. The South followed the national pattern. Thirty-four southern locals were formed in June but only 19 in July, reflecting a brief period of inactivity following the special session of the G.A. But 35 locals were formed in August, surpassing the June total. By the end of 1886, some 483 new assemblies had been organized in the seven states considered in this study. [25]

The Knights' decision to hold the 1886 regular G.A. in Richmond during October reflected the importance of the city and the region to the national order. By that date, Richmond had become the center of the southern order with two district assemblies, the white District 84 and the black District 92. According to figures released at the G.A., the two districts claimed a combined membership of 7,692. Two other Virginia districts, numbers 120 in Petersburg and 123 in Norfolk, had memberships of 576 and 1,174 respectively. In Georgia, Atlanta's District 105, organized in 1885, had over 2,800 members; District 139 in Savannah claimed over 1,000 members; and District 141 in Columbus had an additional 900. District 131 in Key West reported 773 members. Other southern districts organized by the time of the G.A. but after the July reporting date included 187 in Charleston, 193 in Lynchburg, 173 in Birmingham, and 176 in Augusta. Locals in North Carolina and Mississippi, which contained no districts, and locals in most of Alabama, Florida, and South Carolina remained attached to the G.A. Their membership was not reported at the G.A. [26]

Since the memberships of locals attached directly to the G.A. were not reported and since large numbers of southern locals fell into this category, it is impossible to determine the exact number of southern members at the time of the G.A. The total membership of the eight southern districts reported as of July was 14,002. However, some of the locals attached directly to the G.A. were as large as some districts. Local 5030, a textile workers' assembly in Augusta, claimed over 2,000 members. [27] Large locals also existed in such urban areas as Raleigh-Durham, Lynchburg, Danville, Wilmington, Columbia, Charleston, Jacksonville, Pensacola, Mobile, and Jackson. As of August 1886, Lynchburg alone claimed nineteen locals, Danville thirteen, and Jackson, Mississippi, five. [28]

In addition to these urban clusters, by October the order had spread to such small communities as Hiram, Georgia; Henderson, North Carolina; Siddon, Alabama; Darlington, South Carolina; and New Hope, Virginia. In 1885 and 1886, the Knights organized 485 locals in the South, primarily in urban areas. [29] Given the total memberships of the districts reporting as of July 1886, the large number of urban locals not in districts, the increased number of rural assemblies (many of which had fifty to one hundred members), and the continued organization until the General Assembly, it is probable that as many as fifty thousand southern laborers were Knights when the southern order reached its peak late in the fall of 1886.

At the Richmond G.A., General Secretary-Treasurer Frederick Turner observed that "rapid strides have been made in the South, especially in the States of Virginia, the Carolinas, Georgia and Alabama. . . . The colored people of the South are flocking to us, being eager for organization and education." The attendance of forty-one delegates from the seven states considered in this study verified Turner's observations. [30] So, too, did the rapid increase in southern assemblies. Significantly, through 1886 the order's strength lay in the region's urban centers—Richmond, Raleigh-Durham, Atlanta, and Birmingham. Also, the order was not confined to a single industry. By mid-1886, it had obtained a foothold in every major southern industry, especially mining, textiles, lumbering, and the construction trades. With a strong urban base, a growing small town and rural membership, and the prospect of uniting white and black laborers within one organization, the Knights anticipated future southern growth equal to that of any other section of the country. Indeed, the order's southern prospects appeared brighter, for the stigma of the Haymarket affair and the failure of the eight-hour campaign seemed to have little significance in the region. But the position of the southern order was not what it seemed. In the South, as in the nation, the Knights were poised on the brink of collapse.

4 Strikes and Boycotts

ESSENTIALLY reformers dedicated to the abolition of the wage system, the Knights' leadership regarded with a mixture of disdain and fear organized labor's basic economic weapons, the strike and the boycott. Yet in their aversion to tactical economic warfare, the Knights never forbade the use of either the strike or the boycott. Rather, they adopted policies that made the official use of either practically impossible. The order's goal was to restructure industrial society, not the immediate redress of economic grievances. Any activities that detracted from that goal were to be avoided. Because they consumed time, money, and energy that otherwise could have been expended upon educational and cooperative projects which the Knights believed would reform society, strikes and boycotts were viewed as detractions. From the Knights' perspective, even successful strikes and boycotts could do nothing to alter the basic inequities of the laborer's position within society. While they might obtain higher wages or shorter hours, strikes and boycotts were unlikely to return to laborers the managerial and proprietary functions they had enjoyed as master craftsmen prior to the advent of factory production.

This inclination to avoid economic confrontations with capital revealed more than an ideological inflexibility, however. It reflected the experience of many of the order's leaders, including Powderly. They remembered the industrial violence of the late 1870s and the utter futility of the strikes of that decade. As a result, many were convinced that, as Powderly expressed it, "strikes are a failure. Ask any old veteran in the labor movement and he will say the same. I shudder at the thought of a strike, and I have good reason."[1] Since experience supported their theories, the order's leadership saw no contradiction in emphasizing cooperation and education as the means by which to redress economic grievances through social reform, while ignoring the possibilities of reform through the use of strikes or boycotts. Indeed, education and cooperation seemed appropriate methods of reform for an order interested in reclaiming for labor a proprietary and managerial role, while an emphasis upon strikes and boycotts to achieve immediate economic betterment implied the acceptance of an economic system in which a proletariat would be a permanent fixture.

Although it would undergo many revisions, from its inception the order's strike policy reflected the views of its leadership. The first General Assembly established a "Resistance Fund," which was to accumulate untouched for two years. But the delegates failed to make any provisions for the fund's eventual disbursement.[2] In his address to the second General Assembly in 1879, Grant Master Workman Uriah Stephens endorsed the fund, noting that its existence would encourage management to arbitrate with labor. But he also characterized strikes as "the great bane of former efforts in arbitration matters" and expressed the hope that the fund would make future strikes "rare occurrences and irresistible and effectual when they must be resorted to."[3] Powderly was even more hostile toward strikes and believed they were ineffective and largely responsible for the past failures of the trade union movement. In his first address to the General Assembly as Grand Master Workman, he called the strike "that most disastrous of all methods of obtaining a redress of grievance"; and he urged locals to bend their efforts to eliminating the wage system through cooperatives rather than strikes. In 1880, under Powderly's direction, the General Assembly changed the "Resistance Fund" to the "Defense Fund" and allocated 70 percent of its monies to educational and cooperative ventures.[4] Powderly continued his antipathy toward strikes and his emphasis on reform throughout his career as Grand Master Workman, and the order reflected his convictions. In 1886, the General Assembly established a complicated procedure designed to prevent local or district assemblies from initiating strikes. A two-thirds vote was required to call a strike; and at any time during a strike, the General, state, district, or local assemblies could call for a vote on its continuation. If a majority voted against the strike, it had to be settled immediately on the best terms available.[5] Long after the demise of the Knights, Powderly would boast that "not once did I, during my fourteen years incumbency of the office of General Master Workman, order a strike."[6]

Finances as well as ideology prevented the Knights from developing a pragmatic strike policy. The General Executive Board controlled access to the Defense Fund, which was called the Assistance Fund after 1883. The Assistance Fund was pathetically short of funds. In 1885 and 1886, locals contributed only six hundred dollars to the fund. The membership's parsimony forced the order to issue "special assessments" in an effort to obtain funds to aid locals which rushed into strikes the following year.[7]

The order maintained a similar, officially conservative policy on boycotts. At the 1885 General Assembly, Powderly noted that the order had failed to adopt a policy on boycotts. He suggested that local and district assemblies had recently instigated boycotts so frequently that the practice had lost its effectiveness. Boycotting over "every trifling thing, he announced, "was both foolish and dangerous." To prevent "misuse" of the boycott, Powderly suggested that the power to sanction boycotts be placed solely in the hands of the General Executive Board. The General Assembly promptly enacted his suggestion. The legislation adopted allowed local and district assemblies to instigate only those boycotts which would affect no other group outside the local or district instigating the boycott, and then only after making every attempt to arbitrate the matter. All other boycotts required the approval of the G.E.B., which could only be obtained after an official investigation of the problem by a representative of the board.[8]

While the order's leadership opposed strikes and boycotts and sought instead to reform the economic system through education and cooperation, the rank and file demonstrated greater concern for more immediate benefits and a willingness to strike or boycott to obtain them. The general membership exhibited more enthusiasm for economic warfare for two basic reasons, both of which reflected ideological differences with the leadership which resulted from differing experiences. First, and most important, the rank and file confronted the harsh realities of the wage system—low wages, long hours, and adverse working conditions. For them, unlike much of the leadership, whose connections with manual labor had long been severed, grievances were immediate, concrete, and constant. They were, therefore, more inclined to take immediate, direct action in order to obtain relief. Second, the majority of the rank and file had little or no experience with organized labor and had not undergone defeat in the industrial warfare of the late 1870s, as had many of the order's leaders. As a result, they did not fear the use of the strike; rather, it seemed to them a logical method of obtaining desired improvements. This contrast between the attitudes of the rank and file and the leadership concerning strikes and boycotts existed not only at the national level but also within state, district, and even local assemblies.

As a result of the rank and file's greater proclivity for direct economic action against employers to redress grievances, in the South, as in the rest of the nation, local assemblies ignored the leadership's admonitions and instigated numerous strikes and boycotts. Indeed, many of the region's converts to the order in the winter and spring of 1885-86 joined because of the Knights' successful strike against Jay Gould's southwest rail system. Ironically, they undoubtedly believed the national leadership was responsible for the Gould defeat and hoped that leadership could and would produce similar results in their struggles with recalcitrant employers. The excitement of seeing one of the nation's leading financiers humbled by a labor organization convinced southern laborers that the national order was powerful enough to effect immediate change in their economic status. Their enthusiasm led them into strikes for which they were ill prepared and which the national leadership opposed rather than supported. While a few early strikes did achieve minor concessions, overall strike activity proved disastrous to the southern order.

The willingness of the rank and file to challenge management with a strike or boycott was not limited by geography, occupation, or race. In every industry in which the Knights achieved a foothold, strikes occurred. Industrial laborers, miners, artisans, and even agricultural laborers sought to improve their economic condition, or at least prevent its deterioration, through direct action. Blacks, whites, and integrated work forces struck, as did laborers in both the upper and lower South. The Knights' strike activity alone provides ample evidence that southern laborers, like their northern brethren, found their economic status unacceptable and, given some organizational support, would fight to improve it.

Engaged in a rugged and dangerous occupation, the miners had long been among the most militant members of America's labor force. Southern miners proved no exception, for the Knights engaged in more strikes in the mining industry than in any other. Most of the activity occurred in the developing mineral region of Alabama, of which Birmingham was the center. The earliest struggle between the Knights and mine operators occurred in that area in 1882. Over five hundred miners, some of whom were Knights, struck Pratt Mines to protest a wage reduction of five cents per ton. Convicts and scab labor kept the mines open during the month-long strike, which ended in a "compromise." Wages were reduced only two and one-half cents per ton. Two years later, Knights at Coalburg, Alabama, also struck to protest wage reductions. Their four-month struggle ended in failure; convicts and scabs kept the mines working until the strike was broken in August 1884.[9] In May of the same year, miners at Warrior struck over several grievances, including wage cuts and convict labor.

They were most concerned, however, over the introduction of Italian miners. After a year of battling management, the Knights reported a victory. "That terrible curse upon American soil, Italian labor," wrote a Knight in April 1885, had been eliminated. The miners did not obtain the redress of any other grievance, however.[10] But their struggles had only begun. In May, the Warrior Knights struck in an unsuccessful effort to obtain semimonthly payment. In June, they left the mines again to force operators, who had once more begun the importation of Italian miners, to stop the practice. Again, management emerged the victor.[11]

The coal fields were quiet for the remainder of 1885 and 1886, but miners continued to organize. Meeting in Birmingham in July 1886 under the leadership of Nicholas Stack and others, they formed the Anti-Convict League and Union of Alabama. Never a real union, the league existed briefly and was absorbed by the Knights, whose membership increased dramatically during the next year.[12] The increased organizational activity proved a prelude to renewed strike activity.

In February 1887, the Knights of Walker County began what proved to be a rash of strikes in the Alabama coal country. Taking the offensive, they struck over a demand for a 20 percent wage increase. Over thirteen hundred miners left their jobs, closing fourteen mines. Operators remained adamant; and the miners, beaten, returned to work within a month. But that summer, Knights struck the Virginia and Alabama Coal Company in Walker County over a proposed wage reduction. Stack, a state master workman, negotiated a settlement with management; and the workers returned to the mines. Within weeks, however, management violated the agreement; and the Knights went out again. Stack again prevailed upon management to implement the compromise; and in July, management complied. Stack declared the strikers victorious and ordered them back to work.[13] The preceding May, Knights of Corona in Walker County struck in a successful bid for wage increases and a decrease in the prices charged for mining supplies at the company store. In November, Coalburg miners employed by Pratt mines struck to protest the company's retaining the wages of a discharged employee. Again, Stack negotiated a settlement. The men returned to work, and the company agreed to pay the full wages due any discharged miner.[14]

The strikes of 1887 weakened the Knights in Alabama's mining area, especially since the "compromises" Stack negotiated favored mine operators. Alarmed by recent strike activity, mine operators began to take the offensive against the Knights, hoping to destroy the order. By early 1888, operators in Walker County had implemented a policy of discharging Knights. While Stack threatened to "idle every factory, shop, or mine" in Alabama unless the policy was discontinued, in actuality the Knights were in no condition to conduct a successful strike.[15] Partially because of the Knights' ineffectiveness, Alabama's miners sought to create a more viable organization, holding preliminary meetings in Birmingham during May and June. At the time of both meetings, miners, including some Knights, were on strike against the Pratt mines and those of the Tennessee Coal and Iron Company at Coalburg. The miners struck for a wage increase of five cents per ton. At the June Birmingham assembly, delegates voted to support the strikers and to meet in Birmingham in July to launch their new union.[16]

Meanwhile, the Coalburg strike had divided the Knights' membership and created dissension between Knights and miners who had not joined the order. Evidently, one faction of the Knights was seeking a political solution to some grievances and had proposed anti-convict labor bills and mine safety legislation. They believed the striking Knights were hurting the chances of both bills in the legislature. Meanwhile, the majority of the strikers decided to place the strike's direction in the hands of representatives of the miners' convention rather than to continue under the Knights' leadership. The Knights chastised the strikers for this decision, warning that no settlement would be achieved under inexperienced leadership.[17]

On July 20, 1888, over 1600 delegates assembled in Birmingham to determine what organization, if any, should represent them. They decided to create the independent Alabama Federation of Miners. Only 310 delegates voted to remain associated with the Knights. The order's overwhelming defeat undoubtedly reflected displeasure with Stack, who had berated the Coalburg strikers for settling for a wage increase of less than five cents per ton earlier in the month. Stack suggested that he could have obtained a better settlement had the strikers trusted the Knights rather than the leadership of a "professional striker," as they had done.[18] Regardless of their motives, the miners' decision to form an organization independent of the Knights led to a rapid decline in the order, although some miners retained their membership.

After establishing their federation, Alabama miners engaged in a series of strikes in the fall of 1888. Each was an effort to prevent wage reductions, an indication that mine operators believed the miners were too weak to effectively resist. Miners at the Blockton, Henry Ellen, and Pratt mines walked off the job. Some of the strikers undoubtedly remained in the order. All their efforts failed; and the strikers returned to work, accepting wage reductions of up to 20 percent. The editor of the *Alabama Sentinel* noted the miners' disorganized state, which he believed "has steadily progressed from the date of the Pratt Mines' strike last spring [1888] when the miners forsook [*sic*] the Order of the K. of L."[19] Birmingham area miners engaged in three successful strikes in 1889 which again were prompted by wage reductions. Although individual Knights probably participated, the order by this time had little representation among the miners.[20] The three major strikes of that year are not reported in the *Journal of United Labor*.

The Knights also engaged in several strikes in Virginia's mining industry. Coal miners at Pocahontas struck in the spring of 1886 over management's attempt to discharge members of the order. The following year, Knights employed by the saltworks at Saltville had a dispute with management of an undisclosed nature. The G.E.B. sent A.

G. Denny to investigate the incident, and Denny reported that the problem did not require "pronounced action." The following year, however, the Knights employed by the saltworks struck to prevent the firm from enforcing an "iron clad oath" against union membership. Answering the miners' appeal, the G.E.B. sent T. B. McGuire to "arbitrate" the matter. The company president refused to see McGuire, who could only recommend that the order boycott the firm. Although the General Assembly accepted McGuire's recommendation, it afforded no relief for the strikers. [21]

Zinc miners employed by the Bertha Zinc Company of Pulaski City, like the coal miners of Alabama, attempted to use the order to halt the employment of immigrant labor. Although they did not resort to the strike, they informed Powderly of company plans to bring some forty Welsh miners through the port of New York sometime in January 1889. The miners urged Powderly to stop the Welshmen before they could be transported to Virginia. [22]

The order also represented foundry workers in at least four strikes—two in Virginia, one in Alabama, and one in Mississippi. The first Virginia strike occurred at Lynchburg in 1886 when Knights struck for higher wages. Management agreed to meet with a committee of local Knights, and a "compromise" was negotiated whereby the strikers went back to work with no increase in wages. Management evidently agreed not to retaliate against the strikers. In June of the same year, nail makers employed by the Belle Isle Iron Works in Richmond walked off the job to protest a wage reduction of 10 percent. The company justified the reduction by citing similar cuts made by Pennsylvania firms. Only 160 men actually struck, but the significance of their position idled the entire work force of 400. In September, management agreed to talk to a committee of Knights; and a settlement was reached. The company promised to retain the Knights and to raise wages if wages were raised elsewhere on the East Coast; the Knights returned to work. [23]

In the Birmingham area, Knights employed by the Williamson Iron Company complained to Powderly in December 1886 about the employment of nonunion personnel. Powderly advised them to take no drastic action and to continue to organize. The men heeded his advice about continued organization, but they struck both the Linn and the Williamson iron works for wage increases of from $1.00 to $1.25 a day in June 1887. Most of the strikers, over a hundred strong, were black day laborers. White Knights, who held more skilled positions, refused for over a month to go out in support of their fellow members. Finally, Stack ordered them out in late July; and about 150 men left their jobs, closing both establishments. Racial tensions continued, however, and white workers complained that neither Powderly nor the G.E.B. had authorized the strike and that it was therefore illegal. Under pressure from the white membership, Stack tried to negotiate a settlement calling for raises "if merited." Management refused this "compromise" and instead proposed rehiring the strikers "without prejudice" at the old pay scale, while suggesting possible wage increases for "good men" not connected with the strike. By the end of August, white laborers, unable to obtain strike funds and opposed to the venture from the start, returned to work. The strike was broken. Yet despite an obvious defeat, Stack insisted that the grievances had been "arbitrated" and implied that the firms had recognized labor's right to organize. [24]

The Mississippi strike also occurred in 1887 and involved the payment of wages. Knights employed by a foundry and machine shop in Vicksburg sought to obtain prompt payment. The local executive board met with management and presented their request, which management refused. The Knights struck, and management countered by importing strikebreakers. The Knights convinced the strikebreakers not to accept employment, raised some funds, and "sent them out of town." The outcome of the strike is unknown, however. [25]

The lumber industry experienced a rash of strikes, some of which resulted in temporary gains for the workers. Most of the strike activity occurred along the Gulf Coast in northwestern Florida, Alabama, and Mississippi. In this region, large firms, many of them backed by northern and foreign capital, were becoming increasingly dominant within the industry. Like miners, loggers and mill workers followed a rugged and dangerous trade. And like miners, they were inclined to strike in order to settle grievances.

In Florida, the Knights succeeded in rather thoroughly organizing the lumber industry of the Pensacola area. Organized into segregated assemblies, Pensacola area Knights marched between twelve hundred and fifteen hundred members in the July 4 parade of 1887. The industry was organized in such a way that the Knights were apparently able to take the offensive in 1887 and obtain concessions without resorting to a strike. The secretary of Local 5458, one of the lumber assemblies, reported that the Knights "have succeeded in their demands" for increased wages and an eight-hour day. Reports from locals in September 1887 revealed that their position was still strong, with day laborers receiving up to $8 a week and skilled mill workers as much as $3 a day. [26]

Most strikes in the industry occurred in Mississippi, where low wages and long hours reached their extreme. In 1887, Knights in the Moss Point-Pascagoula region struck area mills, demanding recognition and a reduction in the workday of from fourteen to twelve hours. Unprepared for a strike, management granted the twelve-hour day, thus contributing to the order's rapid growth among lumber workers. Encouraged by the success of the Pascagoula Knights, Knights in the Handsboro area struck the following year for recognition and a reduction of the workday from fourteen to ten hours. After a ten-week strike, William Bailey, a representative of the G.E.B., arrived in Handsboro to negotiate a settlement. Again, management conceded, granting the ten-hour day. The successful Handsboro strike prompted the Pascagoula area Knights in 1889 to demand the same workday and weekly payment of wages. This time mill owners stood firm, and again the Knights struck. Over 525 of the area mills' 600 workers, many of whom were black, left their jobs. They survived for nearly a month on a weekly family ration of five pounds of salt meat and a peck of meal. Mill owners, meanwhile, played upon racial divisions among the workers and began recruiting white strikebreakers, who were protected by sheriff's deputies. By the end of March, all the area mills had returned to full production, and the Knights had been routed. At the same time, the Handsboro Knights failed to maintain concessions won in 1888. When management reinstituted the longer workday, the Knights requested that the G.E.B. send a representative to investigate the matter. The G.E.B. refused their request, and the Handsboro Knights were forced to accept the longer hours. The dual defeats destroyed the Knights in Mississippi's lumber industry; and by the end of 1889, nearly 600 men had abandoned the order. [27]

A few months after the Mississippi defeats, the Knights lost a large strike in Alabama. Workers struck the Ray and Lillian lumber mills located in southwestern Alabama in order to obtain prompt cash payments. The G.E.B. sent a representative to investigate the situation. Upon his arrival, he found the strike had already begun to collapse and could only advise the strikers to return to work on the best terms available. The G.E.B. blamed the defeat on the Alabama state assembly, which, the board claimed, "had declared the strike over after the men had practically won it." But the G.E.B. took no action other than to require that a full statement of the relations of this company to its employees be published and circulated "throughout the area of the strike." [28]

Although no strikes are recorded, the Knights were involved in several minor incidents in the tobacco industry. Soon after the order appeared in Durham, the Knights ran afoul of a superintendent at the Duke Tobacco Company. In the fall of 1885, the superindendent had badly beaten a child employed in the Duke factory. Area Knights publicized the incident, seeking to have the man discharged. Their campaign caused the Dukes to confer with the G.E.B. and to promise to see that such behavior was stopped. Two years later, however, a superintendent at a Duke factory assaulted a twelve-year-old male employee. Although tried and convicted of assault, the man was "fined" but $15 and retained his position. The Knights demanded his job, complaining to the G.E.B., which dispatched T. B. Barry to investigate the episode. Barry and a delegation of area Knights, including Broughton of Raleigh, met with management. They received only the assurance that the incident had occurred without management's knowledge and would not be repeated; the superintendent retained his position. Barry noted in his report that only fifteen or so of the factory's several hundred employees were Knights and advised against any further action. [29]

In a somewhat comic episode of the same year, Durham Knights complained to Powderly that the Dukes required young boys and girls, working side by side, to pack cigarette cases with "vulgar pictures." The concerned Knights enclosed in their letter three trade cards depicting young ladies in, for that day, various stages of undress. The Knights had approached the Dukes about the matter, only to be assured that the ladies depicted were some of the finest New York models. Evidently neither Powderly nor the local Knights took any further action to stop the practice. [30]

The Knights employed by the Dukes were cigarette rollers brought to Durham from New York in 1881. After 1884, they had gradually been replaced by the Bonsack cigarette-rolling machine. Although the Knights protested the introduction of the machine, the machine's efficiency made protest useless. In 1888, the Dukes fired the last of the hand rollers, who had numbered over seven hundred in their factories alone. Although it was an impossible task, the Knights' inability to either protect or aid the hand rollers contributed to the decline of the order in the Durham area. [31]

Unlike tobacco factory workers, southern cigar makers engaged in strike activity; but the Knights' participation was limited. The Knights' restricted role resulted from the decision of the 1886 General Assembly to ban from the order all members of the Cigar Makers International, a decision that proved to be the opening round in the Knights' losing battle with the American Federation of Labor. Although the ban was rescinded in 1887, Powderly continued his fight against the cigar makers by forming a cigar makers' trade assembly, District 225, within the Knights. Most cigar makers remained with the international. In 1888, only four shops in the South employed an all-Knights of Labor work force, although individual cigar makers remained within the order, especially in the Key West area. There the Knights were strong enough to obtain a contract with a group of manufacturers in May 1889. But in October, the manufacturers broke their agreement; and the Knights struck, demanding a raise of a dollar per thousand. The Knights claimed the strike threw fifteen hundred out of work, a probable exaggeration. When local efforts to reach an agreement failed, the G.E.B. sent J. J. Holland to obtain a settlement. Holland, arriving in Key West in December, achieved some unreported "concessions" at a meeting with the manufacturers and ordered the strikers back to work. [32]

In the South's urban centers, skilled workers engaged in both strikes and boycotts. Like the miners and lumber workers, they often achieved temporary victories, especially in the early years of the order's existence in the South. The typographers, who had one of the country's oldest trade unions, were also among the most militant of the Knights' skilled urban members. Many typographers held membership in both the Knights and the International Typographical

Union; and until the typographers affiliated with the AFL in mid-1887, cooperation between the Knights and the typographers was common. [33]

One of the urban Knights' first boycotts, however, led to a dispute between the order and the Typographers International. The typographers had struck the *Atlanta Constitution* in 1882 and lost. Until 1885, the paper employed nonunion labor as well as some union members. Late in 1885, the typographers demanded that the *Constitution* recognize the union, pay union scale, and employ only union printers. When the *Constitution* refused, the typographers boycotted the paper. At their request, so did the Knights. When the Knights organized Atlanta District Assembly 105 in 1886, they reaffirmed the boycott but offered their services as arbitrators in the matter. The *Constitution* accepted the offer, but the typographers did not. Nevertheless, on March 9 a committee from D.A. 105 met with Henry Grady and other representatives of the *Constitution*. They reached a settlement which included recognition of the typographers, increased wages for night work, control by union foremen over the firing of union personnel, and an agreement that the union could recruit nonunion employees, a step toward the closed shop which did not quite establish it.

Having reached this agreement, the Knights rescinded their boycott. But the typographers, upset because they had not been invited to attend the conference, refused the settlement and complained to the G.E.B. that D.A. 105 had "sold out" to the *Constitution*. The G.E.B. sent John Hayes to Atlanta to investigate. Hayes found that the chairman of the executive board of D.A. 105, a carpenter, G. F. Fuss, was employed by the *Constitution* after the settlement, although the other Knights had negotiated in good faith. Hayes and the leadership of D.A. 105 met with the typographers to settle their differences. The meeting evidently succeeded, and the boycott against the *Constitution* ended. [34]

In Richmond, the Knights and typographers became involved in a similar situation. While the outcome failed to aid the typographers, it benefited the Knights. Several of the Richmond printers, including William Mullen, were members of both unions. In February 1886, the typographers boycotted Baughman Brothers, at that time Richmond's only nonunion printing firm. The Knights, who had planned to eliminate employment of "rat" printers since late 1884, supported the boycott and circulated a blacklist of Baughman's customers. In July, Baughman's obtained an injunction forbidding the circulation of the blacklist until a grand jury could consider the case. Meeting in September, the grand jury upheld the injunction and handed down criminal conspiracy indictments against Local 90 of the typographers and William Mullen, master workman of D.A. 84 and editor of the *Labor Herald*. Throughout the summer, Mullen had used the *Herald* to support the boycott. The indictments evidently led to an out-of-court settlement, for the incident ended. As a result of the Knights' strong support of the boycott, however, they emerged as the most powerful labor union in Richmond. [35]

Knights of the Birmingham area supported the local typographical union in a struggle with the *Iron Age*. In May 1887, the paper locked out all union employees. Again, some of the printers involved were members of the Knights and the typographers. When Nicholas Stack failed in an attempt to negotiate a settlement, both the Knights and the typographers boycotted the paper and its advertisers. The difficulty with the *Iron Age* continued for nearly a year, with the paper finally agreeing to accept union employees. Upon this agreement, which was not for the closed shop the typographers desired, the Knights ceased their opposition to the paper. [36]

In the spring of 1886, the Richmond area experienced several strikes, most of which probably involved members of the order and some of which were instigated by the Knights. On March 11, the Knights struck the National Cotton Compress Company because it paid black Knights employed there less than white members received. This rare display of racial solidarity ended in defeat. Ironically, the company replaced the strikers with black labor. On April 1, members of a number of trades—among them hod carriers, painters, and coopers—struck for increased wages. The city's contractors met and decided to refuse the demands of the construction trades members. But the strike was effective; and by mid-April the contractors decided that each individual contractor should respond to the wage demands as they saw fit, a clear victory for the strikers. At the same time, nearly two hundred paving stone cutters struck a granite quarry, requesting higher pay. Their efforts, however, proved unsuccessful. [37]

Although striking Knights rarely engaged in violence, a strike by dockhands at Newport News provides a classic example of nineteenth century labor violence. On January 11, 1887, freight handlers, coal stokers, and trimmers demanded that the Newport News and Mississippi Valley Railroad increase their wages from ten to fifteen cents per hour. The railroad, a subsidiary of the Chesapeake and Ohio, apparently owned the docks. Management refused the request, declaring that unless all workers returned to their jobs by January 13, they would be permanently discharged. Management also began recruiting strikebreakers. The strikers responded the next day by marching en masse to the piers to prevent the strikebreakers from working. A riot ensued, resulting in the burning of a hotel and casino across from the docks. Governor Fitzhugh Lee dispatched black National Guard troops from Richmond to quell the disturbance, an action protested by the Knights in Newport News and Norfolk. Lee's use of black troops was probably prompted by the fact that most of the strikers were black.

Meanwhile, the Knights had appointed a committee to negotiate with the railroad. Management consented to the meeting, which was held January 14. Once again the Knights negotiated a "compromise" more favorable to management than to the order. The railroad agreed to retain the strikers "without prejudice" and promised to "consider" wage increases for the poorest paid laborers. The strikers returned to work and the governor withdrew the national guard, although city police and "special deputies" remained on duty. [38]

Black stevedores also engaged in a brief strike in Wilmington, North Carolina, in September 1886. A stevedoring contractor contracted to load a steamer with cotton and pay wages of from four to five dollars per day. The stevedores, members of at least two Knights of Labor locals, refused to work unless the contractor could guarantee their wages. They believed the shipper would fail to pay the wages promised. The contractor refused and brought in Negro strikebreakers from Norfolk. The Wilmington Knights, however, prevailed upon the newly recruited laborers to refuse the job and return home. The contractor then agreed to approach the shipper about wage guarantees, and the Knights returned to work. [39]

In urban areas across the South, skilled laborers other than typographers employed the boycott in their efforts to redress economic grievances. Knights in Raleigh and Durham boycotted a shoe manufacturer who used convict labor. In Winston-Salem, Knights boycotted firms that employed scab labor. Southern Knights also supported boycotts against northern firms which were called by the national or northern district and local assemblies. Richmond area Knights, for example, enforced the order's boycott of the Stetson Hat Company. [40]

Birmingham Knights carried out a long and costly boycott against a local clothier. The order eventually won but paid a high price for the victory. A Birmingham assembly, the Germania, supported the decision of tailors employed by E. M. Costello to refuse wages below those paid in other firms. Costello locked the tailors out, and the Germania Assembly issued a circular accusing Costello of operating a sweatshop. J. J. Holland, sent by the G.E.B. to investigate the matter, reached an agreement with Costello which called for the state assembly to condemn the local for issuing their circular illegally. Costello then claimed the state assembly had exonerated him, which was not the case; and Germania Assembly complained to the state and national executive boards.

When the state board, through the *Sentinel*, notified the membership that they had not in fact exonerated Costello, he filed suit against the board and the *Sentinel*, charging that the *Sentinel* story was a boycott notice and, as such, a criminal conspiracy. His action brought Holland back to Birmingham in July, and he succeeded in obtaining a settlement out of court. Costello agreed to hire Knights at standard wages. The order had won the battle but in the process had created severe tensions between the Germania local and the state offices. [41]

A planned strike by Mississippi fish cannery workers provides an excellent illustration of the dissension created by the strike issue between locals and the G.E.B. and between the rank and file and the national leadership. Cannery workers in the Biloxi area rushed into the order in 1886, hoping it could bring them immediate economic benefits. They found that membership bestowed no economic blessings and so prepared to take more drastic action. Local 10,093 twice requested permission to strike from the G.E.B. and twice received no response. Taking matters into their own hands, local members voted to strike for increased wages on November 1, 1887. Over one thousand laborers left their jobs, many of whom were not members of the Knights. Again, the local requested the G.E.B.'s permission to strike, but after the fact. This time the board responded, sending William

Bailey to Biloxi. Bailey and local Knights met with representatives of the Seafood Shippers and Packers Association but made no progress. Bailey advised the strikers to return to work and lectured the local on the need to "act according to the rules of the Order." In his report to the G.E.B., he simply called for a lecturer or instructor to visit the area in order to better inform members of the order's principles. [42]

The Knights' most spectacular industrial strike occurred in the textile industry. Southern textile workers from Virginia to Mississippi joined the order, but it was in the urban textile centers that the Knights were most successful. Completely controlling the rural mill village, management supplied housing, education, religion, and sometimes medical care. Management doled out the daily essentials of life through the company store. Thus in the more isolated rural villages, management was frequently able to disrupt any union activity before the workers could organize enough to contemplate resistance. But textile workers in urban areas, like skilled tradesmen or foundry workers, were far more independent of management in their daily lives. As a result, they were able to organize more thoroughly than their rural colleagues.

As the principal industry of the New South movement, the textile industry best reflected the extreme laissez-faire and antiunion concepts of southern entrepreneurs. Textile mill owners responded to the Knights with unyielding hostility, determined to crush any efforts by their workers to organize. As a result, textile workers, unlike the Knights in other industries, never achieved even partial or temporary victory in a direct confrontation with management.

The Knights' first skirmish with textile firms occurred in Augusta, Georgia, one of the South's major textile centers, in November of 1884. Smarting from a decline in the price of cotton goods, an Augusta firm initiated wage reductions. Led by a few Knights, the entire work force struck in protest. The mill president locked out the strike's ringleaders and offered to take the other workers back. His divide-and-conquer tactics worked, and the strike was broken. [43] No further trouble occurred between the Knights and textile firms during the following year. But as textile markets began to improve in 1886, management faced an increasingly restive labor force, anxious for restorations of wage cuts experienced in the preceding two years. In April 1886, Knights at Vaucluse, South Carolina, just North of Augusta, unsuccessfully petitioned management for wage increases. The order also continued to recruit members from the textile mills of the southern Piedmont. [44]

Alarmed by the growth of the order, textile manufacturers began planning to "nip in the bud" any "Yankee-inspired" organizational activity which could "demoralize" their labor force. No uniform approach resulted, and the first half of 1886 saw a variety of reactions to the order. In Columbus, Georgia, the Knights obtained a 10 percent wage increase for over two thousand employees without resorting to a strike. Unexpectedly faced with an organized labor force, management, with sales increasing, decided not to fight. Knights in Burlington, North Carolina, sought Powderly's permission to strike for an eleven-hour day. As usual, Powderly advised caution, telling the local to continue to recruit members, in secret, until it could confront management with a thoroughly organized work force. In Wesson, Mississippi, management moved first, discharging members of the order. Again, Powderly advised the workers not to resist but to continue to organize secretly. Faced with an intransigent employer and an unsympathetic national leadership, the assembly in Wesson collapsed. Knights in Alabama and Mississippi boycotted the Wesson Cotton Mills, but to no avail. [45]

The decisive struggle between the Knights and the South's textile firms occurred in Augusta in 1886. Organized and led by the Reverend J. Simmons Meynardie, a former minister from Charleston, South Carolina, the Augusta textile trade Local 5030 claimed over two thousand members. Three mixed assemblies in the city also probably contained a number of textile workers. Throughout the spring of 1886, the Augusta Knights engaged in a series of petty disputes with several of the city's nine textile firms; but beneath the seeming insignificance of the issues involved lay the workers' unannounced expectations of pay increases. Tensions between management and the order increased when Meynardie attended the May special session of the General Assembly in Cleveland and publicly attacked the mills for their low wages, long hours, and employment of child labor. Papers throughout the nation carried his charges, infuriating the owners of the Augusta firms.

On June 11, the discharge of a Knight employed at the Algernon Mills prompted a brief strike. Management agreed to retain the worker involved. The following month, Knights at the King Mill walked off the job, demanding a 20 percent pay increase and claiming they were paid less than employees in neighboring mills. Mill officials responded with a "conditional" 10 percent raise, and the workers returned to their jobs. At this point, Knights in other mills demanded a similar 10 percent raise. On July 9, the president of the Augusta Mills, Charles Phinizy, posted a notice stating that no wage increases would be forthcoming. Rank and file Knights reacted by striking immediately, despite Meynardie's words of caution, throwing some six hundred people out of work. In keeping with the order's antistrike policy, Meynardie attempted to arbitrate the matter. He arranged a meeting between Phinizy, the Knights' local leadership, and William Mullen, sent to Augusta by the G.E.B. Phinizy, however, remained firm in his refusal to grant any wage increases. [46]

With the failure of the arbitration efforts, the situation in Augusta worsened rapidly. Knights at the Enterprise Mills struck for a 10 percent raise but returned to work at Mullen's request. Intending to create a test case, however, Mullen authorized a strike against the Augusta Mills for a 10 percent increase. By sending the Enterprise hands back to work and keeping the Augusta workers out, Mullen was obviously sending mill owners a message of labor solidarity. But rank and file unrest flared again when, in late July, workers struck the Sibley Mills, closing the plant. Meanwhile, mill owners in Augusta and Horse Creek Valley, South Carolina, just across the Savannah River from Augusta, had formed the Southern Manufacturer's Association in preparation for a confrontation with the Knights. On August 7, area mill owners revealed the formation of the association and announced that unless the strikers returned to work by August 10, all Augusta mills would close the following day. [47]

Stunned by the association's announcement, Meynardie and the leadership of Local 5030 nevertheless began preparations for a protracted strike-lockout. Meynardie realized that the strike was crucial to the order in the textile industry and that to win, the local must receive both moral and financial support from the national. He informed Powderly that South Carolina owners had forbidden their workers to aid the Augusta strikers on threat of discharge. He warned that "if they [the owners] force us to disband by starving out our members; and force them to terms by lockouts and boycotts, then we are done. Then with bitter wail may we chant the requiem of our noble—our dearly beloved order, in the South." Meynardie noted that the mills had few surplus goods and could be beaten, and he begged for aid. "Do give us all the help you can—don't let us sink! It will not take a great deal to carry us—we have carried 650 strikers and families on three and four hundred dollars a week." He estimated that over three thousand operatives would be thrown out of work by the lockout. Mullen, who had returned to Richmond, agreed with Meynardie that "the result of this conflict means Knights of Labor or no Knights of Labor in the South"; and he urged Powderly to support the Augusta workers. [48]

Both sides remained adamant. The Knights refused to return to work at the Augusta Mills, and all Augusta factories locked their doors on August 11. A three-month war of attrition followed their closing and gradually broke the order. The G.E.B. sent national Secretary-Treasurer Frederick Turner and Mullen on a second arbitration mission in mid-August. The mill owners held firm; and it, too, failed. Meanwhile, mill owners pressured local grocers to refuse credit to the strikers and laid plans to break the strike. Henry Hammett of South Carolina advised his Georgia colleagues in the association to "stamp out the Knights then and now, and make it amongst them [the workers] discreditable for one to admit that they ever belonged to the organization. When they get good and starved out and miserable and utterly ruined, they will turn upon and murder Meynardie and other leaders of the organization." He proposed a standard wage scale for every mill in the area and an eviction policy to see that the scale was accepted. [49]

Meanwhile, the strikers' position was steadily deteriorating. Their funds were exhausted, and no aid had arrived from the national union. Meynardie appealed to Powderly again, asking that the order issue a circular calling for a special assessment to support the strike. Since the Knights' Assistance Fund was empty, the result of strikes throughout the nation, a special appeal was the only productive action the national could take. The G.E.B. finally approved such an appeal early in September, and $2,000 arrived in Augusta on September 15. It was too little too late. As days passed and no further aid arrived, the strikers' morale plummeted. Sensing weakness in the strikers' camps, the mill owners took the offensive. On September 20, they began a sys-

tematic policy of evicting strikers from company housing while opening several mills to nonunion labor.[50]

At this critical juncture, Meynardie left Augusta to attend the
General Assembly in Richmond. He undoubtedly hoped to obtain
additional funds, but his absence deprived the strikers of effective
leadership. Politics had been injected into the struggle prior to his departure and proved divisive. Some Knights endorsed an independent
labor ticket in the approaching municipal elections as a means of end-
ing the strike. Meynardie, however, endorsed the Democratic slate.
The specter of race raised at the Richmond General Assembly also
provoked dissension in the ranks.[51] Management pounced upon
press reports that the Knights supported "social equality" of the
races, and rumors that Negroes were to be hired swept the mill communities. Faced with social and economic racial fears, some Knights
began to renounce the union and return to work. The Augusta Mills
also began to recruit strikebreakers from South Carolina. Still, the
strikers did not panic. Most workers remained out, and those mills
which opened operated at a fraction of their capacity.[52]

A collapse in leadership soon broke the workers' declining will to
resist, however. Returning from Richmond to an almost impossible
situation after failing in his efforts to obtain additional funds, Meynardie evidently suffered a nervous breakdown. Other leaders proved
incapable of controlling the strikers. Rumors of strikebreakers, Negro
labor, and Meynardie's health flew everywhere. Combined with management's eviction policy and the lack of financial aid, they crushed
the workers' hopes; and increasing numbers accepted management's
terms and returned to work. Additional funds would have revived
morale; and because of the special appeal, these funds were available.
Yet the national had forwarded no funds since September 15, probably because Powderly, in his opposition to strikes, believed the struggle was doomed and wished it to end quickly. Rather than sending
money, the G.E.B. waited until the end of October to send James
Wright to investigate the strike and to achieve a settlement, if possible.[53]

Arriving on October 27, Wright found the strikers without adequate leadership, deeply indebted to local merchants, and without
funds. Many had been evicted from their homes. After agreeing to pay
over $30,000 of the local relief committee's bills, he decided to negoti-

ate the best settlement possible. Surprisingly, the mill presidents met with Wright; and a six-point agreement was reached. This agreement, which meant almost total defeat for the Knights, called for: (1) the abolition of "passes" within the mill and other petty tyrannies, (2) no discrimination against Knights when the mills reopened, (3) no rent on company housing from August 11 to November 6, (4) an arbitration committee of management and workers (not necessarily Knights) to settle future grievances, (5) a promise by workers not to strike or boycott when fellow employees were "fired for cause," and (6) the reopening of the mills on November 8. In a strike-lockout that had lasted nearly three months and cost the Knights, local and national, over $60,000, the order in Augusta had been effectively curbed. [54]

The Augusta strike destroyed textile locals in the surrounding region as well. During the strike, owners of three South Carolina plants summarily dismissed all known Knights in their labor force. The workers, aware of the situation in Augusta, accepted the dismissals without protest. [55] Furthermore, the Augusta defeat generated disruption throughout the southern order. Meynardie and other local leaders felt they had been betrayed by the national leadership. Mullen of Virginia believed Wright had sold out the Augusta strikers and blamed the national order's failure to support the strike financially on an antisouthern bias. [56] The bitterness engendered by the strike made it impossible to rebuild the order in Augusta. And partially because of the Augusta defeat, textile locals in other Georgia towns—including Atlanta, Macon, and Columbus—gradually faded into oblivion. [57]

After the Augusta strike, the Knights never presented a real threat to southern textile manufacturers. The few confrontations that occurred all resulted in disaster for the locals involved. In April 1887, workers struck a mill in Swepsonville, North Carolina, in an attempt to force management to reduce the workweek from seventy-five to sixty-six hours. The strike failed, and the local was destroyed. [58] Knights of Clifton, South Carolina, struck in September 1887 when their employer instituted a policy of discharging all known members. Management responded with the Augusta plan, locking out all employees and evicting Knights from company housing. The G.E.B. ignored the local's appeals for aid, and the strike and the local collapsed. [59] At approximately the same time, management of a Fishing Creek, South Carolina, mill locked out all Knights. T. B. Barry, sent by the G.E.B. to investigate the situation, could only recommend that the order boycott the firm. Management, meanwhile, destroyed the local by encouraging a vigilante organization to attack union members and by evicting Knights from company housing. [60] The following year, management successfully initiated a similar policy against Knights at a plant in Greenville, South Carolina. [61] When, during the same year, Knights employed at a mill in Cottondale, Alabama, protested the actions of a drunken foreman, management responded by locking out union employees and reducing wages. Although the state assembly boycotted the firm, the local was destroyed. [62]

Although urban Knights and those in industries located in rural areas, for example, cotton and lumber mills, engaged in strikes and boycotts, the orders' rural members seldom did. Not a single agricultural strike occurred in the seven states under consideration, even though, especially after mid-1887, much of the orders' membership was rural and black. The only significant strike involving agrarian labor occurred in Louisiana's sugar parishes in 1887.

Knights from New Orleans had organized many of the sugarcane workers of the surrounding countryside, a large majority of whom were black. During 1886, several work stoppages occurred in the low country as Knights struck for increased wages. A series of strikes early in that year forced unprepared planters to increase wages from sixty-five to seventy-five cents a day. But in the fall of 1886, several plantations successfully resisted demands for wage increases, defeating a number of small strikes at harvest time.

The cane cutters' failure to achieve increases in the fall of 1886 did not reduce organizational activity during the next year. By the next harvest season, D.A. 194 of New Orleans, to which most of the plantation workers belonged, felt strong enough to directly challenge area planters. The cane cutters demanded increases to raise their daily wage to at least $1.25. This time planters were prepared; and acting in unison, they refused the demand. The Knights left the fields in early October, and the strike spread through several sugar parishes. By early November, over ten thousand laborers had left their jobs. The planters sought to break the strike by employing white strikebreakers. The strikers, overwhelmingly black, used threats of violence to prevent strikebreakers from working; and the planters turned to the state for help.

In response to the planters' requests, the governor ordered out a company of thirty men from the Louisiana Field Artillery. Equipped with a Gattling gun, the artillery company was also supported by several local militia units and sheriffs' posses. One parish activated eleven militia units. Unleashed against the strikers, the formidable military force produced predictable results. In a series of clashes throughout the sugar country, over thirty blacks were killed, according to "official" records. It is probable that at least twice that number died. [63] The militia's policy of indiscriminate killing crushed the strike by the end of November. The defeat destroyed the order in the sugar country. In a letter to General Secretary John Hayes a year after the strike, a member reported that "all our members has [sic] been squandered ever since the strike here in the sugar districts." [64] The Louisiana cane workers received no aid from the national order. Furthermore, the strike was not mentioned at the General Assembly of 1887.

Throughout the South, the Knights' strike activity followed a general pattern. As the order grew in membership, particularly after the successful strike against the Gould southwest rail system, rank and file members sought to use what they perceived as the strength of the order's reputation in order to achieve immediate changes in their economic status. Rather than being opposed to strikes and docile, rank and file southerners were much more eager to strike than their conservative national leadership, just as were Knights in other regions of the country. A Mississippi Knight expressed the sentiments of many of the rank and file when he wrote Powderly: "we all know that strikes is wrong but what must we do, do just what the factory men say if so it was no use of Organizing a lodge of K. of L. in this place and if we are not recognized any better at the headquarters of our Order, we had better disband." [65]

Several other trends emerge from the strike activity of the southern Knights which, like their willingness to strike, parallel developments within the order in other parts of the country. First, it is significant that southerners engaged in more offensive than defensive strikes, again an indication that they were not docile. That is, most of their strikes were to achieve improved wages, hours, or working conditions rather than to prevent the implementation of managerial policies which would result in a deterioration of the status quo. Of the twenty-two strikes initiated, thirteen were offensive and nine defensive. The larger, more significant strikes—including the 1886 Augusta strike, the 1887 cane cutters strike, and the 1887-88 Mississippi lumber strikes—were all offensive actions. This trend toward aggressive strikes seems even greater when one notes that four of the order's defensive strikes occurred during the depression years from 1883 to 1885, including a series of strikes by Alabama miners, the 1884 Augusta textile strike, and the telegraphers strike of 1884. With but two exceptions, the defensive strikes sought to force management to refrain from implementing proposed reductions in wages. And with a single exception, which did not involve wages, all ended in defeat.

While most strikes ended in failure, offensive strikes fared better than the defensive actions. The Knights won four of their offensive strikes—two in the Mississippi lumber region, the 1886 Richmond construction workers' strike, and the Wilmington longshoremen's strike of the same year. The Augusta strike might be called a qualified success, for it won managerial recognition of the union. These victories occurred largely because the order took management by surprise. They were all, with the exception of the Augusta strike, the first confrontation between management and the Knights. The order's only successful defensive strike, that of Alabama miners to stop the employment of immigrant labor, was also an early contest with mine owners.

After the order's initial success in each industry, however, management closed ranks and moved to destroy the Knights. This pattern is clearly discernible in the mining, lumber, and textile industries. By late 1885, mine operators had resumed hiring immigrants; and miners suffered defeats in their efforts to obtain wage increases in 1887 and 1888. Lumbermen crushed the order in Mississippi in 1889, and textile mill owners acted after the Augusta incident to destroy the order in that industry. Once management decided to move against the order, it did so with force. The lockout, eviction, strikebreakers, and racial prejudice provided them with potent weapons. If violence threatened, or if all else failed, management could always appeal to the state for the militia, as was the case in the Louisiana sugarcane strike and the Newport News longshoremen's strike.

The Knights' temporary successes reveal something about the order's antagonists. Management was more inclined to yield on issues other than wages. Only once did striking Knights force wage increases, in the Richmond construction workers' strike of 1886; and that was a partial victory. Mississippi lumber workers gained shorter hours; Alabama miners briefly halted the employment of immigrant labor; and Wilmington dock workers obtained assurances that wages promised would be paid. But never in the mining, lumber, textile, or iron industries did management agree to increase wages because of strike activity. Management realized that cheap labor was the cornerstone of the region's industrial development and was determined that this foundation be maintained intact.

Their strike activity demonstrates that, like Knights elsewhere, the southern rank and file held no coherent concept of a strike policy. Defensive strikes were spontaneous reactions to managerial policies, usually wage reductions or the discharge of union personnel. Such strikes were essentially emotional responses, void of any planning; and with one exception, these ventures ended in defeat. As such, they conformed to the workers' tendency to react to an immediate economic threat with an immediate, direct response. But the Knights frequently engaged in offensive strikes without serious deliberation and with few, if any, provisions for the long-term requirements of such actions. The Augusta strike, the Louisiana sugarcane strike, and the 1887-88 Alabama miners' strikes all exemplify this tendency. In each case, as soon as the order had organized a relatively large segment of the work force, the new members, hoping for support from the state and national assemblies, initiated offensive strikes. They did so without local financial resources, with no method of curtailing the employment of strikebreakers, with no assurances of support from outside the local or locals involved, and with no detailed strike plan. In each case, not surprisingly, they lost. This propensity of the rank and file for entering strikes unprepared prompts some sympathy for the caution of Powderly and other leaders, although they offered no viable alternative solution to the workers' immediate problems.

The Knights' tendency to strike without adequate preparation, at times in the face of certain defeat, cannot be explained by economic motives alone. Although it is true that economic motives initiated all strikes, both offensive and defensive, the laborers' self-concept contributed to the outbreak of strikes, especially defensive actions. Management would present laborers with policies that hurt them economically and affronted their dignity. To accept without struggle would have further demeaned the workers' sense of individual worth. Partially for this reason, workers struck even in hopeless circumstances. They struck because they believed action had to be taken. Otherwise, management would treat them more harshly, and they would also be deprived of their dignity. [66]

Yet another pattern found in the strikes of the order in the nation at large is to be found in those of the southern Knights. Since the order's national leadership sought long-term rather than immediate solutions to labor's problems, they responded to southern strikes as they did to strikes elsewhere, negatively. The leadership first sought to prevent a strike; and then, if it occurred, they tried to settle it quickly on the best terms available. On several occasions, representatives of the national order called off strikes or boycotts after receiving only verbal promises in meetings with management. Frequently, such "settlements" brought the laborers no real benefits. Thus when representatives sent by the G.E.B. "negotiated" the settlement of a strike or boycott, the locals involved often felt betrayed, and sometimes with good reason. J. J. Holland's handling of the Key West cigar makers' strike or the Costello boycott in Birmingham hardly inspired confidence in the rank and file. Powderly always advised restraint, to the point of urging Knights to disband rather than risk a strike to settle grievances. While usually merited, the national leadership's caution also insured failure when a more aggressive stance may have achieved success. In Augusta, for example, if more funds had been received throughout the strike, morale might have remained high. Under such circumstances, management, in a poor financial situation, might have granted a more generous settlement, even if it had not accepted the Knights' demand for an increase in wages.

Leadership at the state and district levels also sought to avoid strikes. State officers, too, accepted settlements that the rank and file believed were not in their best interest. Settlements negotiated for striking miners and ironworkers by Stack of Alabama proved unpopular with the rank and file; and Alabama Knights criticized the state assembly's role in the 1889 strike against lumber mill owners. Even local leaders advised caution. For example, the local leadership at Augusta and Newport News urged the rank and file of their city to refrain from strike action. However at the district and local levels, once the battle was joined, the leadership fought with all the resources at its command, as is evidenced in the strikes of the Augusta textile workers, the Louisiana cane cutters, and the miners of the Birmingham region.

The strikes and boycotts of the southern order gained few benefits for its members and instead contributed in large measure to the Knights' rapid decline. The combination of repeated failures, even after initial victories, discouragement from the national leadership, and less than aggressive leadership at the state level caused the rank and file to reassess the order's ability to deliver immediate benefits. After making that reassessment, many left the order in disappointment. They, like their fellow workers in other regions, had flocked to the order because it appeared strong enough to combat their employers, to obtain tangible concessions for its membership. Defeat taught them that a reform union led by a man who never called a strike, and was proud of that fact, offered little hope for the immediate advancement of the laboring class.

5 The Knights in Politics

THROUGHOUT the 1880s, the Knights of Labor maintained an official policy of political neutrality. Both ideology and practicality dictated the order's political stance. Many of the Knights' national leaders, including Powderly, believed the old National Labor Union failed because it had attempted to create a labor party. In order to succeed, they felt, a labor union should educate American laborers to economic truths. Once educated, labor could obtain reform legislation through existing political parties, any of which they could control through sheer force of numbers. The Knights were "to educate men first that they may educate parties and govern them intelligently and honestly." From a more pragmatic viewpoint, partisan politics carried an alarming disruptive potential. The Knights' membership contained representatives of practically every organized party. For the order to have endorsed an existing party or to have called for the creation of yet another would have ensured a split within its ranks.[1]

Yet many of the objectives the order sought—land reform, child labor bills, the eight-hour day, trust regulation, and immigration restriction—all required political action. Thus the order faced the delicate task of effecting political change in a nonpartisan manner. The political proclivities of many of the national leaders further complicated the task. Ralph Beaumont, Thomas Barry, and Richard Trevellick were all active Greenback-Labor party members; and in 1888, Charles Litchman resigned as general secretary in order to campaign for Benjamin Harrison.[2] Elected to the first of three terms as mayor of Scranton, Pennsylvania, on a Greenback-Labor ticket in 1878, Powderly was hardly in a position to discourage partisan politics and rarely did so as long as it was successful. On the whole, however, he tried to restrict the order's involvement in partisan politics to essentially educational issues. In 1882, for example, he encouraged locals to lobby for the creation of state bureaus of labor statistics. In 1886, at his suggestion, the order formed a National Legislative Committee, chaired by Ralph Beaumont, to lobby for the passage of congressional legislation favorable to labor. However, during the same period, local assemblies were even forbidden to allow political discussions.[3]

While the national leadership struggled to maintain a distinction between educational and partisan politics, the less ideologically oriented rank and file plunged headlong into the political fray. The "Great Upheaval" of 1886 saw southern Knights, like their colleagues in the North, challenge the established political order in local, state, and congressional elections. In their political activity, as with their strikes, the Knights sought immediate relief from very real economic grievances. Major reform issues received little attention, especially in local and state elections. And, as with their strike activity, the Knights achieved some minor (and in 1886, surprisingly major) victories. Their political triumphs were, however, temporary; before the end of the decade, humiliating political defeats had helped to shatter the order in the South.

With few exceptions, the first surge of political activity by the Knights came in the congressional elections of 1886, when the urban order was at peak strength. Knights in Virginia, North Carolina, and Florida supported labor candidates against incumbent Democratic congressmen and won two of the four seats they contested. In each state, prominent, ambitious Knights, three of whom were newspapermen, used the order to launch or further their political careers.

During the 1880s, Florida had but two House seats and was divided into eastern and western districts by a line that ran from the Keys to the Georgia border. This division placed two of the state's largest urban areas, Pensacola and Key West (at that time, Key West was second in population only to Jacksonville), each with strong local assemblies, in the first congressional district. The strength of the order in the district's two urban centers presented a possibility for political advancement that was recognized by C. B. Pendleton, a leading figure in the Florida Knights. Publisher and editor of the *Equator*, a Spanish-English paper in the Key West area, Pendleton was master workman of Key West Local 4791 and a man of ambition. He was a leader in forming the Florida state assembly, created in Jacksonville in September 1886. Prior to the creation of the state assembly, he served as recording secretary of District Assembly 131, Key West, which was then the only district in Florida. The newly formed state assembly rewarded Pendleton's efforts by electing him chairman of the state executive board. [4]

Hoping to use the Knights as the base for a successful reform coalition, Pendleton entered the congressional lists against the Democratic incumbent, R. H. Davidson, a ten-year veteran of the office. In an effort to maintain a portion of the Democratic vote, Pendleton ran as a "reform Democrat" opposed to railroad monopolies. But he also gained support from the Republicans, who agreed not to field a candidate. However, the Republicans evidently offered Pendleton no financial aid; and his personal resources proved inadequate to finance a campaign. Desperate, in September, Pendleton appealed to Powderly for funds from the Knights. He suggested a general appeal to the order of fifty cents per capita to provide the necessary funds. Powderly met with Pendleton's "representative," probably Mark S. White of Pensacola, at the Richmond General Assembly. His reply was negative; his personal reaction to Pendleton's affrontery can only be surmised. Without funds, Pendleton was never able to mount a serious campaign, and Davidson was reelected by a wide margin. [5]

In North Carolina, the campaign of State Master Workman John Nichols, Independent congressional candidate from the fourth district, thrust the Knights into politics with a stunning upset victory. Comprised of eight counties concentrated about a Raleigh-Durham axis, the fourth congressional district encompassed the political heart of the state. It was also the area of the Knights' greatest strength; locals in Raleigh alone claimed over fifteen hundred members. [6]

A more nearly perfect example of an ambitious, young, shrewd politician than John Nichols could hardly have been found within the order's ranks. Established as a printer in Raleigh before the Civil War, Nichols used his press to print songs and poems for Union troops when the South fell. In the gubernatorial election of 1868, he supported the successful candidacy of William W. Holden, leader of the state's Radical Republicans. Under Holden, his printing firm became the largest in the city. He was also awarded the principalship of the North Carolina Institute for the Deaf, Dumb, and Blind. After the defeat of the Republicans in the 1876 gubernatorial race, Nichols obtained federal appointive offices. He was appointed revenue stamp agent in Durham by President Hayes and postmaster in Raleigh under President Arthur. In addition, he became a leader of the state's Masonic order, serving as grand master. He was also secretary of the state Agricultural Society, whose officers and supporters included several of the state's most influential political figures, both Democrats and Republicans. Nichols almost certainly joined the Knights in 1884 hoping eventually to use the order to enhance his political career.[7]

Grover Cleveland's election left Nichols unemployed; but Nichols's election as state master workman, coupled with the order's strength in the fourth district, presented obvious political possibilities. When the state's Republicans, in an effort to deprive the Bourbon Democrats of the issues of race and radicalism, decided to support Independent congressional candidates, the possibilities improved. Fourth district Democrats, meanwhile, had nominated John Graham, a lawyer and former member of both the state house and senate.[8]

Nichols announced his candidacy in a printed address which stressed the plight of the workingman, rural and urban. He advocated federal and state legislation to limit working hours, outlaw child labor, and facilitate the organization of labor. He also called for federal regulation of railways and currency, the enactment of uniform federal bankruptcy laws, more equitable land policies, and stricter immigration legislation. Citing ignorance as labor's chief enemy, Nichols supported the Blair Bill. He blamed the Democrats for the bill's defeat, noting that southern congressmen had been instrumental in the election of a Democratic Speaker of the House who opposed the bill. He denounced the internal revenue taxes, especially those on tobacco, as major burdens on North Carolina farmers. On the tariff issue, Nichols argued that protection provided jobs for laborers and markets for farmers. His policies were framed specifically for the farm-labor vote, and Nichols often compared the Knights to the Farmers' Alliance and the Arkansas Wheel. He defended his decision to run as an Independent by maintaining that neither of the old parties represented the people. And, he reasoned, if enough Independents were elected to hold the balance of power in the organization of Congress, concessions could be extracted from one of the major parties.[9]

Faced with a potential labor-farm-Republican coalition, the Democrats launched a campaign to hold the Knights within the party. The Democratic party was presented as the workers' true friend, the Republican as the traditional party of big business and foe of labor. Democratic congressional candidate John Graham inveighed against the tariff, internal revenue taxes, and the defeat of the Blair Bill, all of which he attributed to the Republicans. The Democratic press branded Independents "the posthumous bastards of the Republican Party" and amply aired Nichols's association with Radical Republicans. Nichols, charged the press, sought to prostitute the Knights in order to retain the position, power, and income to which he had become accustomed as a Republican political appointee. Some Knights agreed. In their attacks on Nichols, however, the Democrats often expressed sympathy with the Knights' ideals and carefully avoided direct criticism of the order, except for its racial policies. [10]

Sniping at the national order's liberal racial policies began early in the campaign but was usually coupled with criticism of Nichols's support of Negro Reconstruction politicians. As the campaign climaxed, events at the Knights' General Assembly, held at Richmond in October, pushed the racial issue to the fore. When delegates from New York City insisted that Richmond's hotels and theaters accept their black member, the Richmond papers created a furor. North Carolina's Democratic press immediately pounced upon the issue. The *News and Observer* condemned Grand Master Workman Terence Powderly's liberal racial views, warned that Nichols hoped to use the Knights to spread "negrophilism," and asked voters to "repudiate Mr. Nichols and the vile propaganda of social equality." [11]

The last minute racial scare tactics failed. Economic grievances held firm the ranks of Nichols's white labor and farm supporters. Blacks, who represented 30 percent of the district population, voted heavily, especially in the Raleigh-Durham area. The labor-farm-Republican coalition gave Nichols a majority of over fifteen hundred votes, which sharply contrasted with the 1884 gubernatorial candidate's loss of the district by more than four thousand votes. In an astute assessment of the election, Josephus Daniels, editor of the highly partisan Democratic paper, the *State Chronicle*, credited Nichols's victory to the Knights' solid Negro support, continued hard times despite Democratic promises of relief, the retention of excise taxes under Cleveland, and apathy resulting from the fact that neither the governorship nor the presidency was involved. He also declared war on the Knights for as long as they remained in politics, "arraying poor against rich, educated against ignorant . . . and pander[*ing*] to the prejudice against lawyers."12

In Virginia, the Knights supported two congressional candidates in the 1886 elections. Both were Democrats who ran as Independents seeking labor's vote, and both ran in districts with large urban areas containing several local assemblies. In the sixth district, a hill country district with few blacks, Lynchburg and Roanoke provided the nucleus of urban assemblies. Richmond and its environs comprised the heart of the third district. The area of the Knights' greatest numerical strength, Richmond also contained a large and politically active black population. The order triumphed in the sixth district, but it failed to win in the confusing and emotional third district race.

Led by members of the Knights, a convention of Independent reformers in the sixth district met at Lynchburg in September to nominate a congressional candidate. The convention, which included former Radical Republicans, Independents, and Knights, both black and white, nominated Joseph B. Page. This nomination evidently caused trouble among the ranks of the Roanoke Knights, who favored a Democratic candidate. As a result, on October 3, Page withdrew from the race, for he believed it was "sheer folly" for labor to attempt to place an Independent in Congrress.13

The Roanoke Knights' objections to Page probably reflected Democratic charges that Page was a candidate of the "Black Republicans" and the forces of William Mahone. One of the South's railroad magnates, Mahone had formed a powerful anti-Bourbon political force in 1879 based upon the repudiation of the state debt. In an effort to retain his power after being elected to the Senate in 1881, Mahone aligned his organization with the Republicans in exchange for control of federal patronage in Virginia. Although the Mahonites were defeated in the elections of 1883, Mahone remained a power in state politics. Labor in the sixth district believed that a "purer" candidate for Congress was necessary. They decided upon Samuel T. Hopkins, a Maryland native, Confederate veteran, and Lynchburg dry goods merchant. Hopkins, who ran as a "reform Democrat," stressed his loyalty to both the Democratic party and the Knights of Labor.

Meanwhile, the regular Democrats had nominated Samuel Griffen. The Republicans, despite Hopkins's nomination to replace Page, the Independent candidate of their choice, declared in favor of Hopkins. Some Democratic Knights remained disgruntled, however; and although Hopkins's nomination was an obvious effort to attract Democratic Knights to the reform ticket, some members, especially in the Roanoke area, supported Griffen.[14]

A number of factors combined to make Hopkins a contender. With no Republican opposition, he stood to gain the GOP vote by default, as well as most of the black vote. By stressing that "I am for the workingman above all things, but still a Democrat," he hoped to draw support from white Democratic workers, especially the Knights. Democratic apathy also aided his campaign. Despite warnings that apathy could produce an upset, the Democrats expected to win the election by from 4,000 to 5,000 votes. Realizing that a campaign slip might hurt him, Hopkins refused to canvass the district. His assessment proved correct. On election day, Hopkins squeaked into office by a majority of but 505 votes largely because the Democrats failed to create enough interest in the race to turn out the party faithful. In a close contest, the support of the majority of the district's Knights put Hopkins into office.[15]

The congressional race in the third district provides an excellent example of the complexity of postwar southern politics. In the spring of 1886, a slate of Independent candidates swept into office in five of Richmond's six wards in a hotly contested municipal election. The victory was achieved by a coalition of Knights, Republicans, and Independents. The success of the municipal ticket prompted area Knights to consider supporting a congressional candidate in the fall. The reformers' municipal election victory also caused the regular Democrats to revise their strategy. The Democrats nominated incumbent George D. Wise, who, though not a Knight, maintained that he had been such a friend of labor that he had "claims upon the workingmen which perhaps no other aspirant could set up." Third district Democrats also adopted a resolution calling for tax reforms to benefit labor. Frightened by the Richmond election, regular Democrats groomed their candidate and tailored their platform to appeal to the labor vote. As a result, when the Knights called a labor convention for

September 10 in Richmond, the *Richmond Dispatch* speculated that the order would vote to endorse Wise's candidacy. [16]

The labor convention, composed of five delegates from every local in the third district and the two district assemblies, one white and one black, met on September 10 as scheduled. Delegates represented over forty locals, most of which were located in the Richmond area. The majority were blacks. The convention refused to endorse Wise and nominated its own candidate, William Mullen, editor of the *Labor Herald*. Thirty-six years old, Mullen was a Virginia native and, in addition to his membership in the Knights, was also a member of Tyopgraphical Union Local 90. Mullen's nomination came as no real surprise; he had for some time indicated a willingness to run. Some Knights, especially those from the small towns surrounding Richmond, resented the order's blatant political activity; and over thirty delegates walked out of the convention upon Mullen's nomination. [17]

Mullen undoubtedly believed that the Republicans would either endorse him or at least refrain from entering a candidate. But Richmond Republicans, especially blacks, felt that the Knights had mistreated Republican members after their victory in the municipal elections. Leading Republicans called for the nomination of their own congressional candidate, arguing that the GOP had lost the district by less than fifteen hundred of thirty thousand votes cast in 1884. With Mullen drawing support from some Democratic Knights, these Republicans felt their party could win. On September 15, a Richmond Republican convention agreed and decided to nominate a candidate, if they could convince the entire district to do so. In early October, a convention of third district Republicans was held. Delegates refused to endorse Mullen by a vote of sixty-four to twenty-four. They chose as the GOP candidate Edmund Waddill, Jr., a member of Mahone's old Readjuster party, a former United States district attorney, and a member of the Henrico County state legislative delegation. Meanwhile, a group of Democratic Knights, mostly whites, convened in a rump session and voted to support Wise. Speaking to the group, Wise promised to support a bill creating a federal bureau of statistics and to carry his campaign to the working class. [18]

The nomination of a Republican candidate and the defection of some of the Democratic Knights to Wise practically insured Mullen's defeat, but even more trouble lay ahead. On September 28, a grand jury indicted Mullen and other labor leaders for criminal conspiracy in connection with a boycott against Baughman Printers.[19] On the heels of the indictment, the Knights' General Assembly convened in Richmond on October 5. The G.A. destroyed any chance of a Mullen victory. Attended by black and white delegates, the G.A. raised the spector of race among local Knights when a black New York delegate was refused accomodations by local hotels and theaters.[20] The *Richmond Dispatch* seized the racial issue, advising Southern Knights to "get out of it [the order] as soon as possible" before they were contaminated by what the *Dispatch* called the Knights' advocacy of "social equality." Although Powderly tried to quiet the tempest by explaining that the Knights had no intention of violating southern traditions, the damage had been done. Faced with Republican and Democratic opposition, under indictment for conspiracy, and hampered by political and racial dissension within the Knights' ranks, Mullen decided to withdraw from the contest. Three days before the election, on October 30, he announced his decision, citing the impossibility of his election and his desire to prevent a Republican victory. He endorsed George Wise and urged labor to support the Democratic ticket.[21]

With Mullen out of the contest and racial prejudices inflamed by events at the General Assembly, Richmond's labor vote split along racial lines. Black Knights supported Waddill, whites backed Wise. Wise carried the district by a vote of 7,447 to 5,344. The animosity created by the campaign, both political and racial, proved to be the beginning of the end for the Richmond order.[22]

While the Knights' congressional victories were perhaps their most impressive, they succeeded more often at the municipal level. Municipal political activity was spread more uniformly throughout the southern order because neither state nor district assembly organizations were required for local political involvement. A strong local in a small town or several strong locals in a larger one could determine the outcome of an election. Also, Knights in urban areas could, and did, join with other reformers on specific local issues to defeat incumbent city administrations. The political activity of urban Knights demonstrated labor's ability to achieve limited goals and temporarily suppress racial prejudices. Unfortunately, temporary political gains were all too often squandered because victory led to dissension within the ranks of the order.

The Knights achieved one of their earliest and most significant municipal election upsets in Richmond in the spring of 1886. At that time, Richmond was the most thoroughly organized city in the South. Under Mullen's leadership, the order had established two district assemblies, number 84, white, and number 92, composed of black locals. Together they represented over forty locals, twelve of which were in Richmond proper; and each district contained over three thousand members. Buoyed by the rapid growth of the order and disappointed by the failure of the legislature to respond to the problems of urban labor, Richmond Knights were determined to use their potential political strength outside the ranks of the traditional parties in the municipal elections. Democrats feared a bolt by the Knights and made a desperate bid to hold them within the party. As early as February 1886, the *Dispatch*, a Democratic organ, reported that locals had decided not to participate in the election of the city council and noted the Democratic record of support of labor. 23

The Baughman boycott, meanwhile, created further concern about labor among the city's business leaders, so much so that in late February, a group called the Businessmen of Richmond met to discuss the boycott in particular and labor in general. They denounced the boycott and the Knights and issued the usual proclamation about the harmony existing between labor and capital. They also called for a state arbitration law that would be "fair" to all parties, a concept Mullen and the Knights rejected. In an obvious effort to prevent the entry of labor into politics, the businessmen also requested the state legislature to confine the use of convict labor to the upkeep of state roads and railroads, to create a bureau of labor, and to establish a Mechanics Institute in Richmond. 24

The appearance of Richard Trevellick, the Knights' national lecturer, in Richmond on March 8 further aroused the concerns of the business and political communities. Trevellick spoke to the Knights and at a public lecture which was well attended. The incumbent mayor welcomed Trevellick to the city and tried to allay any labor unrest. In a typical politician's effort to carry water on both shoulders, he deplored any clash between capital and labor while maintaining that labor had the right and the duty to speak out for its interests. 25

Despite the mayor's best efforts, hostility between labor and the business community increased rapidly. In March and April, a series of strikes involving foundry workers, typographers, cotton compress workers, hod carriers, painters, coopers, and quarry workers swept the city. That the hostility that caused and fed upon these strikes would spill over into the political arena was inevitable. On May 1, Richmond laborers, led by the Knights, held a preliminary meeting to decide upon a course of action for the upcoming election. They denounced the city council for catering to the interests of the wealthy and called "on all, regardless of former party affiliations, color, religion, or nationality, who labor . . . for their daily bread to co-operate with us in bringing about these much needed reforms." [26]

Responding to labor's call for reform on May 17, the Knights held a "working man's convention" attended by eighty-four delegates, seven from each of the city's twelve locals. Although the meeting was integrated, whites controlled the proceedings. After ratifying an obviously predetermined decision to enter a "reform" slate in the municipal campaign, the convention tackled its real task, the nomination of candidates for the thirty council seats, five from each of the city's six wards, and for the eighteen seats as aldermen, three from each ward. Since the convention contained blacks and whites, Democrats, Republicans, and Independents, negotiations were complicated. But the delegates finally reached an acceptable compromise and endorsed a slate that included blacks and whites, Democrats and Republicans. The majority of the candidates, however, considered themselves "reform Democrats." Most of the Republican slots on the ticket went to blacks who represented predominantly black wards. [27]

The ensuing campaign was a classical New South political contest. The Republicans, especially in the black-controlled Jackson ward, supported the "reform ticket" as a means of ousting the Bourbon Democrats who dominated city hall. The Knights and other labor organizations backed the reform ticket for specific economic reasons. Most important among them was the construction of a new city hall approved by the voters in 1882 but delayed because of political fighting among the incumbents. Organized labor wanted the hall built with "day" labor rather than contract labor, and they wanted to insure an increase in wages paid to day laborers. The labor ticket was also pledged to other labor demands—weekly payment in lawful money to all city employees, including day laborers, the prohibition of foreign contract laborers, the use of Virginia materials in all city construction, and rigid economy in government. In short, labor wanted its share of the municipal budget; and the construction of the new city hall alone called for an expenditure of $300,000. The regular Democrats, however, saw the reform ticket as an extension of the Republican party. Its election, they warned, would turn back the clock to the horrible era of Radical-Negro rule. [28]

Labor failed to respond to Democratic threats of Radical Republicanism, Mahoneism, and "Negro rule." Throughout the city, workers organized committees to support the reform ticket; and on election day, May 27, many in the city's labor force simply quit work to cast their ballots. The reform ticket swept to an easy victory, carrying five of the city's six wards. Two blacks, both from Jackson ward, were elected aldermen; and the ward also elected five blacks to the council. In the council, the reformers captured twenty-one seats; the regular Democrats held nine. Candidates for five of these nine had also been endorsed by the reformers, with the result that the Democrats actually elected only four council members on their own. [29]

Once in office, however, the reformers split into factions and began to squabble over the spoils. White Democratic reformers began to ignore the claims of blacks and Republicans. Blacks objected to the number of police positions they obtained, believing that they had been slighted. "Old Democrats" teamed with "reform Democrats" to return any incumbent appointed officials—including the city clerk, attorney, and engineer—to their positions. New jobs were usually awarded to white Knights of Labor. True to their promise, the reformers adopted the use of day labor in the construction of city hall and increased wages from $1.25 to $1.50 a day. But in the ultimate betrayal of the Republican and black supporters of the ticket, white Democratic reformers voted with old Democrats to ban the use of blacks on city construction projects. Thus racial prejudice, inflamed by the events of the General Assembly and the competition for jobs, demolished the coalition the Knights had constructed in order to capture city government. The black-white coalition that Bourbon Democratic cries of "Radical Republicanism" failed to prevent in the spring fell victim to the greed of white workers in the fall. [30]

Knights in Lynchburg followed their Richmond brethren into the thickets of municipal politics. In the mayor's race of 1886, James McLaughlin, an Irish Knight, challenged the incumbent Democrat, W. C. Mason. Running on an Independent ticket, McLaughlin lost by only 166 votes out of 3,221 cast.[31] Hopkins's election to Congress in the fall provided additional courage to Lynchburg laborers; and in the spring of 1887, the Knights decided to endorse a slate for the fifteen city council positions. Again, a coalition of white and black Knights, Republicans and Independents, defeated the Democrats, winning eleven of the fifteen positions. And again, the coalition broke down when the winners began to distribute the spoils. The new council placed Knights in practically all appointive positions, but aspiring officeholders outnumbered the available positions. Those Knights passed over became resentful. In addition, the council gave most of the positions to whites, embittering the black membership. By the end of 1887, feuds within the order initiated by political issues had become so bitter that one local had expelled a council member for failing to honor campaign pledges. Black and white members were so estranged that the district master workman had difficulty convincing the two races to meet in the same union hall. The internal warfare threatened the very existence of the order, and the G.E.B. finally recognized the seriousness of the problem and dispatched T. B. Barry to Lynchburg in an effort to stop the feuding. Barry arrived in the spring of 1888 and managed to calm the situation. In his report to the G.E.B. he recommended the creation of separate black and white districts, which was not done.[32] Barry's visit kept the order active in Lynchburg, but the disruption caused by its political involvement proved irreparable.

The Knights' most successful venture into municipal politics occurred in Jacksonville in 1887 when, in an election that mirrored the Richmond campaign of the year before, the Knights helped elect a reform ticket. As in Richmond, the election involved local issues and pitted incumbent Democrats against a coalition of reform Democrats, labor, blacks, and Republicans. Once elected, the reform ticket remained united, controlled appointments, and initiated a series of changes. But a combination of political and medical factors ended the reform regime in little more than a year.

Political prompting by civic boosterism and an interstate rivalry created an opportunity for the Knights to test their political influence in Jacksonville, the stronghold of the Florida order. In the winter of

1886-87, California opened tourist bureaus in Jacksonville and flooded the area with agents and propaganda. Jacksonville's citizens retaliated by planning to hold an Exposition in 1888 and requesting the legislature for an improved city charter which would incorporate several suburban towns into the city. Renewed civic pride also prompted the entry of a reform Democratic ticket in the municipal elections of April 1887. Headed by mayoralty candidate J. Q. Burbridge, a leader of the Board of Trade, the reform ticket defeated the regular Democrats. Burbridge's success represented a subdued revolt against "machine politics" and was clearly a part of an effort to create a "better Jacksonville." [33]

Meanwhile, the legislature granted Jacksonville a new charter, throwing the city into political turmoil. Throughout the summer and fall, various political factions sparred over the legality, practicality, and implementation of the charter, which called for elections in December. The city and county Democratic executive committees and the *Times Union*, one of two local papers, opposed the election and argued that the charter was unconstitutional. Reform Democrats, Republicans, the Board of Trade, organized labor, and the *Times Union* supported the charter. The issue became more complex because of the number of groups involved. In addition to the city and county executive committees of both parties, the Young Democrats, the Board of Trade, several citizens' committees, the Knights, and various trade unions contributed their views. Within this confused political situation, the Knights exerted their considerable influence, for they claimed their membership in the eleven Jacksonville locals represented two thousand votes. [34]

Although never an explicit issue, race relations lurked just beneath the surface of the city's frantic political activity. The areas annexed by the new charter were primarily black and gave blacks a majority of about three hundred in the voting population. The white reformers who secured the charter realized that it gave blacks potential control of the city government but hoped to "control" the black vote. Their organ, the *Times Union*, held an equally patronizing view of the Knights, which it praised as an "earnest, honest, just and prudent body of men" who avoided "quixotic agitations or boycotts or the like." In short, the *Times Union* expected both the blacks and the Knights to defer to the political judgment of the "better" people, under whose leadership the city would be purged of corruption and Democratic "ring" politics and would march into the world of progress. [35]

After a series of efforts to halt the implementation of the charter failed, the various political factions began to prepare for the December elections. At a citizens' meeting attended by over eight hundred persons, organized labor endorsed a reform ticket to be determined by a nonpartisan committee. Prior to this decision, the various factions had agreed that in the election, the ward inspectors in each of the nine wards would include a Republican, a Democrat, and a member of the Knights. This agreement recognized the political power of the order, for its choice of inspectors would determine who controlled the polling places. [36]

On December 5, a complex assemblage of warring factions shaped a nonpartisan ticket. Represented in the negotiations were county and city Democrats, county and city Republicans, the Board of Trade, two citizens' committees, the Knights, the cigar makers, and the carpenters. J. J. Holland, a leading figure in the order, was elected secretary of the meeting, again demonstrating the Knights' power. The group formed a twenty-eight-man committee empowered to select a ticket. The committee, comprised of equal representation from Republicans, Democrats, and organized labor, contained at least six Knights, all whites.

The new charter called for the election of two aldermen from each of nine wards. Of the eighteen men the committee nominated, nine were Republicans, nine Democrats. Ten were Knights, four of whom were white Democrats, three of whom were white Republicans, and three of whom were black Republicans. The Republican candidates also included two blacks who were not Knights. As the *Times Union* observed, labor and the Republicans had good reason to cheer the ticket, which was headed by mayoralty candidate C. B. Smith, a local merchant, a Republican, and a member of the Knights. [37]

Disgruntled Democrats, however, announced their own slate, which included some members of the Smith ticket. In an obvious bid for the labor vote, the Democratic slate retained all of the white Knights on the Smith ticket, along with a lone Republican, a black Knight. The other Republicans and the four Democrats on the Smith ticket who were not Knights were all replaced. Frank Pope led the

Democratic ticket, which was endorsed by the *News Herald*, the Young Democrats, and the city Democratic executive committee. [38]

The reform ticket overwhelmed the regular Democratic slate. Smith defeated Pope by a majority of 1,675 votes. Of the five blacks and thirteen whites elected to the council, three were Smith ticket Democrats, two of whom were Knights. All nine Republicans on the Smith ticket were victorious. Two candidates on the Pope ticket were elected, as were four Independents who ran on neither ticket, at least one of whom was black. Only two Knights on the Smith ticket were defeated, both white Democrats. The new council included eight Knights, three blacks and five whites. Organized labor, blacks, and Republicans had routed the Democrats of city hall. Democrats who ran under the Smith ticket fared far better than those on the Pope ticket. Since the Pope slate split the Democratic vote, the failure of some of the Smith ticket Democratic candidates can be attributed to the regular-reform Democratic split. [39]

In a surprise move, the defeated mayor and city council declared the election invalid and refused to surrender their seats. The stunned reform forces immediately initiated legal action to force their removal. After months of appeals, in March 1888, the Florida Supreme Court upheld the election; and the new mayor and council assumed office on March 29, 1888. [40]

Once seated, the new council revealed a remarkable solidarity, especially when the diversity of the membership is considered. The Knights endorsed ten candidates for appointive offices; eight received positions. Seven of the eight Knights on the council supported the three men chosen as police commissioners. But J. J. Holland failed in his bid for the municipal judgeship, receiving the votes of only two Knights, a white Democrat and a white Republican. The Knights on the council also supported Smith's program of reforms. They voted to expand the powers of the city health officer (largely because of past epidemics of yellow fever), to increase the salaries of municipal employees, and to enlarge the police force. Four Knights felt police salaries should be raised to levels above those recommended by Smith and adopted by the council. Voting on more mundane matters throughout the remainder of the year revealed no discernible pattern within the Knights' bloc on the city council, however. Nor did it indicate a partisan split between Democratic and Republican Knights. [41]

In addition to the regular tasks of government, the new council faced a major crisis soon after taking office. In the summer of 1888, a yellow fever epidemic struck Jacksonville, crippling the city's economy and draining its treasury. The local assemblies of the Knights worked to aid fever victims, as did other civic organizations. Jacksonville Knights appealed to the order at large and received several thousand dollars. But the money was slow in coming; and some members, unable to receive immediate support, deserted the order.[42] Several members of the council, all white, fled the city during the epidemic, thereby subjecting the city administration to criticism.

The disillusionment generated by the council's response to the epidemic spread to other areas. Critics renewed the Negro and carpetbagger rule issue. Others charged that the council was inept, that its reform programs would bankrupt the city. The charge of Negro rule undoubtedly hurt the most, for the new council had indeed given blacks a full share of the responsibilities of running the city. The municipal judge, fifteen of twenty-three patrolmen, two police sergeants, and the chairman of the board of police commissioners were black. During the yellow fever epidemic, hundreds of whites had fled the city, while the less affluent blacks remained. A house-to-house survey of the stricken city at the height of the epidemic in September revealed that only approximately four thousand whites remained, compared to ten thousand blacks. Many of the remaining blacks were Knights thrown out of work by the epidemic. In addition, the Knights, black and white, felt that they had been ignored by the relief organizations controlled by the town's "better" citizens, many of whom had departed the city. Thus the fever epidemic exaggerated racial and class distinctions and contributed to the council's growing unpopularity among whites, especially those of the upper and middle classes who had led the reform movement.[43]

Still, the Democratic regulars feared a direct challenge of the Knights-Republican-black reform coalition. Unable to control the election procedure and faced with a continued black majority, Democrats turned for help to the state legislature, which they dominated. They requested a new charter which would disenfranchise the entire population of Jacksonville, and the legislature granted their request. Under the new charter, the governor appointed the council, which in turn chose the mayor and other city officials.[44]

Faced with a fait accompli, the incumbent councilmen chose not to resist the inevitable. J. E. Spearing, a black Knight, expressed the feelings of his fellow council members by publicly announcing his contempt for the legislature's action. But he advocated turning the government over to the appointed council without a fight. On June 4, 1889, the new council took office. [45] The reform council had governed for hardly more than a year. It came to power on the crest of a wave of popular reform, its power derived from blacks, Knights, Republicans, several citizens' groups, and progressive Democrats. Like the Richmond and Lynchburg reform tickets, it failed to survive. The manner in which it met defeat, however, suggests that the coalition which placed it in power was still formidable in 1889.

The Knights also challenged Democratic administrations in smaller towns throughout the South. In Albany, Georgia, which had two assemblies, the Knights supported a successful mayoralty candidate in the spring of 1887. In the same year, the Knights of Athens, Georgia, failed in a determined effort to elect a slate of city officials. [46] Knights in the small towns of North Carolina were especially active in 1887, campaigning for "reform tickets" in Oxford, Burlington, Statesville, and Salisbury. In Oxford, which had at least two locals, one of which was black, a member of the order won the mayor's office. But in Burlington, where white textile workers comprised the single assembly, regular Democrats trounced the slate endorsed by the Knights. In Statesville, another town with at least one black local, the order supported a municipal ticket headed by a Republican candidate for mayor. Although an alderman won election, the Democrats captured the mayor's office; and the venture into politics united white opposition to the order. Rather than endorsing a reform slate, Salisbury Knights evidently supported individuals in both parties who seemed friendly to labor. Their attempt to reward friends and punish enemies at the polls failed and cost the order some support. [47]

In Alabama, where the order was strong in the mineral belt, the Knights achieved considerable success in municipal elections outside the major urban areas. Knights in Anniston, a coal and iron town just outside Birmingham, elected a labor slate to the city council by a large majority in January 1888. Truly representative of the working class, the council included a brick molder, watchmaker, shoemaker, carpenter, butcher, rent agent, and iron molder. The order's mayoralty candidate, a carpenter named F. W. Foster, also won election. In Attalla, another mining community, the Knights elected a labor slate to city hall in 1888. But in Mobile, where the order had become primarily a black organization, the Knights failed in their bid to elect a prolabor slate in the spring municipal elections of 1888. In one of their last excursions into municipal politics, the Knights of Selma, a black belt cotton town, elected E. S. Starr, one of the order's state lecturers, as mayor in the spring of 1889. [48]

Even in South Carolina and Mississippi, states where the order struggled to maintain a foothold, the Knights plunged into municipal politics. In late 1886 and early 1887, Charleston Knights toyed with the idea of backing a reform slate but decided against it. A sharply worded letter from Powderly advising them to purge their membership of "dirty, hungry politicians" probably encouraged their decision. [49] Knights in Vicksburg, Mississippi, were less hesitant and backed a slate in the municipal elections held during the spring of 1888. The Knights, composed primarily of blacks, elected the mayor, an alderman, and a justice of the peace, all members of the order. Again, the Vicksburg election demonstrated the ability of the order to unite the black and urban labor votes. [50]

While the Knights' municipal campaigns attracted the most attention, the order achieved its most significant and enduring political accomplishments in the state legislatures. The Knights never elected more than a handful of members to the legislatures; but especially in 1885 and 1886, when the order was growing and dynamic, it forced many legislative candidates to adopt a more friendly stance toward labor, particularly those from urban areas. In 1888 and 1889, after the decline of the order had become obvious, Knights still campaigned for labor reform bills with some success. The order's efforts to elect legislators friendly toward labor and to influence legislative votes through lobbying tactics represent organized labor's first attempt to speak for the interests of the nonagrarian southern worker. On the whole, the order won few of its legislative demands. But the concessions they won demonstrate the order's substantial, though brief, political threat. Even in defeat, by taking their programs to the state legislatures, the Knights helped lay the groundwork for the reforms of the progressive era.

Encouraged by their 1886 victory in the fourth congressional district, North Carolina Knights determined to exert their recently proven political influence upon the state legislature which convened in Raleigh in January 1887. Raleigh locals made plans for members to entertain legislators in their homes, and state master workman and congressman elect John Nichols called a special meeting of the state assembly in Raleigh to coincide with the opening of the legislative session. Over one hundred delegates attended the state assembly on January 25 and 26, representing a third of the state's counties. They forged an ambitious legislative program headed by a demand for the creation of a state bureau of labor empowered to compile labor statistics. Reform of the convict lease system was next in priority, followed by requests for a ten-hour-day law, a bill to provide for adequate notice of dismissal, and legislation to require the labeling of prison made goods. The assembly also endorsed the Blair Bill. To ensure that their legislative program received a hearing, the state assembly appointed three members to remain in Raleigh as lobbyists. [51]

Meanwhile, a farmers' convention, under the leadership of Colonel Leonidas L. Polk, editor of the *Progressive Farmer*, had also convened in Raleigh in an effort to influence legislative actions. The farmers adopted a legislative program which reflected their interests as employers of farm labor and merchants of the products they grew. It encompassed little of the Knights' program and underscored the basic difference between labor and agrarian organizations. The farmers wanted the Department of Agriculture placed under the control of "practical" farmers, the creation of an agricultural college, and the establishment of a railroad commission. Of the Knights' program, only convict labor reform received support from the agrarians. On some measures, such as immigration restriction, the farmers opposed the Knights. [52]

Legislative debates over the labor bureau bill further emphasized the differences between farmer and laborer. Introduced in the state senate for the Knights by Republican C. P. Lockey of Wilmington, the bill called for an autonomous labor bureau and immediately drew opposition from agrarian forces. Opponents charged that the bureau would be used exclusively for the Knights, would add to the tax burden, would encourage secret societies, and would "cause future trouble." They countered with an amendment offered by Democrat Sydenham B. Alexander, president of the North Carolina Farmers'

Alliance, empowering the Department of Agricultural to compile labor statistics. In the house, agrarians argued that the bill would take funds from the Department of Agriculture. Finally, however, the legislature reached a compromise that established a separate Bureau of Labor Statistics within the Department of Agriculture. A commissioner, appointed by the governor to a two-year term, headed the bureau. The floor debates in both houses of the legislature left little doubt that respect for the Knights' political potential provided the margin of victory. Lockey noted that every local in the state endorsed the bill and claimed that 100,000 voters demanded its passage. In addition to Lockey, the bill's other legislative spokesmen representing counties with active locals included Democrats J. H. Pou and John Shaw of Johnston and Cumberland counties, and Republican C. H. Brogden of Wayne County. [53]

The order achieved one other minor legislative victory. This victory came, however, in an area unrelated to the state assembly's legislative demands. A strike by stevedores in Wilmington in 1886 resulted in the stevedores seeking legislation to guarantee payment of wages. [54] When the legislature convened, John Holloway, a Negro Republican from Wilmington, won passage of a bill requiring owners of ships docked at Wilmington to refrain from paying boss stevedores or contractors of stevedores until they obtained a sworn statement that the laborers had been paid. [55]

Once the legislature had made its gesture of goodwill to the Knights, the remainder of the order's legislative program fared dismally. An unfavorable report from the house agricultural committee killed a ten-hour-workday bill sponsored by the Knights. In the senate, the lieutenant governor broke a tie vote to defeat the Knights' convict labor bill, which had been defended on the floor primarily by Lockey. Other items in the Knights' legislative program failed to receive consideration. [56]

The order's major achievement, the creation of a labor bureau, also proved to be something of a disappointment. The Knights had hoped, even assumed, that the governor would appoint one of their members as commissioner. The state assembly had endorsed J. Melville Broughton, who was a Democrat, for the position. But Governor Alfred M. Scales refused to consider a Knight for the appointment. His selection of a Democratic lawyer for the position was an affront to the order, whose constitution forbade membership for lawyers. The governor's action destroyed the Knights' hope of controlling the labor bureau and infuriated members of the order. [57]

In their legislative struggles, the Knights seemed to be unable to take advantage of the strength of Independent legislators in the state house. The senate was firmly controlled by Democrats; but in the house, eight Independents held the balance of power. An Independent was elected speaker, with Republican support. However, none of the Independents acted as spokesmen for the Knights' program. Rather, the Knights clearly relied upon Republicans from areas with several locals, including such men as Lockey, Holloway, and Brogden. [58]

Disappointed by their lack of success with the 1887 legislature but undaunted, North Carolina Knights determined to remain in legislative politics in 1888, an election year. This time, however, many locals throughout the state attempted to elect legislators friendly to their cause. The order entered full legislative tickets in Gaston and Winston counties; elsewhere, Republicans "endorsed" Union Labor party tickets backed by the Knights. In entering the campaign, and especially by backing a third party, the Knights made a catastrophic error. Their membership was declining; and in a presidential election year, the regular Democrats turned out to vote. A landslide of straight Democratic ballots buried the Union Labor tickets. The legislature of 1889 concerned itself with the problems of farmers, whose Alliance had become a major political power. The Knights and their legislative program were ignored. [59]

Knights in Georgia also entered legislative politics. Early in 1886, W. M. Harbin, the state organizer, informed the *Atlanta Constitution* that the Knights would probably seek legislation to regulate hours of labor, increase taxes on utilities and factories, and abolish convict labor. But he denied allegations that the order would endorse candidates, noting that the order was an educational and not a political organization. [60]

True to their word, the Knights sought to obtain the passage of several bills in the legislative session of 1886. They concentrated their efforts on the enactment of a bill limiting the workday to ten hours for children. Despite the efforts of locals in several cities, the bill never received a hearing. [61]

The failure of their lobbying efforts led Savannah area Knights to develop a legislative program and nominate a three-man legislative ticket for the elections in the fall of 1886. Their program included a bureau of labor statistics, safety regulations for mines and factories, compensation for industrial injuries, weekly payment of wages in cash, the abolition of child and convict labor, and the recognition of labor unions. The Savannah Knights' direct political action angered several members and led to bitter quarrels within area locals between political and antipolitical factions. The latter appealed to and received the support of Powderly in the dispute. 62

The Savannah Knights' ticket was defeated, but the order throughout the state remained determined to continue its efforts to achieve the passage of prolabor legislation. Again, the Knights concentrated their efforts on a ten-hour workday for child labor, and members of urban locals persuaded their representatives to introduce such legislation. Knights supported the bill with petitions from members around the state. They also sent a delegation composed of members from the state's textile centers to testify at hearings on the bill. All their efforts failed, however. The bill was defeated, and the remainder of the order's program received little attention. 63

Despite a decline in urban membership in 1889, the Knights tried for the third time to obtain the passage of a child labor bill. A committee of Knights appeared before the legislature and placed in evidence a survey conducted by locals in Atlanta, Augusta, Macon, Athens, Columbus, Roswell, and other towns. This survey revealed that over eleven hundred children under ten years of age worked for up to twelve hours a day in Georgia's mills and factories. Using the racial tactics common in that era, the Knights argued that since the mills employed only white children, black children were receiving an education denied to whites. In one factory surveyed by the Knights, only two of thirty-two children employed could read. Their statistics failed to secure the bill's passage; it never came to a vote. But on another issue, the Knights won a victory. The legislature did pass an eleven-hour bill, although several escape clauses and a lack of enforcement procedures limited its effectiveness. The remainder of the order's program received short shrift. And by the end of the year, the order, reduced to a fraction of its former membership, practically conceded its political impotence. At the state assembly held in November 1889, delegates ignored state issues, concentrating instead on such national reform issues as the secret ballot, federal control of railroads, and the nationalization of the banking system. The assembly also made plans to affiliate with the Farmers' Alliance, a sure sign of its relative weakness.[64]

The Knights in Virginia entered legislative politics earlier than their colleagues in other southern states, seeking to obtain passage of a convict labor bill in 1885. The legislature ignored their efforts, causing the order to become active in the elections of that fall. Particularly in the Richmond area, the Knights sought to determine the outcome of the election by attempting to make candidates of both parties publicly state their positions on issues of interest to labor, especially the convict labor question. Mullen reported to Powderly that both parties had promised to support the order, "announcing their intentions of abolishing convict labor and declare also in favor of an eight hour law." However, the politically astute Mullen noted that "it remains to be seen what will be the outcome of the promises made by skilled politicians upon the eve of a hot and exciting canvass."[65]

As Mullen had feared, once elected, the new legislature exhibited little interest in labor legislation. Although debated, no convict labor or child labor bills were passed. In 1887, however, Virginia Knights, in cooperation with other labor organizations, scored their single legislative victory. The legislature enacted a requirement that all scrip issued by employers in payment of wages be redeemed in United States currency within thirty days of issue. Like many early labor laws, the scrip law had no enforcement procedures and was frequently ignored by employers.[66]

In Alabama, the order became involved in legislative politics in 1887, after it had already begun to decline. Meeting in Montgomery in July, the state assembly encouraged Alabama Knights to demand legislative reforms. Among the legislative goals adopted by the assembly were a state-supported school in every township with a term of at least six months, no local bills affecting labor, and the abolition of the convict lease system. The last item had been of top priority to the Knights since the order absorbed the Alabama Anti-Convict League in 1886, but the Knights had done little to defeat the system.[67] But in the fall of 1887, under pressure from both Birmingham's *Sentinel* and

Selma's *Vindicator*, the order began to move toward the formation of
a Union Labor party to insure that their programs were placed before
the voters. Birmingham area Knights led in the third party movement, forming a Union Labor party in Jefferson County in August
1887. Once formed, the Jefferson County party took the lead in developing a state organization; and the first convention of the Alabama
Union Labor party was held in Birmingham on September 16, 1887.

Like many other third party movements, the Union Labor party
was "not a success in point of numbers" but "showed great enthusiasm." Convention delegates voted to enter national and legislative politics in 1888, created a state executive committee, and endorsed a
platform. The platform called for an increase in the currency of $60
per capita and the creation of a "peace army" to build the nation.
Otherwise, it stressed state issues. The delegates demanded the abolition of convict labor, the curtailment of scrip wages, and the establishment of a state bureau of labor. Delegates from several reform
groups, including the Farmers' Alliance and the Agricultural Wheel,
attended the convention; but Knights from the Birmingham area
dominated its proceedings. J. C. Jeffers, a prominent Birmingham
Knight, chaired the convention; and three of the four members of the
state executive board were members of the order. [68]

The order's drift toward active political involvement was apparent
at the state assembly held in Huntsville in January 1888. The assembly
attempted to maintain its political neutrality by voting to support the
friends of workingmen rather than a third party. But it also adopted
an aggressive ten-point legislative program whose demands mirrored
those of the Union Labor party. Among the demands of the assembly
were the abolition of convict labor and scrip wages, the payment of
wages within two weeks, the creation of a state bureau of labor, the
passage of a mine safety law, and the repeal of all conspiracy laws that
applied to labor organizations. [69]

A "convention of workingmen" held in Montgomery in March
again demonstrated the order's politicization. Eighty delegates from
seven of the state's eight congressional districts attended, representing the Farmers' Alliance, the Agricultural Wheel, the Knights, and
four trade unions. Again, the Knights dominated the proceedings.
Delegates took pains to secure black support, placing Negroes on all

committees. However, differences between agrarian and labor forces surfaced immediately. Labor, especially the Knights, favored backing the Union Labor party statewide; the agrarians objected. The convention compromised, calling for the creation of the Labor Party of the State of Alabama, which was to enter candidates in as many races as possible. The agrarians wanted to name the *Montgomery Advertiser* as the party organ. The Knights objected, both because they preferred the *Sentinel* and because, they claimed, the *Advertiser* used scab labor and was under a boycott by the order. Delegates sidestepped the issue, tabling the endorsement of a paper. Agrarian forces also killed efforts by labor to place a strong child labor plank in the party platform.

The platform finally adopted combined the specific legislative proposals of the Knights' state assembly with the vague federal reforms favored by the agrarians. It called for state legislation to reduce hours of labor, to provide for the inspection of tenements, mines, and factories, to require payment of wages in legal tender within two weeks, and to stop the abuse of conspiracy laws. At the federal level, the convention supported government-owned railroads and telegraphs, postal savings banks, and federal issue of currency. The platform called for unity among reform groups, and the convention urged counties to form their own party structure and place legislative candidates in the field. [70]

Across the state, locals responded to the convention's call for active political involvement. Their participation was undoubtedly encouraged by the legislature's failure to consider three bills which the Knights managed to get introduced. The bills—a convict labor bill, a mine safety proposal, and a requirement that wages be paid in cash—never came to a vote. Locals nominated their own legislative tickets, frequently endorsing members. In Jefferson County, for example, A. J. O'Keefe, one of the state's most active members, received a nomination for a house seat. In Bibb County, a local master workman was nominated. Knights were also on the ticket in Clifton, Mobile, and Baldwin counties. In addition to legislative candidacies, Knights in Baldwin, Mobile, Jefferson, and other counties stood for election to county and local offices. [71]

The Alabama Knights' venture into politics in 1888 cost the order dearly. In a presidential and gubernatorial election year, Democrats humiliated their opponents in the state elections. The *Sentinel* blamed the staggering defeat administered to the labor candidates on corrupt Democratic election officials; but it was forced to admit that laborers, "by their supreme prejudice and indifference to the cause of labor," aided the Democratic sweep "in no small degree." The 1888 campaign proved to be the Knights' last hurrah in Alabama. Already on the decline, the order now began to disintegrate. Even loyal members sensed the significance of the defeat. Thomas White, editor of the *Sentinel*, announced after the election that while the paper would continue as the official organ of the Knights, "it will not be confined as organ to this organization alone as in the past, but its columns will be for the use and welfare of all bodies of organized labor." [72]

Elsewhere, the Knights lost their two congressional seats in the campaign of 1888. In North Carolina, John Nichols stood for reelection from the fourth district. The Democrats responded to his decision with an attack based on racism and economics and executed with the vigor and vulgarity common to the era. They charged that in voting against the Mills Bill and tariff reform, Nichols ensured both higher living costs for the worker and the continuation of excise taxes. They stressed his past associations with Radical Republicans and blacks, branding him a "southern man with Northern principles . . . a black Republican, foisted upon the people as a friend of labor," whose political ambitions had driven white members from the Knights. Although his opponent, Major Benjamin H. Bunn, a lawyer and cotton mill owner, seemed a perfect target for a labor candidate, Nichols never gained the offensive. And when the fourth district Farmers' Alliance leaders joined in the condemnation of Nichols, all hope was lost. Bunn carried the district except for Wake County. There, because of the large black vote in Raleigh, the Republican-Negro-Knight coalition gave Nichols a slender majority. [73]

In Virginia, too, the Knights failed to hold the sixth congressional district. The incumbent, Samuel Hopkins, had angered Republicans by voting for tariff reform and remained unforgiven by the Democrats for bolting the party in 1886. As a result, in the elctions of 1888, he found himself opposed by both Democratic and Republican challengers. The Democrats appealed to labor for their votes on the grounds that Hopkins was "confessedly out of the race" and that by continuing to support him, labor could only hope to elect the Republican. Their approach worked; the Democratic candidate, P. C. Edmunds, won the district over his Republican rival by a majority of over three thousand votes. Hopkins finished a poor third. [74]

The Knights made little impact upon southern presidential politics. In 1884, the order had just to begun to organize; by 1888, it had already begun to decline, as is evidenced by its poor showing that year in local and legislative races. In addition, the order realized that it was practically impossible to break the grip of the major parties in a presidential race. No local, district, or state assembly endorsed a presidential candidate in 1888, including the Union Labor candidate, Alson J. Streeter. But several prominent Knights campaigned for Streeter, and both the *Alabama Sentinel* and the *Fayetteville Messenger* endorsed his candidacy. However, in North Carolina and Alabama, Streeter polled a negligible vote; and many of the votes he did receive came from Knights who supported the Union Labor ticket primarily because of local candidates. [75]

On national issues, the stance of the southern Knights reflected that of the national order. Southerners generally backed the Blair Bill, for they saw it as an opportunity to improve the region's inadequate school system. On other national issues, resolutions adopted by the North Carolina state assembly illustrate basic southern positions. The assembly endorsed the Blair Bill, called for the direct election of senators, and approved of government-owned railways and telegraphs. Other assemblies, such as that of Alabama, added postal savings banks and other items to the list. [76]

Except for voting for friends of labor for congress and urging the national order to lobby for the passage of federal legislation, southern Knights could do little to advance their cause at the national level. And both these methods proved ineffective. In 1887, for example, the order's national legislative committee, with headquarters in Washington, failed to obtain an appointment with House Speaker John Carlisle to discuss the Blair Bill and a bill requiring railroads to return all lands obtained from the federal government, among other issues. Ralph Beaumont, committee chairman, then attempted to obtain an appointment with Carlisle through the good offices of congressman and Knight John Nichols of North Carolina. Carlisle again refused, and Beaumont conceded defeat. [77] Lobbyists for a national organization who failed to obtain an appointment with the Speaker of the House through the efforts of a congressman who was a member of the organization could have little hope of influencing national legislation.

The national order, under Powderly's leadership, attempted to refrain from overt political activity because American laborers held strong ties to both major parties, making political activity a disruptive tactic. Yet Powderly's personal response to the order's political activity was considerably more ambivalent than his public stance. Privately, Powderly encouraged political activity when it succeeded, damned it when it failed. For example, he gave John Nichols detailed advice on political strategy in North Carolina after Nichols's election to Congress. After the Knights' success in the 1887 Jacksonville municipal election, he wrote J. J. Holland that "it afforded me genuine pleasure to know that thirteen of the eighteen aldermen elected in your city are members of the K. of L., such a gain as that cannot but produce good results if all prove true to the principles of our order." On the other hand, when a Charleston Knight wrote that the question of politics was disrupting the local and district assemblies, Powderly replied that such letters made him sick and ordered the man to "do everything in your power to keep dirty, hungry politicians out of the order, they are a curse wherever they get an entry." [78] The ambivalence of Powderly and the national order reflected an essential dilemma. The reforms the Knights desired at both state and national levels were political in nature. Yet to enter the political arena assured disruption of the order.

In the South, political complexities magnified the danger of disruption. The Knights sought to mount a serious political offensive in a region where politics were so convoluted that a noted historian has observed that the average man, faced with the absurdity of the situation, retreated into "political nihilism." [79] Too few in numbers to be a political power themselves, the Knights had no natural allies. Bourbon Democrats catered to industry and ignored labor yet claimed to represent the workingman. They controlled the votes of rural blacks to prevent the adoption of reforms beneficial to labor while simultaneously denouncing the Knights' appeal for political and economic cooperation between the races as a threat to white supremacy. Republicans, though willing to ally with the order to oust Democrats, held sound money and laissez-faire principles diametrically opposed to those of the Knights. After 1886, the agrarians increasingly found the industrial and urban workers' demands for labor bureaus, child labor laws, and wage and hour legislation inimical to their interests as employers. Thus any coalition formed by the order had to be for specific, short-term goals and carried with it the possibility of offending a large segment of the membership.

In addition to facing regional difficulties, like their fellow members elsewhere, southern Knights' political efforts were hampered in two ways by the ideology of the national order. First, the ambivalence of the national leadership confused the rank and file. Political action was condemned or praised from on high according to the degree of its success. Not even in the Great Upheaval of 1886 could the national leadership agree to officially endorse partisan political activity, although the leadership encouraged local efforts to elect Knights to a variety of offices, including the Congress. Because of this ambivalence, members could never be sure that their political plans would not draw the ire of national leaders, including Powderly himself. Second, the Knights lacked a political program that could galvanize labor into a cohesive political unit as a third party or within one of the two major parties. Cooperation and arbitration, the heart of the Knights' ideology, were to be achieved through nonpolitical means. Monetary reform, land reform, and rail and trust regulation, all political goals, offered few concrete benefits to the average worker and probably would not have inspired political action even if it had been endorsed. The Knights never found a single issue to unite its membership. The Southern Farmers' Alliance provides an interesting contrast with its subtreasury program, a concept that addressed farmers' two most serious economic problems, the inability to obtain long-term credit and to control markets for their crops. [80] Because the Knights had no meaningful political program for the rank and file, political activity tended to stress such state and local issues as convict labor, child labor, scrip wages, and a share of public construction monies.

The order's inability to find an issue that affected most of the membership reflects a difference between the agrarians and urban and industrial workers perhaps as significant as the disparity in their numbers. Practically every farmer, landowner, or tenant suffered from a lack of credit and marketing control over his crop. But child labor, convict labor or scrip wages did not affect all workers, not even within a single industry. The agrarians adopted a logical approach to the problems of credit and markets—have the federal government provide relief through the subtreasury program. For the Knights to have addressed the common problems of its members, of which wages and hours were the most universal, would have required a change in ideology. Either the order had to accept the wage system and stress the use of direct action to obtain economic benefits, as did the AFL, or adopt a political program which dealt with the members' problems, as had the Farmers' Alliance. The Knights could have advocated cooperation as a political program, for it proposed definite solutions to most of the members' basic concerns. Such action would have meant, essentially, an endorsement of socialism. The Knights' impractical reform ideology, however, kept them from adopting either course.

Despite the handicaps the southern order faced, its political activity does not compare unfavorably to that of the Knights in other sections of the country. In 1886, the two Knights elected to Congress from the South equaled the national total of successful candidates within labor parties. The region also had unsuccessful candidates in Florida and Virginia. Gerald Grob notes that in 1886, labor obtained victories in at least six cities, two of which, Key West and Richmond, were southern. Yet he states that "labor made its poorest showing in the South" in the 1886 campaigns. Without specifying, Grob notes that nineteen localities elected labor tickets in 1887. A look at the record reveals that southern Knights backed at least nine municipal tickets that year and were successful in four races, including those in Jacksonville and Lynchburg. In 1888, the southern order, like the order nationally, met defeat at the polls, as exemplified by the failure of Nichols and Hopkins to obtain reelection and the poor showing of legislative tickets in Alabama, Georgia, and North Carolina. Nevertheless, when the percentages of urban and industrial workers, North and South, are compared to the total populations, the political achievements of the southern Knights appear more impressive. At the very least, they once again demonstrate that southern laborers did not differ from their colleagues elsewhere in their willingness to attempt to improve their status.[81]

The achievements of the southern order, compared to its failures, offer another measure of the political significance of the Knights. Again, the southern order fit a national pattern, for despite their activity, few reforms were achieved. The Knights elected two congressmen, one from North Carolina and one from Virginia. Neither proved an effective representative of the Knights' national legislative program. At the municipal level, the Knights placed, or helped place, reform tickets in office in Richmond, Jacksonville, Lynchburg, and several smaller towns. Immediate gains, including the slight increase in wages for Richmond city laborers and political offices for members, were limited. Only in Jacksonville did the reform ticket carry out a program designed to benefit the entire working class of the city, and there the state legislature halted the city reforms. In state legislatures, the order obtained the creation of one state bureau of labor, passage of one bill requiring payment of wages in cash and one eleven-hour bill, and enactment of some minor legislation. They did not obtain child labor bills, mine or factory safety laws, convict labor bills, or repeal of conspiracy laws.

The order paid a high price for these few achievements. In almost every case, when local or district assemblies entered politics, they lost membership. Correspondence to Powderly from southern members after 1886 is filled with complaints about political activity. J. Melville Broughton, one of the pillars of the order in North Carolina, expressed the sentiments of thousands when he wrote to Powderly in December 1886, "Politics! Politics! Seems to be the one idea of many locals in this state."[82] Even their victories created dissension. In Richmond and Lynchburg, competition among Knights for political appointments weakened the order; and in North Carolina, prominent Knights openly fought for the appointment as commissioner of labor, which neither received.[83] Because the Knights contained blacks and whites, Republicans and Democrats, they naturally sought the votes of blacks and Republicans. This fact opened the order to Democratic charges of "social equality" and Radical Republicanism, causing further dissension in the ranks.

By the fall of 1888, partially because of the disruption caused by political activity, membership had declined dramatically, rendering the order politically impotent. The Knights' entry into the legislative races of that year in North Carolina and Alabama represented a desperate gamble by an already disintegrating organization. Campaign results destroyed the hopes of even the most optimistic that the order would again wield significant political influence. The

Knights' official organs in both states acknowledged that the humiliating defeat at the polls practically destroyed what remained of the order. The *Messenger*, the official paper in North Carolina, ceased publication a month after the elections; and the *Alabama Sentinel* ceased to speak for the Knights exclusively. [84] The debacle of 1888 conclusively demonstrated the order's overall decline. After that date, its efforts to become a political ally of the Farmers' Alliance, discussed later, are more a part of the order's final collapse than of its political activities and only serve to underscore the weakness of the order after 1888.

What, then, other than a few pieces of legislation and the spoils of victory in an occasional municipal election, were the political accomplishments of the Knights? Essentially, their major contribution was to squarely place, for the first time in the New South, questions involving urban and industrial laborers in political debates, especially in state legislatures. In every state, even Mississippi, the Knights forced public consideration of such issues as convict labor, child labor, workers' safety, scrip wages, and more reasonable hours of labor. They also forced, if briefly, legislative candidates to listen to the voice of nonagrarian labor. Although concrete, immediate achievements were small, the Knights laid the foundation for political reform affecting southern labor upon which the Progressives would build. As with their strikes, the Knights rushed into political action because the rank and file demanded that they do so. And also as with their strikes, they suffered defeats, resulting in the disillusionment of some of those who had originally demanded action. But their very challenge to the political establishment of the New South was their most important political contribution.

6 Education and Cooperation

THE ideology of the Knights was essentially middle class, and at its heart were the principles of education and cooperation. Both were positive concepts representing that which the order hoped to achieve rather than what it wished to avoid, as with strikes or political action. In this sense, the positive elements of the Knights' ideology were based on theory, while the negative elements were based, at least to some extent, on experience. The Knights sought to avoid strikes in part because they believed strikes had been proven ineffective during the 1870s. The order also believed that political action had contributed to the demise of the National Labor Union. Education, on the other hand, was too general a concept to connect with specific setbacks; and cooperation was untried. Thus both seemed to offer promise, while other measures had been tried and, at first appraisal, seemed inadequate for the task of acquiring for labor its just rewards.

Both education and cooperation reflected the order's essentially middle-class viewpoint and its ideological connections with antebellum reform movements. The AFL accepted the concept of an industrial working class, worked to organize it, and then proceeded to nourish within it middle-class values. The Knights insisted upon adopting a middle-class program for an American labor force which they refused to contemplate in industrial, working class terms. Like most middle-class reform movements, the Knights were convinced that educational programs would lead to needed reform. If only "the producers" could see basic social and economic "truths," they would act to correct the system's inequities. For the Knights, cooperation provided the obvious answer to an enlightened producing class. Cooperation would restore the worker to a proprietary status and, if administered democratically, would insure an equitable distribution of profits and provide the worker with a voice in the decision-making process in an industrial society. In short, cooperation would return the laborer of the industrial world to a status similar to that held by the craftsmen and master workmen of preindustrial society.

The Knights saw no contradiction in creating a labor organization to implement a middle-class reform program. In the first place, the order did not see the work force as a collection of industrial wage earners. It sought instead to unite all "producers." Producers included not just laborers or craftsmen but all members of society who were not what the Knights deemed parasites (for example, financiers and industrialists). The Knights considered most white-collar workers as members of the "producing" class. Professionals, except for lawyers, also fell into this category. In other words, the Knights held a preindustrial concept of the work force they wished to organize. Thus the Knights' essentially middle-class goals fit the concept of the work force held by the order's leadership.

But if ideology presented the order with no problems, its implementation did. The Knights believed their first task was to educate the producing class to basic social and economic "truths." But education was a continuing process requiring tremendous expenditures of time, energy, and money; enlightenment did not come overnight. To succeed, the Knights had to retain their membership. To do that, they needed to succeed in other, less ideological areas, in order to provide the membership with some immediate benefits. This the order failed to do. And in the South, a successful educational program was crucial because so many of the new members were sorely in need of an introduction to even the most basic concepts of organization.

The Knights faced other problems in their efforrts to implement a cooperative program. Cooperation on the scale envisioned by the Knights was simply beyond the order's resources, both human and capital. In addition, cooperation required a commitment to action and dedication to specifics, not debate and generalizations. The Knights proved much better at the latter. The national order made no serious attempt to instigate a cooperative movement, as did the Farmers' Alliance. Nor did the order come to the aid of cooperatives established at the local or district assembly level. Its cooperative program, which originally held great appeal for urban southerners, produced only a series of failures. By the end of 1888, southern Knights had abandoned most of the cooperative ventures they had initiated and had drastically curtailed their educational efforts.

The order's educational program involved three distinct yet overlapping areas, each of which required different strategies and techniques. First, the Knights sought to introduce all laborers or producers to their principles and then recruit them as members. Once the worker joined, he was continually indoctrinated in the order's beliefs, ritual, and purpose. Finally, the Knights attempted to enlighten those outside the order to its nature and purpose. This effort frequently coincided with the order's first education priority, for, given the Knights' liberal membership qualifications, most Americans were potential members.

The South presented each aspect of the order's educational program with handicaps peculiar to the region. To introduce their principles to the southern workers, the Knights had to overcome several impediments. Many southerners believed unions were a Yankee concept, a part of the enemy's culture. Management and their spokesmen encouraged the belief that labor organizations robbed the worker of his individuality, that virtue perhaps most cherished by members of a society still dominated by preindustrial, agrarian values. Few of the South's work force had any previous experience with organized labor, except for a handful of skilled tradesmen in urban areas, such as the typographers. Thus as the first labor organization in the region on a major scale, the Knights faced the problem of introducing the very concept of organization to the labor force in addition to the task of explaining their principles and program. Finally, especially in the isolated lumber camps, cotton mill villages, mines, and plantations of the South, the Knights had to avoid the attention of intransigent owners. Cotton mill owners, for example, constantly watched their labor force for signs of organization and maintained correspondence with other owners to learn of organizational activity within the industry. Knights from northwestern Florida's lumber regions reported that "a hawk does not watch chickens" closer than opponents watched the order, and some rural organizers resorted to secrecy when introducing the order to agricultural laborers.[1]

Many who joined the order had but a brief exposure to its principles and programs and understood but vaguely the concept of organization. Thus the Knights first had to indoctrinate new members in the most basic beliefs of the order and then attempt to encourage the membership to begin the implementation of the order's programs.

This task of indoctrination was made the more difficult because most of the rank and file expected immediate material benefits and were only secondarily concerned, if at all, with union ideology. Yet if the order was to make any progress in its efforts to improve the workers' status, the membership had to understand and support its principles. Southern leaders were aware of this dilemma, and their corresponddence to Powderly graphically illustrates their concern that the membership receive the sorely needed education in union principles. "The fact that labor has been so long disorganized in the South," wrote John Ray in 1885, "makes it very hard to organize Assemblies and harder still to hold them together." An early Alabama organizer complained of "a great amount of ignorance" among workers and cited the need for education. John Power of Mississippi informed Powderly of "a great need of a speaker who would instruct in the principles of our order." A year later, in 1886, another Mississippi organizer complained of "the gross ignorance that pervades every nook and cranny of our state." The following year, Power again requested an instructor, observing that "a majority of our members . . . seem to know as little of our principles, aims and objects as a Hotten Tot." As late as 1888, local officers in Georgia and Florida requested instructors from the national order, stressing the memberships' need for "education in the principles of the order."[2]

The rapid growth of the order further complicated the problem of an uneducated membership. As was seen in the first chapter, local assemblies frequently formed almost spontaneously. Banding together to seek relief from some economic problem, such groups appealed to the order for official recognition. An organizer would appear, take their money, and give the new members their first instruction in the principles of the order. Unfortunately, the organizer often knew little more about the order which he represented than did the new members.[3]

To combat this problem, the order constantly sent national officers into the field to explain the order's principles, programs, and practices to new members. The South received its share of such visits, but the touring officers shared the disadvantage of being nonsouthern. Powderly's tour of the region in 1885 and Trevelick's tour of 1886, discussed in chapter two, were the first such visits. In 1887, Ralph Beaumont, general lecturer, toured the upper South; and John Hayes, secretary of the G.E.B., accompanied by Tom O'Riley, traveled through the lower South, concentrating on Alabama and Georgia. Under a barrage of unjustified criticism for neglecting the region, Powderly appointed John O'Keefe as a permanent southern lecturer in mid-1888. O'Keefe set out on his first southern tour in the fall of that year.[4] In the spring of 1889, Mrs. Leonora Barry, head of the order's women's department, toured the South on behalf of the G.E.B., swinging down the East Coast and then turning westward into Alabama, Tennessee, and Kentucky.[5]

National officers touring the South followed a pattern set by Powderly in 1885. Arriving in a town, they held a public lecture on the order's principles. On her 1889 tour, for example, Leonora Barry lectured on the evils of child labor and the need for shorter hours, especially for women. After the public address, the lecturer would meet with members of local assemblies. In these meetings, closed to the public, the visitor instructed the membership in the order's teaching and ritual and tried to correct misunderstandings about the order's beliefs and practices.[6]

The effectiveness of the lecturer program is questionable. In 1885 and 1886, as the order was expanding, visiting national officers drew large crowds. But by 1889, Leonora Barry attracted few spectators, drawing an audience of but four people at Montgomery. The appearance of a lecturer momentarily lifted the spirits of the faithful, but his departure led to an inevitable letdown. After praising the O'Keefe tour and the enthusiasm it created, a South Carolina Knight wrote, "One thing I regret—that is the shortness of his stay in our midst, and I hope that . . . we will again be visited and instructed by Bro. O'Keefe."[7]

State assemblies, organized in North Carolina, Alabama, Florida, and Mississippi by early 1887, attempted to complement the national order's program of visiting instructors. But state organizations, chronically short of funds, could afford few full-time lecturers. As a result, the task of indoctrinating the membership fell to officers in state assemblies and to state organizers. John Ray of North Carolina is typical. The state's first organizer and later secretary of the state assembly, Ray spent over two years traveling the state to work with newly formed locals. Nicholas Stack, Alabama's first state master workman, "traveled the Alabama labor field and counseled with and encouraged to the best of my ability some of the most oppressed people on the continent. So long as I had a dollar of my own to travel with." In Mississippi, John Power led in the formation of a state assembly so that it could be used as "the means of strengthening and cementing the order throughout the state as I find from conversation and inquiry amongst the Representatives [at the state assembly] many things being done very loosely." Although some state assemblies appointed lecturers, lack of funds prevented them from performing effectively.[8]

Local assemblies also recognized the need to instruct the membership and attempted to do so. Pioneer Assembly 3606 of Raleigh, for example, was constantly concerned about instruction for its members. The local received the usual visits from touring national officers. Trevelick appeared on March 6, 1866; Beaumont spoke on May 30, 1887. The assembly subscribed to several papers published by the Knights, including the *Journal of United Labor* and the Durham *Workman*. Pertinent articles were read aloud from these publications. Members established a library and reading room in their union hall and stocked it with labor publications. They discussed the order's constitution and gave "addresses" on such topics as "hard times and its causes." They also held open-air meetings at which members spoke to the public about the order.[9] This educational activity occupied an increasing portion of the local's schedule, eventually reducing the assembly to a discussion group. Like state and general assemblies, the local engaged in endless conversation but found it difficult to take action on specific issues.

The ineffectiveness of the Raleigh local's educational program reflects more than the magnitude of the task involved; it demonstrates serious flaws in the order's structure and ideology. Like most southern locals, the Raleigh local was a mixed assembly. Its membership included professionals, white-collar workers, craftsmen, factory workers, and shopkeepers. While they could agree that times were hard, such a diverse group had little in common and could hardly be expected to support the program of a single labor organization, unless that program proved so generalized as to be meaningless. Again, the Farmers' Alliance provides an interesting contrast. The alliance not only appealed to a much larger constituency, but the great majority of its members were farmers with precisely the same economic problems. Both numbers and common grievances allowed the suballiance, unlike the local assembly, to act as a schoolroom which forged its members into a cohesive unit. But even if local assemblies had achieved perfect harmony on the order's principles, those very principles made the implementation of a program impossible. Prohibited from political action and discouraged from entering strikes or boycotts, locals lacked both the financial means to inaugurate cooperative ventures and the numbers from any single occupation to insure arbitration. Thus local assemblies became consciousness-raising groups for workers who had joined primarily because they already perceived their economic plight and hoped the order could help.

In addition to their efforts to indoctrinate the membership in the order's beliefs and principles, local assemblies also sought to improve general educational opportunities for the worker and his children. The membership was fully conscious that niggardly funding crippled the region's public school system and deprived their children of an adequate education. Realizing that federal money would provide the funds required to upgrade public schools, most southern locals, including the Raleigh assembly, endorsed the Blair Bill and lobbied for its passage. Locals also sought to provide practical education for their members. The Raleigh assembly, for example, established a night school, staffed by members, for "young mechanics and apprentices." Knights from assemblies in the Norfolk area also founded and operated two night schools "for the boys." [10]

The Knights' press supplemented the educational efforts of the general, state, and local assemblies. Like their northern brethren, southern Knights read the *Journal of United Labor*, the order's national paper. Southerners also wrote to the *Journal*, and their letters provide insight into the workings of the order. [11] In the locals, members pondered *Journal* editorials on such national issues as the currency, cooperation, government run railroads, and land reform. Issues demanding state action discussed in the *Journal* included child and convict labor and the creation of state bureaus of labor. Because it carried items from other labor publications, the *Journal* acquainted southerners with labor papers such as *John Swinton's Paper*. It kept members abreast of developments within the order, indoctrinated them in the principles of Knighthood, and supplied them with general information about organized labor.

Perhaps more important to southern members was the order's local press, for it dealt with problems peculiar to labor within a state and provided specific information about local strikes, the condition of the order within a state or region, and state and local politics. Because printers joined the Knights early, a number of Knights of Labor papers, all weeklies, were established throughout the South. Undoubtedly, many were established by printers who saw in the order a chance for economic and perhaps political gain. Papers falling into this category include Richmond's *Labor Herald*, published by William Mullen, Durham's *Workman*, published by Hiram Paul, and Key West's *Equator*, published by C. B. Pendleton. Other Knights papers included Florida's *Palladium*, Charlotte's *Weekly Craftsman*, Raleigh's *Workman*, Lynchburg's *Labor Record*, Greensboro's *Craftsman*, Savannah's *Evening Call*, Selma's *Vindicator,* Wilmington's *Daily Index*, Montgomery's *Master Workman*, Atlanta's *Working World*, Fayetteville's *Messenger*, and the *Alabama Sentinel*, published in Birmingham.[12]

Most of the papers were short-lived, succumbing to the harsh economic realities faced by papers with few subscribers. The Montgomery *Master Workman*, for example, folded early in 1877, within a few months of its first issue. The publisher claimed that he ceased publication to aid the *Sentinel*, which honored subscriptions to the defunct *Master Workman*. But obviously the publication failed because Alabama Knights could not support papers in both Birmingham and Montgomery.[13] The mortality rate for North Carolina papers was extremely high. C. K. King, editor of Greensboro's *Craftsman*, ceased publication of his paper in November 1887. Other papers that failed during the same year included Durham's *Workman*, Raleigh's *Workman*, and Wilmington's *Index*.[14] Begun amid the euphoria produced by the order's rapid expansion in 1886 and early 1887, the Knights' papers, like other projects, proved unable to survive. The urban laboring class, to whom the papers were originally addressed, was hardly large enough to support five papers in a state as rural as North Carolina. With the decline of the order in urban areas after 1886, the papers collapsed.

Copies of two of the Knights' weeklies, the *Alabama Sentinel* and Fayetteville's *Messenger*, are extant. Both survived for over a year, and both were official organs of state assemblies. Edited by C. W.

Ezzell, the *Messenger* ran from April 1887 to November 30, 1888. Founded by Alfred Taylor and later edited by Thomas White and J. F. H. Mosley, the *Sentinel* also began publication in April 1887 and continued until 1889, although it ceased to speak exclusively for the Knights in August 1888. Together, the two papers provide an excellent record of the Knights' local press.[15]

The basic function of the various papers published by the Knights was to educate their readers in the principles of the order. Both the *Messenger* and the *Sentinel* performed this task admirably, with editorials on cooperation, land reform, tariffs, trusts, and other reform topics. Like many critics of the new industrial order, they viewed the federal government as an agent for reform. They urged that treasury surpluses be expended on education and construction projects, called for a nationalized banking system, and advocated government ownership of railroads and the telegraph. They decried dissension in the ranks and expounded the gospel of solidarity, reminding laborers that organization was the only means of receiving a fair share of the wealth they created. "Individual efforts for justice," wrote Alfred Taylor of the *Sentinel*, "are of no further use to cope with the powers of a society that extort an unjust share of what by right should belong to you [the worker]." Only when labor organized and demanded change would it be forthcoming. C. W. Ezzell joined the attack, condemning laws that "treated combinations of capital as citizens and combinations of labor as conspiracy."[16]

Like the order's educational programs, the efforts of the local press to propagandize the membership were less than an unqualified success. In the first place, the content of the papers reflected to a high degree the opinions of the editor-owners, not necessarily those of the rank and file. Most editors were typical spokesmen for middle-class values and reform programs, often politically ambitious or at least possessed of a keen interest in politics. Thus the reforms they suggested usually required political action of some sort, with the exception of cooperation. While the rank and file generally supported the order's broad principles of land reform, trust regulation, and tariff and monetary reform, which were all endorsed by the Knights' local press, they were more interested in obtaining immediate economic benefits. The press could explain the order's general goals but could not demonstrate how they were to be achieved. This was because, in fact, the order's principles made their achievement impossible. Yet if no action were taken to meet the demands of the rank and file, membership would decline and subscription lists dwindle. This paradox eventually forced both the *Sentinel* and the *Messenger* in 1888 to advocate that the Knights enter politics, a decision that countered the order's policies.

Labor papers also attempted to counter the prevailing antilabor sentiment of the southern press and to convince the general public of the worth of labor organizations in general and the Knights in particuliar. This was no mean task, for the press, frequently controlled by industrialists such as Daniel Tompkins or their proponents, including Henry Grady and Francis Dawson, staunchly opposed unions. The *Messenger* editorialized for a stronger labor press to refute antiunion charges by the majority of the southern press. Ezzell maintained a constant feud with papers he believed unfriendly to labor, including Raleigh's *Chronicle* and *News and Observer* and Wilson's *Advance*. The "subsidized press," Ezzell charged, deliberately sought to misrepresent the Knights and give the order a bad reputation.[17] The *Sentinel* criticized other Alabama papers for their antilabor position and flayed the *Atlanta Constitution* for its efforts "to curry favor with the capitalistic class."[18]

Although critical of the antiunion bias of the press, both the *Sentinel* and the *Messenger* advocated industrial development to capitalize on the region's natural riches with the verve of a Henry Grady or a Francis Dawson. Alfred Taylor believed Alabama's "coal, iron ore, stone, clay, timber, good soils, and navigable rivers" would make her the wealthiest state in the union and "Mobile the rival of New York." Ezzell envisioned coal from North Carolina mines carried on North Carolina railroads to power factories throughout the state. Excellent waterpower sites awaited development, and mineral deposits held promise of sudden wealth.[19]

To capitalize on these resources, Ezzell urged the construction of railroads, cotton and tobacco factories, and city services. He promoted the formation of cotton exchanges and chambers of commerce. The *Messenger* regularly urged local merchants to be more aggressive. Supporting the reformers' major nemesis, the railroads, Ezzell urged the construction of a line to give Fayetteville merchants direct access to a deepwater port. In a burst of boosterism, he endorsed a plan to lure northern plants by sending manufacturers descriptions of state assets, including labor forces, power sites, and possible sources of capital. The *Sentinel* also regularly carried articles boasting of Birmingham's industrial potential. "With the development of an industrial sector," editorialized Alfred Taylor, "the South is on the right road to prosperity. It is not only on the right road . . . it is dead earnest in its intent to acquire wealth." [20]

In format neither paper differed greatly from other weeklies. They carried local news, editorials, letters to the editor, and clippings from other papers. Both emphasized news items of interest to labor. They covered local strikes in detail, something the antilabor press frequently failed to do. They also informed subscribers of boycotted firms, conditions of labor within many industries, and employment opportunities at various towns throughout the state and region. Of course, they carried news of the order's activities at the district, state, and national levels. If other papers published by the Knights compared favorably to the *Sentinel* and *Messenger*, the order briefly enjoyed a remarkably capable press. But unfortunately for the order, the press could not provide the immediate benefits its members expected.

The *Sentinel* and *Messenger* also illustrate the financial problems encountered by the labor press. Subscription lists were small. In October 1887, the *Messenger* reported a circulation of 578 copies. Subscribers paid only a dollar per year. By January, its subscribers had increased to just over 600. Advertising revenues must have been low, for both papers relied on ads from local grocers, inexpensive clothing shops, patent medicine distributors, and so forth. Advertising income was so badly needed that despite the Knights' strong temperance stand, the *Messenger* ran frequent ads for liquor dealers, one of whom proclaimed "Pure North Carolina corn whiskey a specialty." [21]

A fundamental goal of the Knights' educational efforts was to convince workers to initiate cooperative programs. The order rejected the wage system because it felt the system separated the laborer from the means of production and cheated him of the just rewards of his labor. Through cooperation, the Knights sought to turn back the clock and once again make the laborer a proprietor. Goods made in cooperative factories would be distributed through consumer cooperatives. Powderly revealed his opposition to the wage system in his first address to the G.A. as master workman in 1880. Cooperation, he maintained, offered the most viable alternative. From its inception, the *Journal* urged the adoption of a cooperative system, portraying cooperation as "the only means whereby the poor can obtain a just share of the profits and honors of advancing civilization." [22]

The national order did little to implement its cooperative theories, however. In 1880, the G.A. reserved 60 percent of the Assistance Fund for cooperation, but failure of the membership to support the fund made this an empty gesture. In 1881, the G.A. established a Cooperative Association governed by an elective cooperative board. But the following year, the G.A. made participation in the cooperative program voluntary. The voluntary program generated a thunderous lack of response. By September 1884, the cooperative board had less than a thousand dollars at its disposal. Still, the discouraged board sought to encourage the development of cooperatives by local and state assemblies, although it could offer such projects no financial assistance. [23]

Southern Knights supported the cooperative ideal. Both the *Messenger* and the *Sentinel* carried frequent editorials on the need for cooperation. Ezzell believed it the only plan "to save the farmers from the Irish tenant system and the wage worker from the slave driver's lash." He urged locals to employ money that would otherwise be "wasted" on cigars, whiskey, and beer to establish cooperatives and believed that once established, they would generate the profits necessary for expansion. [24] The *Sentinel* declared cooperation "the answer to the labor problem . . . the inspiration of the future." Its editor argued that if given a fair trial, cooperatives could succeed, restoring the laborer to his rightful place in society. [25]

Leading southern Knights also endorsed cooperation. J. Melville Broughton, a stalwart of the Raleigh order who was elected to the cooperative board at the 1886 G.A., was an ardent supporter of cooperation. The national order's unwillingness to tax the membership to support cooperatives frustrated him. Writing to Powderly late in 1887, he asked that the order reevaluate its stand on the issue. If it concluded that cooperation offered no hope, it should be abandoned. But, he continued, if cooperation were practical, and he believed it was, the order should "give us [the board] a chance to do some real good work next year." [26]

Despite the lack of financial support from the national order, Knights attempted to establish cooperatives throughout the South.

Their earliest and most successful ventures were established by strong urban locals. Although varied in nature, these urban cooperatives produced a product, unlike the consumer cooperatives that were established later in small towns and rural areas. Of the urban co-ops formed, two were manufacturing firms, two were newspapers, and one was a combined real estate development and manufacturing enterprise. All suffered common problems of inadequate capital, restricted markets, and improper management. Only one survived the decade of the eighties as a cooperative.

The most successful of the urban co-ops was the National Knights of Labor Co-operative Tobacco Company, incorporated in Raleigh on January 1, 1886. The cooperative began production on March 1, after raising $1,000 of its $10,000 capital authorization. It began with seven workers but employed twenty-five after a month's operation. The firm manufactured two grades of smoking tobacco, the "K of L" brand and a cheaper brand called "Noble Order." At the end of June 1886, the co-op had sold over $5,000 worth of tobacco, paid out $1,000 in wages, and had over $4,500 paid in capital. The officers, including Secretary J. M. Broughton and President John Nichols, urged members to invest, believing the venture had proven its economic feasibility. [27]

Operating capital remained a problem, however. As of June 15, 1886, the firm had nearly $3,000 in accounts receivable and less than $400 cash on hand. [28] The cooperative turned to the national cooperative board for financial aid in late 1886 and again in May 1887. Its officers proposed turning the firm over to the board for an investment of $4,000 to $5,000 to be used to hire salesmen to develop markets in the North and West. The board sent G. G. McCartney to examine the cooperative in July 1887. After a year's operation, the firm had over $1,600 in accounts receivable and only $400 in cash on hand. It had, however, acquired assets of $3,400, exclusive of accounts receivable, while expending over $8,000 for wages, tobacco, and other operating expenses, and showed a profit of $208.74. McCartney recommended that the board accept the cooperative's offer, but the board had neither the authority nor the funds to do so. At the board's request, the 1887 G.A. issued an appeal for members to buy the firm's products. [29]

The tobacco co-op continued its efforts to compete with the Dukes and other major tobacco manufacturers of the Raleigh-Durham area despite the lack of aid from the national order. Largely because it lacked capital, the firm never obtained cigarette-rolling machines. Nevertheless, it struggled through the decade, producing the two brands of smoking tobacco. In 1890, it remained a cooperative and continued to be plagued by inadequate capital. That year, the firm requested members to invest at $2.50 per share. George Tonnoffski, recording secretary of the state assembly, had replaced Broughton as company secretary; and B. H. Woodell, a prominent Raleigh Knight, had replaced Nichols as president. [30]

Knights in the Birmingham area initiated an even more ambitious project. The brainchild of Emil Lesser, a German Jew and local restaurateur, the project reflected the boom mentality of the mineral region in the 1880s. Lesser, like coal barons Henry Debardeleben and Enoch Ensley, decided to establish a town complete with homes, factories, stores, and a commuter rail line; only he proposed a cooperative town to be settled by Knights. In December 1886, Lesser and two other Knights, N. Lowenthal and L. N. Schmid, formed the Mutual Land and Improvement Company, capitalized at $7,500. The three men purchased all 120 shares and acquired thirty-seven acres of land for $9,000. They then laid plans for a cooperative town, which they named Powderly. The town contained 175 lots, each 50 by 120 feet. Corner lots were reserved for businesses, interior lots were to be sold as homesites to members of the order. Purchase of a lot made a Knight a member of the cooperative. [31]

The project proved an immediate success. Within six months, fifteen homes were constructed and thirty more contracted. Valued at $700, the homes sold to cooperative members for $350. In April, Lesser and other Knights organized the Co-operative Cigar Works, capitalized at $10,000. The cooperative began production in Birmingham but in October moved into a new factory at Powderly. Four hundred shares in the firm were sold to members at $25 each; miners in the region purchased over half of them. In March, the Knights established the T. V. Powderly Cooperative Association, a general store capitalized at $5,000. By February 1888, Powderly boasted twenty-six houses, with an additional twenty-five scheduled for completion within two months, a depot and post office, a general store, the cigar works, a school, and a hall for the local assembly, the Girard Assembly. [32]

Encouraged by their success at Powderly, Lesser and others attempted to duplicate it. They formed a second firm, the Beneficial Land and Improvement Company, and purchased forty acres some two miles west of Powderly. Here they laid off another town, Trevelick, named for Richard Trevelick, the Knights' general lecturer. Although Trevelick experienced some growth, it failed to meet its founders' expectations. Evidently Birmingham area Knights could only support one town.[33]

Powderly also began to encounter difficulties. Despite rapid growth, some of its plans were unfulfilled. Lesser had difficulty obtaining trolley connections to Birmingham. The cigar factory badly needed operating capital. In 1888, the state assembly urged its members to buy the co-op's products, observing that the firm "has had a hard struggle since its organization." The town fathers failed to attract the heavy industry, especially a steel mill, which they had hoped would locate in Powderly. Finally, like the Raleigh co-op, Powderly appealed to the G.A. for aid. In 1888, its leaders requested the G.A. to invest $10,000 in a cooperative factory to be located in Powderly, an investment which they proposed be raised by a compulsory assessment on the membership. The G.A. ignored their request. Without capital, the cigar factory and general store failed; the town lost its cooperative status. But it remained a surburb of Birmingham populated by the white working class, continued to grow, and was eventually incorporated into the city. Powderly remains today an identifiable neighborhood, one of Birmingham's postal substations, zip code 35221.[34]

Virginia Knights met with less success in their cooperative ventures. In Richmond, members of the area's two district assemblies established a cooperative soap factory. The firm manufactured a soap called "K of L" (the Knights displayed no originality in naming their products), which was described as a "first class product." Although the *Journal of United Labor* urged members to purchase its product, the cooperative encountered immediate financial problems. Charges by local Knights that the co-op manager, Henry Mente, converted its funds to his personal use further complicated matters. Mente's accusers appealed for an investigation by the G. E. B. The board queried Mente by letter on several occasions and requested that he appear before them to answer the allegations against him. Mente ignored their requests, and the cooperative failed.[35]

Of the cooperatives established by the Knights, two were news-

papers, both in Georgia. The cooperative board's report to the 1887
G. A. listed the *Savannah Evening Call* as one of eleven cooperative
Knights of Labor papers in the country. The other cooperative paper,
the *Working World*, was published in Atlanta. Several members
established the *World* early in 1886, but it soon fell under the control
of one member who found himself and his paper at odds with Atlanta
D.A. 105, of which the *World* was the official organ. As a result, the
D.A. decided to purchase the paper and assessed its members for
funds to do so. Members received a share of stock in return for payment of the ten-dollar assessment. The paper, with over 3,500 subscribers and assets of over $2,500, prompted visions of vast financial
returns in the minds of D.A. officers. As one officer, Ben H. Doster,
expressed it, "With proper management the possibilities of such a
paper are incalculable." [36]

Some locals, including those in Macon, disputed Doster's optimistic forecast and refused to pay the assessment. They also complained
to Powderly about the purchase, and he ruled that the D.A. could not
collect the assessment because all Knights' cooperatives had to be voluntary. Infuriated, Doster countered that the Macon locals led the
movement to acquire the paper and then reneged on their commit-
ments. Thus, like other of the order's projects, the *Working World* fell
victim to petty jealousies, perhaps an inevitable fate given the district's motives for acquiring the paper. [37]

The struggles and failures of urban cooperatives had little effect
upon the enthusiasm of rural and small town locals for cooperation.
Rather, as the order became more rural in 1887 and 1888, interest in
cooperation increased. But rural and small town locals emphasized
consumer cooperatives rather than manufacturing firms. The ideal of
many small town locals was to build a two-story building, use the
upper floor as a meeting hall, and establish a cooperative grocery or
general store below. [38] Small town and rural Knights undoubtedly
avoided more ambitious cooperative ventures because they lacked
capital resources and knowledge of the manufacturing process. The
preference for small consumer cooperatives also reflected the influence of the Farmers' Alliance, the order's major competitor for membership in the rural South. Like the Knights, the Alliance proclaimed
cooperation a potential cure for the farmers' financial woes. But the
Alliance concentrated on merchandising cooperatives, especially cooperative cotton markets, as a method of destroying the crop lien sys-

tem which had dragged so many of the region's farmers into tenancy. They also encouraged the formation of consumer co-ops in an effort to lower prices paid by farmers for supplies, staples, and equipment. [39] In short, rural Knights, like rural Alliance men, emphasized consumer cooperatives because they better fit their needs.

More so than their urban brethren, rural and small town Knights plunged into cooperative ventures because they appeared to offer the only glimmer of hope of escape from economic disaster and the accompanying sense of sheer frustration. Many had no real understanding of the concept, let alone devotion to it. They realized, however, that some action must be taken so that they could purchase supplies, tools, fertilizer, and other items at lower costs. Otherwise, they would continue to live at the mercy of the local merchant or banker. As one Knight admitted, his assembly was ignorant of the principles of the order but was "awakening to the benefits of cooperation." Another rural Knight, even more ignorant of the order's principles, asked Powderly to aid his local's cooperative general store so that the local might acquire funds in case it had to strike. [40]

A cooperative established by Knights in the rural Alabama community of Knightville typified many such ventures. Members of the Knightville local invested $500 in a two-story building. The upper floor was used as a meeting hall, while they converted the lower into a cooperative grocery which they stocked with goods valued at $100. Many of the members, with good reason, were skeptical of the cooperative's chances for success. But its supporters believed the venture would succeed and help cultivate the virtue of thrift within the membership. [41]

Some more imaginative rural Knights attempted to apply the principles of cooperation to the problem of obtaining land. In a pathetic letter to Powderly, Knights in the rural community of Scotland Neck, North Carolina, probably members of a black local, appealed for financial aid. The local had established a cooperative which had purchased one hundred acres of land for $1,000. The members planned to farm the land. But the assembly had paid only $25 down on the purchase and saw no prospects of raising the remainder. Perplexed, its members asked Powderly to assess the general membership a cent per member to help them pay off their indebtedness. "If we can't get no assistance from our brothers," the local's recording secretary explained, "we will be forever lost." [42]

The educational and cooperative programs of the southern Knights reflect the nature and state of the order within the region from its inception through its decline. Prior to 1887, the order was essentially urban, and so were its educational and cooperative efforts. The national officers who toured the South, with few exceptions, concentrated their efforts on the region's major cities and towns. The labor press was located almost exclusively in major urban areas. The *Labor Herald*, the most successful of the Knights' papers, was established in Richmond in 1885 and served the order in the Richmond metropolitan area. The *Alabama Sentinel*, although the organ of the state assembly, was primarily the voice of the Knights in Birmingham and the state's mineral region. Until the order's political defeats in 1888, both the *Sentinel* and the *Messenger* primarily addressed the concerns of urban laborers. All of the manufacturing cooperatives established by the order were located in urban areas. The Raleigh tobacco factory and the Powderly venture capitalized on economic trends in their specific regions—tobacco manufacturing and real estate development. They met with some success because each locality possessed locals with a large urban membership, competent leadership from the ranks of the middle class, and members with enough capital to establish the cooperatives. But even the larger urban assemblies lacked the capital to sustain cooperatives once begun or the numbers to provide a market large enough to generate the capital required.

As the order began to decline in the cities, its urban members disillusioned by the Knights' failure to procure for them immediate economic benefits, its programs began to reflect the needs of a more rural membership. The Knights newspapers still in existence began to emphasize programs designed to meet problems peculiar to an agrarian constituency, as exemplified by the *Sentinel* appealing to both Knights and Alliance members. Small rural locals, composed, unlike the Farmers' Alliance locals, of tenants and rural day laborers, sought to found consumer cooperatives without capital, managerial skills, or even a basic knowledge of the principles of cooperation. Their efforts imitated those of wealthier alliance assemblies, whose members were primarily landowning farmers. Among an increasingly rural, impoverished membership, the Knights could maintain neither educational nor cooperative programs without assistance from the national order. The G.A. simply did not have the ability to lend such assistance, and the programs formerly supported by an urban labor force collapsed.

7 The Knights of Labor and Southern Blacks

SO COMPLEX, ambiguous, and contradictory were patterns of race relations in the South of the 1880s that historians continue to debate their nature.[1] Laws, economics, social mores, and the percentage of the total population that was black all helped to determine the relationship between the races. Each factor varied from state to state and even from region to region within a state. Yet in this chaos, one constant remained. The white southerner's determination to preserve his region as a "white man's country" had been tempered by neither the Union victory and the end of slavery nor Radical Reconstruction's challenge to white concepts of the place of the Negro in society. Apparent differences among whites over the "Negro question" only reflected disagreements over the degree to which blacks were to be subjugated and the tactics to be employed to keep them so.

The Noble Order of the Knights of Labor, like any organization seeking to build a southern membership in the 1880s, was compelled to confront the complex, emotionally explosive racial issue. The order could not ignore blacks, for their presence was a major determinant of labor economics, as were the prejudices of whites. To succeed, the order had to formulate a workable approach to the racial problem. For the Knights, as for so many other organizations, the task proved to be too difficult.[2]

To be effective, the Knights' racial policies had to offer hope to blacks, overcome some of the prejudices of white laborers, and blunt the inevitable criticism of those who opposed the order. The Knights' leadership sought to meet these requirements by implementing two separate strategies. Although somewhat contradictory, they were implemented simultaneously. On the one hand, the order tried to circumvent the issue by maintaining that it sought to redress purely economic grievances. Race had no relation to economic questions and should not be allowed to interfere with the work of the order. On the other hand, the Knights recognized the racial problem and sought to solve it in a manner that would betray neither the order's northern antebellum reform heritage nor the more ardent prejudices of the white southern laborer. Both approaches proved inadequate, resulting in a system of modified segregation within the order. Opponents sucessfully used the order's liberal policies against it, while white members failed to overcome their prejudices and unite with black members on economic issues. As racial attitudes hardened in the South, whites began to leave the order. It became increasingly the refuge of the most downtrodden blacks—the tenant, the rural day laborer, and the domestic worker. They clung to the Knights with a hope and faith born of desperation.

The national leadership of the Knights espoused racial policies decidedly more liberal than those accepted by white southerners. Like many of the Knights' national policies, they reflected the influence of antebellum reformism, including abolition. The order's first Grand Master Workman, Uriah Stephens, came from a Quaker background and was educated for the Baptist ministry. An abolitionist, he supported Fremont in 1856 and Lincoln in 1860.[3] Stephens advocated the recognition of blacks as economic but not social equals. In a reply written in 1879 to a white organizer in Alabama, Stephens ruled that Negro and white locals should be treated equally. He noted, however, that no integrated locals existed in the order and, rather, that blacks were organized into separate assemblies. Despite his approval of segregated locals, he believed that "in labor there is no distinction of Race. We all stand or fall together."[4]

Terence V. Powderly, who succeeded Stephens as Grand Master Workman in 1879, held even more advanced views about race.[5] Younger than Stephens, Powderly had not engaged in antebellum politics. But he remembered supporting the views of his mother, "a pronounced abolitionist," rather than those of his father, "a pronounced Democrat."[6] While in office, he expressed the belief that the abolitionists and organized labor were both "revolutionary in their character. . . .[Their] ends in view were the same, viz.: the freedom of the man who worked."[7] His second official opinion as Grand Master Workman declared that "the [outside] color of a candidate [for membership] cannot debar him from admission: rather let the coloring of his mind and heart be the test."[8] In his first memoirs, Powderly devoted an entire chapter to the race question. He noted that "in the field of production," blacks and whites were equal. Poor whites were held in bondage by their beliefs of racial superiority. He chided white southerners for breaking their own racial taboos, stating that "the slave owners of long ago leveled the distinction between races."[9]

Yet Powderly's racial concepts were not so advanced as to prevent his accommodating the views of white southerners. Although he did not oppose integrated locals, Powderly believed segregation was the only practical way to organize southern members. An 1887 reply to an inquiry about the organization of blacks contains an excellent example of Powderly's willingness to compromise. "Our Order," he wrote,

> does not recognize any difference in the rights and privileges of the races of mankind. Colored men are regarded as entitled to the same treatment as whites, they may be admitted to Assemblies having white members, but the best way is to organize them in Assemblies of their own and allow the work of education to do away with the prejudice now existing against them.[10]

Powderly even stood ready to curtail the organization of blacks if it threatened the existing southern order. In 1885, a dispute among locals in the Raleigh-Durham area of North Carolina over the propriety of organizing an assembly of black women prompted Powderly to advise the locals that "I think it better to postpone the work, at least for a time under the circumstances."[11]

Powderly also neglected excellent opportunities to increase the order's popularity among urban blacks as late as 1889, at a time when the southern order was becoming increasingly an organization of rural blacks. Charles H. L. Taylor, a black attorney in Atlanta and a former minister to Liberia, requested an audience with Powderly during that year's General Assembly, which was held in Atlanta. "Your grand order is able to do more good for them [blacks] than any organization I know of on Earth," he wrote. Powderly stamped his request "No answer required." He affixed the same stamp to an offer by C. E. Yarboro, editor of the *Southern Appeal*, a black Atlanta paper, to use his paper in a manner that might "prove beneficial to the order amongst the Negroes in Georgia."[12] As Powderly stated in his memoirs, he did not seek "to interfere with the social relations of the races in the South, for it is the industrial, not the race, question we endeavor to solve."[13]

The order's southern leaders endorsed, with varying degrees of enthusiasm, the racial policies of Stephens and Powderly. Their relative liberalism can be accounted for by a number of factors. Some, like Nicholas Stack of Alabama and John Power of Mississippi, were not natives of the South. Others, such as John Nichols of North Carolina and W. P. Russell of South Carolina, were Republicans of long standing. Still others, such as J. Melville Broughton of North Carolina and William Mullen of Virginia, were Democrats concerned about the plight of blacks.

Whatever their reasons, southern leaders exhibited a racial liberalism that created problems within the rank and file white membership. Nicholas Stack protested the hypocrisy of those who ignored crimes of whites but lynched alleged Negro rapists. Southern sheriffs, wrote Stack, justified lynchings by shouting "I didn't like's niggers no how!" Stack encouraged racial solidarity within the Alabama ranks, even at the temporary expense of white members.[14] C. W. Ezzell, editor of the *Fayetteville Messenger*, the Knights' official state paper in North Carolina, defended the order's racial policies. Race, he believed, should not be considered in attempting to solve economic problems. In "matters of civil rights," the Knights should see that "justice is meted out."[15] Few southerners, however, were willing to go as far as J. A. Bodenhamer of Jacksonville. He proposed that the Knights concentrate on organizing blacks, since southern whites could never overcome their racial prejudices.[16]

The structure of the southern order revealed the inherent tension in the policy of accepting the blacks as economic equals while regarding whites as socially superior. At the local assembly level, segregation was the accepted practice. Although some integrated locals existed, they were rare. Letters from southern locals to John Hayes, the order's secretary-treasurer, Powderly, and the *Journal of United Labor*, leave no doubt that the overwhelming majority of southern locals were segregated. There is also little doubt that the national order acted upon the advice of southern whites in developing its racial policies. And with few exceptions, whites demanded a segregated structure at the local assembly level. John Power, Mississippi's state master workman and a champion of the organization of blacks, recognized that integrated locals would defeat the order's efforts to organize the South. He informed Powderly that "the colored race for the present at least, had better be formed into separate assemblies."[17] Blacks would acquiesce in this arrangement but not without protests of unequal treatment.

Integration was the rule at the district assembly level; but powerful forces for segregation existed, primarily among blacks. Organized in 1885, the all-black District Assembly 92 of Richmond contained thirteen locals at the time of that year's General Assembly.[18] As the order recruited more blacks, D.A. 92 added locals as far East as Portsmouth. The black Portsmouth locals chose affiliation with District 92 rather than District Assembly 123, organized in Norfolk in 1886, despite the fact that District 123 invited the black tidewater locals to join.[19] Black locals at Savanah, Pensacola, and Petersburg also expressed the desire to form black districts; but opposition from the districts to which they were attached prevented them from doing so. [20] Black locals wished to establish segregated district assemblies in order to give blacks control of the district offices. Black districts would insure more black representation at the state and General assemblies, for districts elected delegates to both bodies. Thus, to some extent, segregation at the district level was initiated by blacks and reflected a sense of black pride. But blacks also felt that white districts, although wishing to retain their black locals, were less than equitable in their treatment of them. In this sense, their support of segregated districts illustrated mistrust of whites, as well as a desire for a power base of their own within the order.

Except for the locals in District Assembly 92, all southern black locals not directly attached to the General Assembly were members of integrated district assemblies. Most southern districts contained black locals, although District Assembly 85 of Richmond evidently did not, for the black locals of the region were attached to District 92. Blacks were active in the affairs of integrated districts, attending meetings and holding offices. [21]

Both the state assemblies and the General Assembly were integrated. All southern state assemblies contained black locals, and blacks participated fully in state assembly activities. State assemblies also insured that blacks obtained some state offices. [22] Since the state assemblies met only once or twice a year, the offices blacks held were more important than positions as delegates to the assembly. Most of the major state offices, however, went to whites. The annual General Assembly was attended by blacks who represented black locals directly attached to the General Assembly, District Assembly 92, or, occasionally, integrated district and state assemblies. Blacks from Georgia, Florida, Virginia, North Carolina, and Alabama represented the southern states at the 1886 General Assembly in Richmond. In addition, Maryland, Pennsylvania, New York, and the District of Columbia each had at least one black delegate in attendance. [23]

The Knights adopted an integrated structure above the local level for the same reason that the Populist party would integrate its party structure in the 1890s. That is, the leadership of the order, both North and South, believed that to organize only the white worker would be an exercise in futility. They had to appeal to blacks as well, because economic improvement for whites could not come without improvement for blacks. But they could not appeal to blacks simply on economic terms, for blacks were as interested, if not more so, in the order's social and racial concepts. Yet to grant the blacks' demand for equality would surely drive white members out of the ranks. The order therefore opted for segregated locals and an integrated structure above that level in an attempt to satisfy all factions.

In most southern states, white organizers accomplished the original organizational work among blacks. In North Carolina, for example, John Ray, the state organizer, established the first black local in Raleigh in 1884. [24] H. F. Hoover, a roaming organizer, led in the organization of blacks in South Carolina and Georgia. William Mullen organized the first black locals in Virginia. [25]

As blacks' interest in the order grew and the number of black locals increased, a demand for black organizers developed. Originally, whites anxious to build the order's southern membership voiced the demand for black organizers. A resolution introduced at the 1885 General Assembly called for "colored organizers" to be placed in each of the old slave states. [26] Thereafter, entreaties to Powderly for the appointment of black organizers poured in from the South. [27] Early in 1887, the North Carolina state assembly recommended the appointment of eight state organizers; four were white, and four were black. [28] Among the black organizers appointed by Powderly in 1886 and 1887 were W. A. Brooks, W. J. Campbell, J. W. Robertson, and Alexander Walker of Alabama; Frank Johnson and W. J. Woodward of North Carolina; Andrew Allen of Georgia; and Lee Nelson of Virginia. Black organizers were also in the field in South Carolina, Florida, and Louisiana. [29]

The Knights used black organizers in an effort to ensure continued black recruits by appealing to racial pride. Blacks made it clear that they expected to be treated with dignity and respect and that they were entitled to a share of the order's patronage, including organizers' positions. Black Knights from Savannah informed Powderly in 1886 that "we want a colored organizer where there is this kind of preduce [*sic*] against us" and noted that "we can't mix in Masonic and Odd Fellows and that is why this preduce [*sic*] is still kept up." Charleston Knights expressed the same sentiments. Members of a lapsed black local sought to have their assembly reorganized. But they wrote to John Hayes that "this assembly is composed of colored men who do not want the white men to re-organize there [*sic*] assemblies." When Frank Johnson and Alexander Walker, black organizers in North Carolina and Alabama, respectively, found their credentials challenged by whites, they appealed to Powderly to sustain them. To do otherwise, they argued, would damage the appeal of the order to blacks. [30]

Those southern whites who believed that the Knights had to appeal to blacks if they were to effectively address the region's economic problems also realized that if the order were to attract blacks, it must recognize their desire for equal treatment. A feud over the credentials of a black organizer prompted John Ray, in defending the organizer, to tell Powderly in a letter that the blacks were "growing impatient and suspicious and watching every move to confirm their suspicions that they are not treated just as their white brothers are." [31] Such concerns on the part of the state assembly's leadership certainly prompted the North Carolina state assembly's 1886 decision to distribute organizers' commissions equally to members of both races.

On the other hand, the reluctance of whites to organize blacks also contributed to the use of black organizers. When a white organizer near Richmond delayed the organization of area blacks, the blacks appealed to Powderly for the appointment of a black organizer. [32] A black member from South Carolina complained to Powderly that "our white brothers down South is not eager to organize the Negro race that is why we appeal to you for a colored organizer."[33]

Finally, blacks mistrusted white organizers, often with good reason. "As a general thing," wrote an Alabama black, "the colored people of the South do not understand the white, and the white organizer can not do just what is necessary for the upbuilding of the order." W. S. Rudd, writing to Powderly in 1885, stated the blacks' distrust of white organizers even more forcefully. A member of a white local, Rudd urged Powderly to appoint someone to work among the blacks of the Richmond area, for "Taking every thing into consideration, the political differences between the white and blacks and the general opinion held by them, the colored man in this state, that the white man is his enemy, places this assembly in the light of wishing to retard their progress in organizing."[34] The conduct of some white organizers did little to discourage the blacks' distrust. Powderly revoked the credentials of white organizers in Alabama and Georgia for failing to forward fees and dues collected from newly organized black locals. The *Journal of United Labor* demanded their expulsion from the order for endangering its growth among blacks.[35]

Black members of the Knights, just as the whites, represented many occupations. They included miners, stevedores, lumber and sawmill workers, ironworkers, cannery hands, railroad laborers, barbers, merchants, farmers, day laborers, and a few professionals. Most black locals were mixed assemblies, as were most white locals. A number of women's locals were also organized and were usually comprised of domestic workers. The first black members, usually laborers and domestics, came from such urban areas as Atlanta, Richmond, Durham, Raleigh, and Jacksonville. On his 1885 tour of southern cities, Powderly found blacks extremely receptive to the order. But by 1887, the order's black recruits came primarily from rural areas. This trend toward a rural black membership ceased only with the demise of the order and was perhaps most evident in North Carolina and Georgia.[36]

Southern blacks rushed into the order for two basic reasons. The first was economic. Landless in an agrarian society, barred from the textile, bright leaf tobacco, furniture, and other industries, blacks sought an escape from the deadening poverty in which they lived. The

Knights seemed to offer this means of escape. A black member from North Carolina, after noting the prevailing low wages and the notion that farm labor was demeaning, expressed the hope that the Knights could "enlighten the mind of men to the dignity of labor." A Florida Knight expressed the belief that since God helped those who helped themselves, laborers should exert themselves to obtain freedom from the "sharks and shylocks." [37]

Blacks, however, sought more than better economic conditions and dignity as laborers. They sought acceptance by society and dignity as men. The Knights, more than any other organization of the era, appeared willing to extend to blacks a measure of both acceptance and dignity. The racial incidents at the Richmond General Assembly of 1886, which will be discussed later, significantly increased the interest of blacks in the order. A South Carolina black sought to join the order because "we are bond to join something what will to led to better rights then [sic] we have. I read of your convention in Richmond makes me feel more interest in it." Another black expressed the hope that the racial barriers would be overcome and that both blacks and whites could be "brought into the fold of the Knights of Labor." [38]

Timing also played an important part in the order's success among blacks. Not since the collapse of the Reconstruction programs of the Radical Republicans had a national organization offered southern blacks the opportunity to both improve their economic status and gain recognition of their worth as individuals. Reconstruction dreams of forty acres and a mule and social independence, if not acceptance, had been shattered. Instead, tenant farming, domestic service, and hard manual labor became the harsh economic realities of blacks in the postwar South. And by the end of the 1880s, it was obvious that racial lines were beginning to harden, that blacks were to be treated as a people apart, an inferior population. No other organization seemed to offer hope. The Farmers' Alliance had banned black members. Not until March 1888 was the Colored Farmers' National Alliance formed; and for nearly a year it remained primarily an extension of the black Texas State Alliance, which had been created in December 1886. In addition, blacks were well aware that the Southern Alliance represented landowning farmers who looked upon blacks as a source of cheap labor and were unlikely to take any action which would jeopardize that labor supply. [39]

As economic conditions worsened and racial lines were drawn more sharply, southern blacks turned to the Knights with a hope born of the desperation that precedes resignation. "The colored people of the South are flocking to us, being eager of organization and education, and, when thoroughly imbued with our principles, are unswerving in their fidelity," reported Secretary-Treasurer Frederick Turner to the 1886 General Assembly. The blacks' faith in the order, and in Powderly, seemed unshaken by the order's failure in 1886 to win several strikes of national importance. Many saw the Knights as something of a religious organization and Powderly as a high priest who possessed powers approaching the supernatural. A South Carolina member penned a typical expression of such devotion while reporting the deplorable conditions encountered by farm laborers and domestic servants in 1887. Little could be done, he wrote, "except trust in the God of our salvation and in our order." Tom O'Riley, who toured the South with John Hayes in the spring of 1887, vividly portrayed the Negroes' response to the order. Writing to Powderly, he observed that "the order is making wonderful headway in the South, but the colored assemblies are the most perfectly disciplined. You possess, in a marked manner, the fealty—the very hearts of the Southern people. The very mention of your name sets them wild with enthusiasm. The poor Niggers believe that 'massa Powderly' is a man born to lead them out of the house of bondage." [40] The Negroes' faith proved to be misplaced, for Powderly and the Knights failed to deliver them from either the economic or social "house of bondage."

The Knights failed partially because race provided an effective, emotionally charged issue for their opponents. Critics of the order could always attack its racial policies rather than its economic concepts, a step that might have caused them embarrassment. Such opposition always resorted to two basic issues—economic interests and social mores. They sought to show that organization of blacks threatened whites in both areas. Of the two, economic interest aroused the most violent opposition. And, as has always been the case in the South, social mores were manipulated to serve economic ends.

The Knights encountered their most violent opposition from white planters and large farmers, who saw the organization of blacks as a threat to their labor supply. Like most nineteenth century employers, they believed in complete control of the labor force. Violent reaction to efforts by the Knights to organize black farm laborers began in 1886. In that year, an isolated local of cotton plantation workers near Little Rock, Arkansas, attempted to strike for higher wages. A gun battle between a sheriff's posse and the striking blacks crushed the attempt. Several blacks were wounded in the melee.[41] Increased activity by the Knights among blacks the following year led to a surge of violent opposition in the lower South. H. F. Hoover, who organized blacks in western Georgia and South Carolina, was killed by an enraged mob of whites near Warrenton, Georgia. Armed whites in South Carolina disrupted locals of black farm laborers, questioned members separately at gun point, and threatened them with violence if they remained in the order.[42]

Planter violence against the order culminated in one of the largest strikes in which the southern Knights engaged. Organizers from New Orleans had recruited many of the sugarcane workers in Louisiana's low country. A large majority of the workers were black. Just before the 1887 fall harvest, District Assembly 194, to which most of the workers belonged, threatened to strike if the planters refused to raise wages. The planters, determined to have a showdown with the union, refused to grant wage increases; and the Knights struck. The strike lasted into November, involving thousands of workers, including many nonmembers who nevertheless supported the strike. Workers walked off the job in several parishes. Unable to defeat the strikers, the planters appealed to the governor for aid, and the militia was sent. Working with local sherriffs' posses, the militia shot down the striking blacks throughout the sugar region. At least thirty blacks were killed, and it is possible that twice that number actually died.[43] The militia's policy of indiscriminate killing not only crushed the strike but destroyed the order in the sugar country.[44] As in South Carolina and Georgia, the whites justified their methods by maintaining that black locals were secret societies plotting armed insurrection.

In the upper South, planters and farmers reacted less violently to the Knights; but they also resisted the organization of their farm laborers. Many letters from black locals of farm workers appeared in the *Journal of United Labor*, complaining of resistance offered by white farmers.[45] White members of the Farmers' Alliance, which was supposedly working with the Knights, resented the organization of their day laborers just as did farmers who were not in the Alliance. A

black member of the Knights believed the Alliance was a major threat
to the black farm laborer, offering him nothing but "oppression and
death." Another blamed Alliance members for the economic plight of
blacks. Alliance members, the writer charged, had pledged not to hire
day laborers unless absolutely necessary. Then they hired fifteen-
year-old boys and paid them a child's wage for a man's work. The Alliance, the writer continued, had a "law" against lending or giving a
Negro anything. A North Carolina member charged that "the land-
lords in this section are bitterly opposed to the Knights of Labor, so
much so that some of them have said that no member of the Order
should stay on his land. But we [tenants] intend using every honorable
means to spread the light of the principles of our Order." [46]

Perhaps because black labor was less essential in urban areas, economically motivated oppositon to the organization of blacks was not
as pronounced in the cities as in rural regions. But it was evident,
sometimes forcefully so. Florida State Master Workman T. J. Mott, a
painter, was fired for his "insurrectionary movements among the
Negroes." Negro Knights in Oxford, North Carolina, were accused of
setting fire to the town. Whites nearly lynched the local master workman, who escaped physical harm only to be jailed on a "trumped up
charge." In the lumber regions of eastern Georgia, whites explained
to Victor St. Cloud, an organizer from Savannah, "that it would not
be healthy for me to tamper with the hands." The hands St. Cloud
attempted to organize were primarily blacks, whom he described as
"more of a slave than they were before the war." St. Cloud reported
that he "was also threatened with a shot gun (the South's favorite)
near Beaufort, S.C." because of his work among blacks. [47]

The Knights encountered less violent but more universal opposition because of their perceived threat to the South's racial mores.
Present from the order's initial efforts to organize blacks, such opposition was largely responsible for the development of the segregated
local assembly. A letter written to Powderly in late 1884 by Charles
Miller, organizer in the Richmond area, candidly addressed the problems the Knights might expect to encounter if they sought to organize
blacks on a major scale and recommended a policy of segregation.
The membership of Miller's Local 3380 had discussed the possibility
of organizing area blacks, who had expressed a willingness to join.
Some members staunchly opposed any effort to organize blacks if

black members would be able to attend the meetings of white locals. Miller noted "that there is yet in a large portion of our country a strong objection on the part of the whites to mix with the colored race." But he believed this was the whites' only objection to organizing blacks, for "As to helping the colored man in any attempt to benefit himself or to advance the interest of labor or to call on him to assist us in time of trouble we do not object." He hoped that Powderly would "suggest some way to overcome this trouble and so arrange it that all matters of interest to both white and colored assemblies can be done through committees and that no visiting [of blacks to white assemblies] be allowed except by invitation."[48]

While the Knights' early organizational activity among blacks aroused some criticism, it was the 1886 Richmond General Assembly which focused the attention of the South on the order's racial policies. At the Richmond General Assembly, New York District Assembly 49 insisted upon equal treatment for its Negro member, Frank J. Ferrell, in the city's hotels, restaurants, and theaters. The district's delegates left their hotel when the hotel refused to admit Ferrell. To salve the district's injured feelings, Powderly chose Ferrell to introduce him to the General Assembly. The introduction followed immediately after Governor Fitzhugh Lee's welcoming speech. Ferrell castigated the South's segregationist philosophy, declaring that the Knights sought the "abolition of those distinctions which are maintained by creed or color." He presented Powderly as a man "above the superstitions which are involved in these distinctions." After the addrress, District Assembly 49 and Ferrell initiated a row by attending a local theater. The following night, a mob of armed whites assembled outside the theater to prevent the entry of more Negroes, should any attempt to attend the performance.[49]

Armed with the Richmond incident, the opponents of the Knights leaped to the offensive. The southern press led the attack on the order's social indiscretion. The *Atlanta Constitution* warned its readers that "this agitation over the color question is a side issue, but it is big enough to wreck the Knights of Labor. The Southern members of the order are not likely to submit to the insufferable conduct of a gang of radical cranks." The *Charleston News and Courier* saw even darker clouds on the horizon. The activities of the Knights in Richmond demonstrated the order's support of "social equality." And, continued the paper, "Social equality means miscegenation," which would inevitably "leave the Southern country in the possession of a nation of mongrels and hybrids." Savannah's *News* wondered if the Knights proposed "to settle social as well as labor questions," while Raleigh's *News and Observer* noted that "our people should be warned of the new and vile use to which the Knights of Labor organization is to be put." Southerners, the editorial declared, would reject such usage. Richmond's *Whig* suggested that the Knights were greater champions of social equality than the Radical Republicans and asked "Is this the feast to which that order invites the working people of our nation?"[50]

Continuing long after the Richmond incident, such tirades began to take their toll. Rumors about the Knights' racial policies spread; it was even rumored that a Negro headed the order. The few integrated locals that remained and even segregated locals of whites that shared meeting facilities with black locals found difficulty in obtaining places to meet. Black locals increasingly resorted to secrecy. As one black member expressed it, by 1887 in much of the South, "Nigger and Knight have become synonymous terms."[51] White members began to leave the order, and an increasingly smaller proportion of the new members were white.

Opponents of the Knights' racial policies within the order also severely handicapped its efforts in the South. Although they did not resort to violence, white members exhibited the same racial prejudices as did nonmembers. They, too, refused to accept the more liberal views of the order's leadership. They refused such ideas for both economic and social reasons. Perhaps the use of segregated locals and infrequent meetings of the district, state, and General assemblies would have enabled white members to cope with the social problems if they had been convinced that the economic problems of blacks and whites were mutual. But southern whites were not so convinced, and their lack of conviction led to racial problems within the order.

The inescapable conclusion is that white members refused to accept a breach in the South's racial etiquette. Many whites demanded outright segregation. Whites refused to be organized by blacks. A Virginia member requested that Powderly appoint a white organizer for his area because whites refused to be organized by the only commissioned organizer in the region, a black. Other letters to

Powderly echoed this complaint. Local assemblies of whites also denied membership to blacks.[52] Whites withdrew from locals which admitted blacks and either formed new locals or joined existing segregated locals. Others simply left the order. Whites resented the growing influence of blacks at the district and state assembly levels and hoped to see segregation established at these levels. A white member from North Carolina complained that the 1891 state assembly was three-fourths black. His local sought to sever its attachment to the state assembly in order to prevent being "ruled" by blacks.[53] Elsewhere in the South, the Knights sponsored segregated social events. The white locals of Birmingham invited Powderly to attend their July 4 celebration of 1887. The invitation was addressed to "all white members of the order and their friends." Such events held by Mississippi Knights were also segregated.[54] The *Alabama Sentinel*, official organ of the order in that state, despite an occasional good word for blacks, carried the usual lurid reports of the captures and lynchings of alleged Negro rapists.[55] After the Richmond incident, a white member of a segregated Montgomery local wrote to Powderly that "I cannot believe that our colored brothers will be set up by our grand order as our social equals . . . when the social problem comes in, public sympathy is to emphatically against it for our order to hold up its head this side of Mason and Dixon line."[56] The gentleman knew his region well.

The membership of a few whites in integrated locals and the integrated structure of district and state assemblies did not alter the fact that white members had no intention of removing blacks from their subservient position. Indeed, the development of black district assemblies resulted partially because of white members' racial prejudices. When black and white assemblies met together, whites usually dominated the meeting. In some instances, whites denied Negro members the privilege of speaking. A letter from Alexander Walker to Powderly vividly portrays the indignities to which white members subjected black members:

I take it opon myself to ask you is it wright that a colored members cannot speak in the white assembly last meeting the white man they was discussing labor one of the colored members ask the master workman could he speak a word or two on labor. He told him he could not speak in this assembly and when they come to our meeting they speak as long as they say in the meeting i have no more to say at this time present please send me answer as son as you can i like to have it by next meeting night.[57]

White assemblies also refused to allow officers from black assemblies to fulfill certain duties within the courts and offices of the district assembly.[58] Such open displays of white supremacy understandably led to friction between the races within the order.

The Knights also failed to overcome the fears of white members who saw the blacks as economic competitors. When the Knights elected a majority to the Richmond City Council in 1886, the council refused to hire blacks for the construction of a new city hall.[59] In North Carolina, textile workers questioned the candidacy of a Knight for county office because they had heard the order would place Negroes in their jobs. The beleaguered candidate vowed he did not favor the use of Negroes in the mills, at least "not in competition with white labor." He denied that blacks had any desire to obtain positions in the mills.[60] An 1886 strike by the Knights against textile mills in Augusta, Georgia, collapsed partially because striking white operatives believed rumors that mill owners planned to hire Negroes. The *Evening Call*, a Knights of Labor paper in Savannah, refused to hire black printers, even if they were Knights.[61]

A strike by black ironworkers in Birmingham in 1887 illustrates in classic simplicity the inability of whites to grasp the truth that their long-term economic interests were identical to those of blacks. Black Knights struck three ironworks that summer, seeking higher wages. White members, most of whom were more skilled and better paid than the blacks, refused to go out in their support. State Master Workman Nicholas Stack worked for weeks before convincing the whites to support the striking blacks. The whites finally left the ironworks on the direct orders of Stack, but dissension in their ranks continued. One white local refused Stack admittance to their union hall. Many sided with an opponent of Stack who argued that it was foolish for a $3-a-day white worker to strike in support of an unskilled black laborer. Shortsighted self-interest prevailed; dissension in the ranks forced Stack to call off the strike.[62]

Blacks protested the prejudiced and shortsighted actions of the white members of the order, but to no avail. The *Savannah Tribune*, a black newspaper provides an excellent example of black criticism of racism within the order. The *Tribune* had praised the order for its actions at the 1886 Richmond convention and expressed the belief that it offered great hope to blacks. But when Savannah's *Evening Call*, paper of the city's white Knights, refused to hire black printers in February 1887, the *Tribune* advised blacks to "ponder over and reflect when they continue to furnish aid and support to a cause that recoils and strikes them down." When whites criticized the *Tribune*'s editorial on labor and race, the paper made its position even clearer. Powderly and the national order, the *Tribune* believed, recognized no color line; "But the organ of the Knights of Labor [the *Evening Call*] in this city, cowardly forsakes the principles of the Order, and demands the elevation of white men at the expense of colored men; indeed it commended the decision of the Central Railroad management to employ none but white men."[63] Such protests did little, however, to dispel the white members' fear of economic and social competition with blacks.

An assessment of the Knights' racial policies and their implementation depends somewhat on the assessor's point of view. Some historians have seen the Knights as a liberal organization which proved that the southern color line could be broken. Others have expressed the belief that the racial liberalism of the order has been overrated, as have its accomplishments in breaking the color barrier.[64] Both views can be substantiated. As with many of the problems in the South's complex racial history, much depends on whether the viewer sees the bottle as half-full or half-empty.

The positive contributions of the Knights are undeniable. They made the first serious effort to recruit black laborers and were the last labor organization to do so for the rest of the nineteenth century. They succeeded in obtaining a large number of black members, especially in rural areas. The order's announced liberal racial policies clearly brought many blacks into its ranks. The Knights gave blacks positions within the order, utilized a partially integrated organizational structure, and espoused the doctrine that the economic interests of blacks and whites were identical. Some southern leaders, including Stack of Alabama and Mott of Florida, championed the cause of social justice for blacks, at least to a degree. The order's racial policies were more advanced than those of the Farmers' Alliance, which adopted a rigidly segregated structure once white Alliance members decided that blacks should be organized at all. It is also evident that rural blacks, many of whom were day laborers, favored the Knights and mistrusted the Alliance members, many of whom were employers of farm labor. The landowners' desire to maintain a supply of cheap black labor helps explain why blacks, especially those in rural areas, turned to the order. For economic reasons, an alliance between white urban and industrial laborers was more likely than one between white landowning farmers and black tenants and rural day laborers. But it should be noted that the Knights' racial policies were also more liberal than those expressed by southern leaders in the American Federation of Labor at the turn of the century. [65] However, much of the Knights' apparent liberalism might be explained by C. Vann Woodward's assertion that southern racial patterns did not solidify until the 1890s.

Despite the Knights' accomplishments, it is evident that the racial views expressed by both the national and southern leaders of the order were far in advance of those held by the majority of southern white laborers. It is also clear that white members continued to discriminate against their black fellow Knights and to feel economically threatened by them. In the contest between economic interest and racial prejudice, prejudice won, as usual. The order's southern leadership realized that the racial problem had to be controlled if the Knights were to be successful in improving the lot of the workingman. But they could not overcome decades of racial fear and mistrust. J. A. Belton of Mississippi wrote to Powderly in 1886 that "unless by means of organization we [white and black] can be brought to co-operation, our cause is lamentable, and will be perpetuated by the gross ignorance that pervades every nook and corner of our state." Opponents, he cautioned, would inaugurate "the social equality principle, knowing that social principle is so odious to many of the white people that they will be deterred from the order." [66] Belton was only partially correct. Opponents did use the "social equality principle" against the order, and it did hinder the order's growth among whites. But racism did more than stop the order's growth. It caused friction within the order and finally drove many whites from its ranks. The organization became basically a black union in the South and one composed of the economically weakest blacks. Once this change occurred, for all practical purposes, the order ceased to exist in the South.

8 Internal Problems of the Southern Order

WHEN the General Assembly convened in Richmond on October 4, 1886, the Knights of Labor appeared, even to opponents, as a formidable advocate of the southern worker. The Knights had locals in every southern state and were establishing state assemblies in North Carolina, Florida, and Alabama. The order was active in congressional and municipal elections throughout the region. At that moment, it was conducting at Augusta, Georgia, the largest strike in the history of the southern textile industry; and sporadic strikes continued to hamper industries throughout the region. The very presence of the national convention of the country's largest labor union in a southern city, the capital of the Confederacy, and the large number of southern delegates it attracted indicated that the Knights might, indeed, sweep the "producers" of the region into one organization which would possess the power to drastically alter the region's political and economic establishment.

The Knights' outward appearance, however, belied the actual state of the order. Rather than a vital, powerful, expanding organization, the Knights of Labor was a dying institution already on the decline at the national level. Although not at peak numerical strength, the southern order, too, was floundering. Built upon the hopes and dreams of the economically powerless, lacking a solid foundation, and plagued by internal weaknesses, the southern Knights were on the brink of collapse. Internal problems, or those problems over which the order had some control, were the primary factors in what would soon become the order's rapid disintegration.[1] While the southern order faced some internal problems that were also encountered by the order nationally, some were unique to the region.

Ironically, the Knights' large membership, which so alarmed southern industrialists in 1885 and 1886, led the list of the order's in-

ternal difficulties. Because of the virtual absence of membership
requirements, the Knights' membership was a polyglot mixture of
rural and urban, black and white, male and female, laborers and
white-collar workers, salesmen and small businessmen. Large mixed
urban assemblies frequently contained representatives of many occupations, social classes, and religious and political persuasions. Farmers (both landowning and tenant) day wage workers, and "mechanics" composed most rural assemblies. Coming from such disparate
backgrounds, members had little in common except the desire to improve their economic standing. The order's liberal membership
policies created confusion among local officials concerning who could
join the union. Wage laborers in Richmond resented efforts to organize city officials, whom they regarded as politicians. The secretary of
a Danville local requested Powderly to define the term *wage worker*
because, he wrote, "we have men in our midst who are engaged in a
small business on their own account. Such as bakers, merchants, sew-
ing machine agents . . . contractors . . . etc." [2] Such diversity of membership and confusion about eligibility made specific, tangible goals
difficult to define, let alone achieve.

Many of those who joined the Knights were ignorant of the principles of the Knights of Labor in particular and organized labor in
general. White-collar members knew little more than wage workers.
Both understood only vaguely the principles and programs of the national order. The ambiguity of the order's principles compounded the
problem. The Knights condemned strikes yet maintained a strike
fund; they opposed political action yet called for the election of workingmen. Their program of arbitration, education, and cooperation,
however, was explicit in theory. But the order lacked any but the
vaguest, most general plan of implementation. As a result, an inexperienced membership encountered difficulty in grappling with the
order's ideology. A contractor, for example, had so little understanding of the concept of cooperation that he asked Powderly to explain
the 1885 General Assembly's decision that contractor members share
their profits with member employees. Should he share profits before
or after the payment of wages? If the latter were the case, he wrote, all
contractors would be forced to depart the order's ranks. [3] John Power
of Mississippi informed Powderly late in 1885 that "there is a great
need of a speaker who would instruct in the principles of our Order."

Nearly two years later, Power expressed the same concern, one shared by the Knights' leadership in other southern states. He wrote to Powderly that "the great majority of those composing the order here are very illiterate and many of the organizers have been little better, knowing but little of the organization they were spreading and but imperfectly explaining the objectives of the order."[4]

The task of molding such a diverse membership, composed of persons largely unlettered in the concepts of organized labor, into a viable union capable of sustained growth would have been difficult given the best leadership and the most favorable circumstances. The South of the 1880s hardly presented a healthy environment for an institution dedicated to changing the region's economic and political structure; and the Knights were woefully short of able, experienced leaders. Lack of effective leaders, in fact, ranked as one of the southern order's most serious internal weaknesses.

The leaders of the southern order fall into three major categories— politicians or the politically ambitious; professional men and small businessmen; and the true believers, those who felt a need to give their all to the "cause" and can be called the martyrs. Most influential within the order were the politically ambitious, many of whom attempted to use the Knights to advance their political careers. Among this group were C. B. Pendleton of Florida, John Nichols of North Carolina, and William Mullen and Samuel Hopkins of Virginia, each of whom entered congressional campaigns in 1886.[5] Lesser figures used the order in an effort to obtain election to municipal and county offices and are typified by J. J. Holland of Jacksonville, a major figure behind the scenes of the 1887 municipal election in that city.[6] No matter how genuine his concern for the worker, the politician ultimately failed as a labor leader because the American laborer, especially the southern laborer, was not prepared to seek a general political solution to economic problems. While many laborers could support specific state and local reforms—for instance, the abolition of convict labor, child labor, and script wages—they were divided over such national economic issues as trust and railway regulation, the tariff, monetary policy, and taxation. Laborers were also divided over noneconomic political issues, race being the most prominent in the South. Under these conditions, the leaders' political activity inevitably caused dissension within the ranks and diverted energy from more potentially productive procedures, especially economic ones. On the other hand, the Knights' refusal to endorse economic actions against capital no doubt led some members to experiment with political activity.

The second major category was composed of professional men, small businessmen, and merchants who understood the inequities of the distribution of wealth within their society and sought ways to remedy the situation. Typical of this group was J. Melville Broughton of Raleigh, who was convinced that cooperation held the answer to the economic problems of the day. His work within the order exemplified this belief, for he served as a director of a tobacco cooperative in Raleigh and as a member of the national cooperative board. John J. Power, state master workman of Mississippi, also fit into this category. The manager of a gas company in Natchez, Power, like many of the order's national officers, believed that education and cooperation could lead to a workable accommodation between capital and labor. A reformer to the core, Power, again like many national leaders, was involved with a number of causes, including the Irish-American Land League. [7]

The third category of leaders can be labeled the martyrs. Neither ambitious politicians nor contemplative professionals or businessmen, members of this group were totally dedicated to the "cause" of labor. John Ray of North Carolina and the Reverend Simmions Meynardie of South Carolina are typical members of this group. Ray, who helped introduce the order to North Carolina and served as a state officer, worked himself into a state of nervous exhaustion trying to build the order. Writing to Powderly in 1886, he revealed the frustration of one who had labored for the cause only to be rejected by the organization he had helped to build. "I walked over a greater portion of this State," he told Powderly,

and have gone nearly two days and nights without tasting food; have stood up before mobs congregated to take my life, and have had to flee for my life and sleep in the mountain forests alone for the cause, while pampered big-bellied hypocrites were drawing a salary from the proceeds of my work. . . . Today while the Knights of Labor are rejoicing over a victory I have not a penny in the world and no work, while my family are suffering for the necessaries of life.

Meynardie, who led the 1886 Augusta textile strike, collapsed under the burden of leadership. His letters to Powderly during the strike reveal the same frantic dedication to the order as that expressed by Ray.[8] Nicholas Stack, state master workman of Alabama, wrote to Powderly in 1889 that "I have travelled the Alabama labor field & counseled with & encouraged to the best of my ability some of the most oppressed people in the continent. So long as I had a dollar of my own to travel with. . . . Now my race is run."[9]

The Knights' leadership shared certain characteristics which handicapped their efforts to organize and lead southern laborers. Most significant of these handicaps was the fact that most of the order's leaders were not laborers. Rather, they were small entrepreneurs, businessmen, printers, contractors, teachers, almost everything but wage laborers. While printers might have been wage laborers (that is, employed by a press), most printers who obtained positions of leadership within the order owned their own printing firms. Numbered among this category were William Mullen of Virginia, John Nichols of North Carolina, C. B. Pendleton of Florida, and T. M. White and M. A. Thomas of Alabama. John Power managed a gas works at Natchez, and Nicholas Stack was employed as a superintendent by a Birmingham coal company.[10] J. J. Holland of Florida owned a dray and contracting business. Emil Lesser, prominent in the founding of Birmingham locals, operated a restaurant and boarding house. J. Melville Broughton was a bookkeeper and merchant and, in 1888, established one of Raleigh's more successful insurance and real estate agencies.[11] At the 1887 General Assembly, only three of the ten southern representatives—a nailer, a carpenter, and a plumber—could be considered wage workers; and the plumber could have been a contractor rather than a wage laborer.[12]

Because they were not laborers but were, in many cases, small businessmen, the leadership supported the order's programs more tenaciously than did the rank and file. They did so because arbitration, education, and cooperation held meaning for them. The programs offered, in theory, solutions to the leadership's concerns, one of the most important of which was the retention of their proprietary status. The Knights' programs, in short, promised to preserve what many of the leaders already had and to do so without the specter of class divisions and conflict of the European type. Members of the leadership, especially at the state level, also exhibited a high degree of ego involvement with the order. Their positions gave them status and a sense of accomplishment, even though they were big fish in a small pond. On the other hand, the rank and file member, whether white-collar, blue-collar, or agrarian day laborer, had nothing and wanted that situation changed. Membership per se conferred no status, no sense of accomplishment; and the rank and file member would support the order only as long as it seemed to promise to help him directly and immediately. Given the order's programs and the nature of leadership, such changes were not forthcoming.

Perhaps almost as detrimental to the efforts of the leadership to rally southern workers to the cause was the fact that many of the leaders were not natives of the South. Others who were native southerners were not natives of the states in which they were active as Knights, a fault not quite as grievous as being a Yankee. Nicholas Stack illustrates the "foreign" origins of some of the southern order's highest officials. Born in Ireland, Stack immigrated to New York and then moved to Ohio where, in 1870, he began mining coal. Bitten by the gold bug, he traveled to the Rockies, eventually drifting into Mexico by way of Tombstone, Arizona. In 1884, he returned to the United States through New Orleans. There he read of Alabama's booming iron industry and headed for Birmingham. He obtained employment at the Cahaba Mining Company and a year later helped found the Anti-Convict League of Alabama, serving as secretary of that organization until it merged with the Knights.[13]

John Power's biography reads remarkably like that of Stack. Born in Ireland in 1848, he immigrated to America as a young man and obtained employment as a railroad laborer. He later secured a position as assistant superintendent of a gas works at Middleton, Connecticut. Forced to resign because of ill health, he moved to the South and accepted a position as manager of the Natchez gas works in 1884. Like Stack, Power had joined the Knights in the North and continued his association with the order upon moving South. The growth of the order in the mid-1880s allowed both men to renew their activities as Knights.[14]

The career of J. J. Holland of Florida fit the same pattern, with the exception that Holland was a native of the United States. A carpetbagger, Holland, a former union officer, settled in Jacksonville. He became a contractor, leading citizen, and a major figure in the Republican party. He served as city clerk, alderman, fire chief, and sheriff of Duval County. [15] John Ray took the principles of Knighthood to North Carolina from Massachusetts; and William Oree, organizer in the Richmond area, was a native of New York. [16] Lacking experienced southern union members, the Knights relied upon leadership from outside the region. This reliance made the order suspect to xenophobic southerners. It also afforded business and industrial spokesmen an opportunity to denounce unionism in general and the Knights in particular as both un-American and alien to the southern way of life. The Knights' opponents failed to allow such an opportunity to go begging.

While northerners played a major role in the organization and leadership of the southern Knights, they were far too few in numbers to provide more than a fraction of the leaders needed. The great rush of members into the union after its initial success in 1885 compelled the development of native leadership. That leadership had to come from the ranks of a people almost totally ignorant of the most fundamental concepts of organized labor. As a result, leadership was frequently incompetent at the local and often district levels. Ignorant of the Knights' structure, procedures, and principles, local officers deluged Powderly and other national officers with trivial procedural questions. Inexperienced local leaders also encouraged the membership's already unrealistic hopes. Their ignorance and excessive optimism led locals to adopt untenable positions and to attempt projects far beyond their means. Locals plunged into strikes with no preparation, only to be humiliated by defeat. Others sought to establish cooperatives with little or no capital and less managerial skill. [17]

In the face of harsh reality, local leaders often reverted to quoting platitudes about the virtues of labor's cause. Their faith in the eventual triumph of the Knights over the injustices of society approached religious conviction. The order would triumph because it stood for justice. Neither the numbers and power of the opposition nor the inexperience and numerical and financial weakness of the membership could stay the ultimate victory. In 1887, a Virginia Knight reported that his assembly members were "full of love for the brotherhood and great confidence for our General Master Workman Powderly." A Georgian believed "the idea of the Knights of Labor will be to the working classes what Christianity has been to the world." A North Carolina member felt that the "wisdom, love, and justice" of the order would prevail. As a result of their will to believe, local officers consistently relayed overly optimistic reports to the national leadership well into 1888. Even in 1889, when the deterioration of the order was obvious to all but the most ardent believers, local officers stressed the dedication and resolve of the "true" members who remained.[18]

The order in the South also failed to prevent internal feuding or to suppress those feuds that were begun. Southern Knights shared this problem with their northern brethren, for intraorganizational wrangling was the bane of the national order. Except for the racial issue, southerners argued over the same issues as did northerners. Their interminable feuds involved petty pesonality conflicts, race, politics, procedural and jurisdictional disputes, and other matters, some unbelievably trivial. Members invested considerable time and energy in the most petty disputes, whether at the local, district, or state assembly level. So intense was this internal warfare that from 1885 to 1890, Powderly received at least thirty-one letters concerning feuds in Georgia locals alone, despite the fact that many letters concerning procedural and jurisdictional disputes were sent to the national secretary-treasurer rather than to Powderly.[19]

Poor leadership and a surplus of prima donnas and "leaders" in search of a following encouraged the order's internecine warfare. Bitter personal clashes rent the order in every southern state, and letters filled with invectives directed at fellow Knights poured into Powderly's office. An Atlanta member complained that a local organizer was spiteful, argumentative, jealous, and incompetent. John Ray described a foe in the order as being "as selfish and hypocritical as it is possible for human [*sic*] to be." Florida Knights described their colleagues as "arbitrary and dictatorial," "dead limbs and trash," and "blackguards." A Charleston member described a brother as "a political schemer of the deepest dye, a man who has had his brightest hopes and aspirations dashed to earth time and again by his unbridled tongue and fierce, ungovernable temper," a man who had "no bright side." A Virginia Knight complained of "brothers who had been so unkind to me and whose personal conduct had been such that there was no place for me in their association."[20]

Local, district, and state assemblies seemed incapable of coping with procedural questions that varied in the slightest from the order's constitution and bylaws. Instead, they forwarded an endless stream of trivial questions to Powderly. Could the local master workman fine a member? What authority did a master workman have to overrule a member? Could a local delegate be elected to a district assembly before his local joined the district? [21] Some of the procedural squabbling was pathetically comic. The recording secretary of a South Carolina local complained that his master workman had requested him to notify a member of his expulsion. This was an absurd request, the recording secretary maintained, since the expelled member was in attendance when the local voted to expel him. Members of Savannah District 139 spent hours trying to determine whether women would "spread broadcast" the order's secrets, in the event that they were organized. Failing to reach an agreement, the assembly sent a five-page brief of the case to Powderly, asking his decision. [22]

Jurisdictional disputes raged between locals, between districts, between locals and districts, between district and state assemblies, and occasionally between local and state assemblies. Trade locals resented mixed locals that admitted members from occupations represented by organized trade locals within a given area. An Atlanta local of railroad car builders felt they should have jurisdiction over all carpenters, who frequently joined mixed assemblies. A carpenters' local in Birmingham complained when mixed assemblies in that city accepted carpenters. [23] Most jurisdictional disputes, however, were over more mundane matters. Members of Charleston Local 8225 "seceded" to form four other locals, an action which Local 8225 protested to the General Executive Board. The board upheld the local, allowing it to use its own discretion in welcoming seceding members who might wish to return. The board received similar protests from locals in Lynchburg and Wilmington. [24]

Relations between locals and their district assemblies were often poor. Many locals resented the formation of districts, for district assemblies reduced the ability of locals to communicate directly with the national organization. Locals resented per capita dues for district membership, assessments levied by districts, and what they considered arbitrary treatment at the hands of district officers. Such provocations, whether real or imagined, prompted aggrieved locals to appeal either to Powderly or to the General Executive Board for permission to leave the district and affiliate directly with either the state or the national assembly. Invariably, the board denied the locals' appeals, replying that as long as district or state assemblies were in good standing, permission for locals to disassociate must be obtained from them. Among locals and district assemblies involved in such disputes were Local 722 of Macon and District 105 of Atlanta; Local 5431 of Atlantic City, Virginia, and Norfolk District 123; Hephzibah, Georgia, Local 8979 and Augusta District 176; Local 9095 of Brunswick and Savannah District 139; Local 6700 of Charleston and District 187 of the same city; and Local 6271 and District 139, both of Savannah. [25] District Assembly 193, Lynchburg, Virginia, found it particularly difficult to control member locals and constantly appealed to Powderly to restore order. [26] Jealous of their autonomy, locals paid little attention to the nominal authority of district assemblies. In a plea to Powderly "to promote peace and harmony where now exists discord," Victor St. Cloud of Savannah District 139 complained that members of an expelled local "don't care a damn for D.A. 139" and continued to meet and initiate members. [27]

Locals attached directly to state assemblies seemed no happier with this arrangement than those attached to districts. The Florida state assembly constantly fought with member Pensacola locals, a situation resulting primarily because of the dominance of Jacksonville locals within the state assembly. Some locals, formed long before state assemblies were organized and originally attached directly to the national assembly, regretted ever joining state assemblies. Several, such as Local 4106 in Durham, sought to disaffiliate from the state assembly but were denied permission to do so by the General Executive Board. [28] Powerful older locals, such as Local 5009 in Birmingham, frequently challenged state assembly policies. [29] Many locals received few, if any, benefits from state assemblies yet were taxed by them. Members of Huntsville, Alabama, locals lamented that they were "in the worst condition you ever saw anything and it is all on the account of being attached to the State Assembly." [30]

Once organized, state and district assemblies jealously guarded their powers, seeking to stifle the development of additional districts within the area of their jurisdiction. State assemblies dominated by locals of a single urban region—including the Florida assembly, dominated by Jacksonville locals; the Alabama assembly, controlled by Birmingham area locals; and the North Carolina assembly, dominated by locals of Raleigh-Durham area—opposed the creation of new districts. Since the officers of state assemblies usually came from the dominant urban locals, the urban assemblies controlled the order statewide, especially in 1885 and 1886, before the Knights began to recruit heavily in rural areas. The creation of additional districts would have diminished their control of the order within the state. Thus District Assembly 84 in Richmond, which acted much as a state assembly through 1886, sought to block the chartering of a district in Petersburg and Lynchburg. [31] Furthermore, the Florida state assembly prevented the creation of a district in Pensacola in 1888; the North Carolina state assembly stymied efforts to establish districts in Durham and Dallas; and District Assembly 105 of Atlanta opposed the creation of a district in Macon. [32]

Political action also contributed heavily to the order's internal feuding. Fierce political conflicts erupted within the Florida state assembly in 1887 and finally led the General Executive Board to revoke the state assembly's charter in 1892. [33] Politics prompted most of the chronic internal difficulties which plagued Lynchburg District 193 and Savannah District 139. Politics also accounted for much of the trouble encountered by Charleston locals in District 187 and bedeviled the order in North Carolina. [34] Many of the political difficulties arose, as might have been anticipated, from the efforts of politically ambitious Knights to use the order to further their own ambitions.

The ever present racial issue combined with politics to contribute to the Knights' failure to achieve internal stability. J. J. Holland of Jacksonville and W. P. Russell of Charleston both sought to associate the Knights, especially black assemblies, with local Republican organizations; and their attempts were naturally resented by white Democratic members. [35] Blacks also resented white dominance of state and district assemblies, so much so that they attempted to form black districts in Virginia, Florida, and Georgia. Whites resisted these efforts, just as they resisted attempts by white locals to create competing district assemblies. [36] Blacks also complained of high-handed treatment by white members who visited black assemblies; and whites expressed the fear that the relatively liberal racial policies of the national order might promote "social equality," despite the fact that nearly all local assemblies were strictly segregated. [37]

In an effort to solve the order's internal difficulties, both Powderly and the General Executive Board dispatched national officers to the scene of particularly disruptive quarrels. The South received its share of such visits. In 1887, Mrs. L. M. Barry traveled to Lynchburg, G. G. McCartney sought to smooth ruffled feelings in Wilmington, and Tom O'Riley attempted to quell a dispute among the ranks in Charleston. [38] The following year, T. B. Barry journeyed to Lynchburg, T. B. McGuire attempted to restore order among black locals in Pensacola and Savannah, and William Bailey sought to settle difficulties among the Knights of the Birmingham area. [39] In 1889, J. J. Holland traveled to Birmingham on a second peace mission; and in 1890, A. W. Wright traveled to Savannah, while John Devlin drew the task of bringing peace to the conflict-ridden Florida order. [40]

The incessant conflict within the southern order, as within the order nationally, occasionally overcame Powderly's patience, as is revealed by a scathing letter he wrote to locals in Lynchburg. "For some reason or other," Powderly wrote, "since the district was organized, it has failed to conduct itself as a District Assembly of the Knights of Labor. Bickerings, dissensions, and jealousies have characterized the actions of both officers and members, until it would be better to turn over the property of the entire District and cease to work than to continue in such a foolish manner." [41] Powderly could have easily written such a letter to almost every district and state assembly in the South.

Dissension within the order in the South did not prevent quarrels between the southern order and the national leadership. From local master workmen to state officers, southerners complained, at times with some justification, that national officials and policies "slighted" their region. Powderly treated such complaints seriously, and they were promptly and courteously answered. [42] When William Mullen of Virginia wrote to Powderly that "I get hundreds of letters asking me why it is that the Southern wing of the Order is entirely ignored by the Board, while it is continually travelling, laboring, and calling for assessments to sustain the Order in the North and West," Powderly replied that the South had not been and would not be slighted. [43] John McDonald, elected state master workman of Mississippi in 1889, criticized the board for not sending lecturers of national prominence to work in the state. Members in Alabama also chided Powderly for failing to assign lecturers to that state, thus restricting the order's growth. [44]

Such criticism from the South led Powderly to appoint John O' Keefe as a general lecturer in the South in mid-1888. This action failed to appease Mullen, because O'Keefe was not from the South. Other Knights in the South, however, found O'Keefe quite acceptable and welcomed his appointment. [45] But O'Keefe's tour of the South in the fall of 1888 did not end the sense of alienation felt by many Southern Knights. At the 1888 General Assembly, the Alabama State Assembly introduced a resolution calling for the order to place at least one southerner on the General Executive Board. Miffed by the assembly's past failures to place a southerner on the board, the Alabamians prefaced the resolutions with the statement that the General Executive Board's abuse of the South had seriously injured the order in the region. Although the resolution was rejected by the assembly, J. J. Holland of Jacksonville was elected to the board. [46] The resentment expressed by the southerners also probably led the General Executive Board to send Mrs. Leona Barry on a tour of the region early in 1889. [47] Still, some southerners, including Nicholas Stack, complained that Mrs. Barry, as head of the order's "woman's work," lacked experience in the South, which had a high percentage of women and children in the labor force. [48] Quite clearly, Stack would have preferred the position to have gone to a southern lady.

On the whole, southerners avoided power struggles within the national order. The most serious of such national disputes involved Powderly and his supporters, including New York's "Home Club" after 1886, on the one hand and both the trade unionists and the fundamentalists who wished to return the order to its early policies of secrecy and anti-Catholicism on the other. Generally, southern delegates to the General Assemblies backed Powderly for several reasons. The order developed in the South after the Knights had dropped its secrecy and some of its ritual, and their was little support in the region for a return to such policies. The northern trade unionist element within the order received little encouragement from southerners because few southern members, who were organized primarily in mixed assemblies, had trade union backgrounds. Nevertheless, southerners were occasionally drawn into both struggles to the detriment of the order within the region. Nothing better illustrates the impact of these national feuds upon the southern order and the enormous amounts of time and energy wasted upon such disputes by the national leadership than the exploits of Victor E. St. Cloud of Savannah, Georgia.

The St. Cloud affair began at the 1888 General Assembly in Indianapolis. At Powderly's request, the assembly combined the offices of general secretary and general treasurer and elected John Hayes, the past general secretary, to the new post. General Treasurer Frederick Turner, defeated by Hayes, received no national office to compensate for his loss. A leading figure in the Knights after 1873, Turner did not take defeat graciously. He bolted the order and, in conjunction with several other prominent "old" members, early in 1889 initiated a rival group called the Founders' Order of the Knights of Labor, which advocated a return to secrecy, elaborate ritual, and anti-Catholicism. [49]

Powderly's response to Turner's rival faction revealed his talent for intrigue as well as his enormous ego, both factors in the eventual failure of the Knights. In February 1889, he asked Mrs. Leonora Barry, head of the order's "women's department" and about to embark upon a tour of the South, to pick "some good, true Knights of Labor in the south" to write the Founders' Order expressing sympathy for their cause. These persons could then relay to Powderly any information obtained. "I would not advise you put [*sic*] anything concerning it on paper," Powderly wrote, noting that "you must have implicit trust in whoever you broach that subject to and have them well instructed in what to do and write." [50]

One of the southerners Mrs. Barry selected to implement Powderly's scheme was Victor E. St. Cloud, a carpenter, member of the order for seven years, and recording secretary of District Assembly 139, Savannah, Georgia. St. Cloud entered the conspiracy with alacrity. Writing under the pseudonym "George Jones," he requested information from the Founders' Order and received a circular in reply, which he forwarded to Powderly. Excited by the success of his intrigue, Powderly urged St. Cloud to "keep the matter up and report a healthy growth of sentiment in favor of the improved order of the Founders' Order of the Knights of Labor; make the most flattering reports to Turner so that you will be in shape to receive future communications, circulars, &c. which may be sent out from the Founders' office." [51]

From this point on the St. Cloud conspiracy becomes increasingly complicated, melodramatic, and farcical. Following Powderly's instructions, St. Cloud began to relay to Powderly letters from Turner, circulars, and other documents obtained from the Founders. He even forged fifteen signatures in order to acquire a charter for a fake Founders' "local" which he "established" in Savannah. To further his efforts, Powderly forwarded to St. Cloud $100 and agreed to pay the per capita tax of the fifteen "members" of St. Cloud's "local." St. Cloud even became an "organizer" for the Founders, while actually working as an organizer for the Knights throughout eastern Georgia. After several months of correspondence with Turner, St. Cloud reported in mid-July that the Founders' Order seemed inactive. Powderly urged him to maintain his correspondence with Turner, adding that "so long as there is any life in the concern we will see you through." [52]

Meanwhile, St. Cloud's efforts on Powderly's behalf got him into trouble with some locals and the district assembly. The secretary of one local complained to Powderly about the money St. Cloud was spending on "educational" work and his refusal to account for his activities to the district master workman. Powderly defended St. Cloud, asking the irritated Georgia Knights to "trust me" and informing them that St. Cloud was engaged in "special work against the Order's enemies." In a reply to an inquiry about St. Cloud from General Secretary-Treasurer Hayes, prompted by complaints from angry members of District 139, Powderly noted that "we cannot very well afford to fall out with him now for he is our agent in the Founders' Order." [53]

Powderly's assurances failed to squelch the protests of St. Cloud's fellow Georgia Knights over the secrecy surrounding his activities, which continued to become more involved. By mid-October, St. Cloud had become Powderly's spy in a second splinter group, the Brotherhood of United Labor, founded by Thomas Barry, an expelled member of the Knights' General Executive Board and a trade unionist. [54] The master workman of District 139, infuriated by Powderly's evasion, demanded to know what was going on. Otherwise, he informed Powderly, St. Cloud's activity "will be the downfall of the order in this locality without satisfaction is given immediately." At this point, Powderly replied that he had authorized St. Cloud's work, the expenditure of funds by him, and the secrecy involved, including St. Cloud's refusal to inform the district master workman of the nature of these activities. The district accepted Powderly's less than complete explanation "with feelings of regret that Same was not given when first asked." [55]

By this time, Powderly had St. Cloud corresponding with P. J. McGuire of the American Federation of Labor's Brotherhood of Carpenters and Joiners in an attempt to determine the actual strength of that organization. [56] By the late fall of 1889, St. Cloud was reporting to Powderly on Turner's Founders' Order, Barry's Brotherhood of United Labor, and the AFL carpenters' union. Eventually, however, St. Cloud's enemies, angered by and somewhat jealous of his "secret work," succeeded in bringing him up on charges of misrepresenting the order. He was tried and convicted by the district court and appealed to Powderly for aid. St. Cloud requested that Powderly verify that he had never requested funds in the name of the district, that he always acted on Powderly's orders. Without such statements, he informed Powderly, his seven years of service to the order and Powderly would be destroyed. Powderly stamped his appeal "NO ANSWER REQUIRED." [57] While southerners rarely became involved in the politics of the national order to such an extent, the St. Cloud episode typifies the pettiness consistently displayed by the national leadership. It also reveals much about the leaders' inability to prevent or control internal feuding at the state, district, or even local assembly levels.

Insufficient funds also contributed substantially to the internal weakness of the order in the South, where even the order's minimum financial requirements presented members with a serious problem. A number of factors made the southern order's financial plight more drastic than that of the national order, although its financial situation was far from stable. The South lacked large numbers of skilled industrial workers, whose relatively higher wages could, to some extent, offset the low wages paid to the unskilled laborers. Also, southern wages in almost all fields, skilled or unskilled, were significantly below those paid to northern laborers in the same occupations. And in the South, the use of scrip wages was still a common practice. Scrip was used in the cotton mills, the mines, the lumber industry, the tobacco factories, and, in some cases, even by plantation owners. As a result of these factors, southern locals were continually in financial difficulty. Many functioned sporadically; when enough members paid dues, locals reported in good condition. Otherwise, they lapsed from the active roles, sometimes to be revived, sometimes not. Because local assemblies were so poor, district and state assemblies encountered even greater difficulties in their efforts to maintain an adequate treasury.

The general poverty of the southern laborer, rather than unreasonable financial policies or an unwillingness to pay, caused members difficulty in meeting dues requirements. The national order deliberately established low dues, as did southern state and district assemblies. A low dues policy was adopted partially to encourage the organization of both the skilled and unskilled laborers into one big union and partially because the order's national leadership, in its opposition to strikes, saw no need to create a large strike fund. Under the national order's original constitution, national dues were set at only one and one-half cents every three months. Local assembly dues were required to be not less than thirty cents for three months. In 1883, the Knights approved an assessment of five cents per member in order to establish a strike fund, only to abandon the fund, called the Assistance Fund in 1887. At the same time, however, state and district assemblies were authorized to establish their own strike funds by assessing their memberships. Initiation fees were minimal. In 1887, for example, the General Assembly adopted an initiation fee of a dollar for males and fifty cents for females.[58] Thus even when dues paid to state and district assemblies were combined with local dues, the average Knight in North Carolina, where the state assembly levied a per capita tax of five cents per quarter for males and two and one-half cents for females, paid less than twenty-five to thirty cents in dues per month, including special assessments.[59]

Despite such minimal dues requirements, members of southern locals consistently failed to meet their financial obligations to the order, as many letters to Powderly and the G.E.B. from southern locals attest. The recording secretary of a Virginia miners' local complained that many members neglected to pay their dues, although some managed to find money for whiskey. However, he blamed the local's financial problems primarily on low wages and the use of scrip. A member of a North Carolina local observed that the prevalent low wages paid in his region kept the order from expanding. A Mississippi Knight complained that his local faced continual financial strain caused, in part, by the necessity of aiding destitute Knights who drifted through the area. Late in 1887, the Atalla, Alabama, local underwent "a reconstruction process." suspending eighteen members for nonpayment of dues; and a member of a Marietta, Georgia, local reported the lapsing of a number of locals in the vicinity because of financial difficulties early in 1888. [60]

Increasingly after 1887, letters from southern assemblies told the same story of low wages, the inability of members to maintain dues payments, and the demise of locals. Nicholas Stack informed Powderly in October 1888 that he could no longer visit locals in the state assembly. He had exhausted his private funds for travel expenses; and, he reported, "the S. A. has had none for many a month." By the middle of the year, locals in major urban areas were struggling to stay alive. Local 6736 in Charlotte, for example, was suspended for nonpayment of dues early in the year but managed to obtain dues payments for the second quarter and asked for reinstatement.[61] By the end of the year, the North Carolina state assembly faced a financial crisis. Its officers implored Powderly to "extend a little degree of liberality" to "several" lapsed locals in an effort to revive them. Some locals, in an attempt to survive, simply "cancelled the indebtedness of all that were in arears,"without asking permission from the national order. [62] This inclination to fail to enforce even a minimal dues policy resulted from an internal weakness shared by the national and southern order. The Knights, in their determination to unite all laborers into one organization, measured success by membership roles and not by the strength of the treasury. Their failure to stress finances was one of the most significant factors in the eventual collapse of the order.

Unable to meet local and national per capita dues, southern locals contributed little to the national "Defense" or "Assistance" funds or to the special assessments which the G.E.B. levied in 1886 in an attempt to support the rash of strikes sweeping the order, some of which were in the South. Typical of southern attitudes toward the Assistance Fund were those contained in a letter to Powderly from a member of a Winston, North Carolina, local. In 1887, the secretary of the local requested exoneration from payment of the assistance tax because "The hard times here with the class of people who compose our assembly is such that none of them scarcely are paying dues & we had the misfortune of loosing too of our brothers this spring creating considerable expense on us which expense we have not been able to meet yet & unless times get better or our members pay up I am afraid we will have to go to the wall yet." Requests from locals in the South and in other regions to be relieved of the Assistance Fund tax, or to have an extension of time for its collection, filled the G.E.B.'s report to the 1887 General Assembly. The failure of the southern locals to support the fund reflected a national problem, however, and was not peculiar to the region. Between 1885 and 1886, when the national order was at its peak, the Assistance Fund received only $600, prompting the General Assembly to abolish it in 1887.[63]

The financial problems of the southern order were compounded by the financial irresponsibility and outright dishonesty of the leadership at all levels. Complaints of theft and embezzlement by officers were numerous, even at the peak of the order's strength. The financial secretary of a Macon local absconded with the treasury and fled to Cincinnati, and a Birmingham local expelled an officer for embezzling funds. Locals in Richmond; Waycross, Georgia; and Dallas, North Carolina, also reported expulsions of sticky-fingered members. Nicholas Stack attributed part of the financial woes of the Alabama state assembly to the "rascality" of the membership. In Mississippi, a newly elected master workman accused his predecessor of making a $157 error in his favor and charged that "the financial secretary has robbed us of about three hundred dollars, our treasurer of about $150."[64] Charges of fraud against organizers were common, and some resulted in bitter feuds because locals organized by an individual frequently defended the organizer against charges of corruption.[65]

In undertaking to organize southern workers, the Knights of Labor accepted a Herculean task. The southern laborer was impoverished, lacked the most elementary understanding of the concept of organized labor, and was polarized by race. The diversity of the order's membership defied any coherent approach to the laborers' practical problems. The Knights faced an environment hostile to the development of any institution that threatened the economic and political power of the region's new industrial elite. To build a successful union under these conditions would have required superior leadership, financial stability, and unity of purpose; and even then, the chances for success would have been remote. Rather than displaying a united organization, however, the Knights in the South were plagued with poor leadership, financial instability, and incessant internal squabbling. Under such circumstances, the destiny of the southern Knights was all too predictable. By 1888, the order was in serious decline; and within another year it had almost ceased to exist, except among the black day laborers and domestics of the rural South who still hoped that Powderly and the Knights could provide some miracle of economic salvation. The white urban laborers who had given the order strength in 1885 and 1886 had deserted its ranks, disillusioned by the order's inability to effectively address their grievances, an inability that resulted in large part from weaknesses within the order.

9 The Decline and Legacy of the Southern Knights

IN THE three years between the two General Assemblies held in the South, the Knights of Labor declined from its position as the largest, most powerful labor organization in the United States to become an ineffectual shell of its former self, struggling for survival. At the Richmond General Assembly of 1886, the order appeared strong and vigorous, capable of consolidating its rapid growth and dominating the American labor movement for years to come. But by November 1889, when the General Assembly convened in Atlanta, the order was in disarray. Its leaders were fighting among themselves, its membership was less than a third of the 1886 figure, its treasury was empty, and its position of leadership within the labor movement had been preempted by the American Federation of Labor. At Atlanta, in a desperate attempt to reestablish the Knights' influence among the nation's "producing classes," the General Assembly voted to join forces with the agrarian reformers of the South and West, thus taking the first step toward political action, a policy which would culminate in support of the Populist party and the destruction of the Knights of Labor.

At the time of the Richmond General Assembly, the Knights had passed their peak numerical strength nationally but were still expanding in the South. And in the South, which had few strong trade unions, the Knights did not face a strong challenge from the AFL, which contributed so significantly to the decline of the northern order. Yet the order's pattern of growth in the South had begun to change, presaging difficult times ahead. Through most of 1886, the Knights had experienced their most rapid growth in the region's urban areas. By October, when the General Assembly was held, the order had begun to obtain the majority of its new recruits from the ranks of the rural poor, especially the blacks. This shift in membership resulted from a decline in urban membership and the success of various farmers' groups in organizing the landholding and relatively more affluent white tenant farmers. In their drive to continue to build membership, it was inevitable that the Knights would turn to black agrarian laborers, whom the agrarian organizations for a time virtually ignored, and that the blacks would respond. This trend was even more inevitable once the Knights' urban recruits began to decline. The Knights' appeal to agrarian blacks would hurt the order among urban whites, however, expecially after the racial incidents of the Richmond General Assembly.

Not only did a change occur in the type of assembly organized after mid-1886, but the rate of organization slowed drastically as well. As in the nation, organizational activity reached a peak in the South in 1886, with 393 assemblies formed in the seven states under study. In 1887, the number fell to 201; and the following year, the Knights organized but 113 assemblies. In 1889, the order organized only 25 locals in the seven states, over half of which were comprised of blacks from small rural communities in eastern North Carolina. In Virginia, the state with the largest urban membership, the Knights failed to organize a single local in 1889. The order managed to form 69 locals in 1890, but the increased number of locals organized did not reflect an increase in the Knights' numerical strength. Again, over half the new locals were located in the poorest regions of rural North Carolina and were comprised of black agrarian laborers. Alabama and Georgia recorded a brief revival of miners' locals; but only in Georgia did the order make any gains in urban areas, with nine assemblies organized in Brunswick and Savannah, probably among black laborers.[1]

Unable to continue to recruit members in urban areas, the southern order eventually experienced a decline in membership, just as did the national order. Nationally, the Knights' membership reached its highest point in mid-1886. In the South, peak membership probably occurred sometime early in 1887 and then fell rapidly. Table 3 illustrates the sudden drop in membership experienced by southern district assemblies. Membership cannot be determined after 1888, the last year in which the order released detailed figures for district and state assemblies.

Membership figures for the southern order clearly indicate a grow-

TABLE 3
Knights of Labor Southern Membership, 1885-1888

	Location	Membership as of July 1*			
		1885	*1886*	*1887*	*1888*
DIST. ASSEMBLY					
84	Richmond	1,619	3,125	1,675	495
92	Richmond (colored)	1,285	3,567	1,132	343
105	Atlanta	———	2,827	1,370	365
120	Petersburg, Va.	———	576	230	Lapsed
123	Norfolk	———	1,174	940	225
131	Key West	———	773	258	115
139	Savannah	———	1,037	945	347
141	Columbus	———	926	405	Lapsed
176	Augusta	———	———	987	452
187	Charleston	———	———	209	Lapsed
193	Lynchburg	———	———	1,545	176
215	Pulaski City, Va.	———	———	———	143
227	Spartanburg, S.C.	———	———	———	885
STATE ASSEMBLY					
Ala.		———	———	3,951	1,978
Fla.		———	———	2,402	1,454
Miss.		———	———	1,660	2,925
N.C.		———	———	3,928	7,391
NATIONAL MEMBERSHIP			729,677	548,239	259,518

*SOURCE: Compiled from *G.A. Proceedings, 1885*, 174; *G.A. Proceedings, 1886*, 327-28; *G.A. Proceedings, 1887*, 1847-50; and *G.A. Proceedings, 1888*, "Report of the Secretary-Treasurer," 2-5.

ing, healthy urban order in 1886. By mid-1887, however, the urban areas were in trouble; and growth had shifted to the rural areas, as is indicated by the newly formed and relatively large state assemblies in Alabama and North Carolina. This trend continued into 1888, as is evidenced by the almost total collapse of the urban order. On the other hand, the membership of the North Carolina and Mississippi state assemblies nearly doubled. In both states, this rapid growth occurred almost entirely in rural areas. This pattern was especially evident in North Carolina, where the vast majority of the new locals were organized among the black rural poor of the agricultural counties of the northeastern corner of the state. The spectacular growth reported by the North Carolina state assembly is somewhat suspect because the figures recorded are total membership and not membership in good standing. Nevertheless, the North Carolina order experienced a real increase in members between July 1887 and July 1888, making the North Carolina state assembly larger than the state assemblies of Iowa, Illinois, Ohio, Michigan, and several other northern states.[2] Despite its increase in members, the order in North Carolina actually lost strength because of the decline of the stronger and more concentrated urban locals. And in the South as a whole, the order's gains in rural areas failed to offset its decline in urban membership.

Although some urban locals remained in good working order, a decline in urban assemblies was evident by mid-1887. For example, a member of a Rome, Georgia local informed Powderly in August of that year that "we had at one time about 225 members, was in good working order and doing well." But internal disputes and political differences had nearly destroyed the local; "Now we have got scattered to the four wind Now we are behind with rents and dues unpaid."[3] From Charleston came news that questionable financial practices and personality conflicts among the leaders of District Assembly 187 had seriously injured the order in that city. One local could get only 7 members to attend meetings, and another failed to obtain a quorum in two of three scheduled meetings. The correspondent's observation that "the order here is not in a very flourishing Condition" seriously understated the district's problems.[4] In Lynchburg, a center of union activity, the order was in serious difficulty by the fall of 1887. A member implored Powderly to "send some one down here to get us straight as the order is on the eve of breaking up."[5] Correspondence from other urban locals indicated that while the problems of Lynchburg locals were more serious than those experienced elsewhere, they were far from unique.

By the following year, problems had spread to the more recently organized rural assemblies, while organizers struggled to keep the order viable in urban areas. It was becoming increasingly evident that the Knights were fighting a losing battle. The plight of the order in North Carolina, the state in which the shift from urban to rural membership was most pronounced, indicated the extent of the southern order's decline. A member of a rural local reported that members had become discouraged and that interest in the Knights was difficult to maintain. The master workman of a local in the rural northeastern section of the state complained that members had abandoned the local because it failed to produce the expected immediate benefits. Other rural locals failed to meet dues requirements, lapsed, and returned their charters. The lapsing of local assemblies became so prevalent by the end of 1888 that George L. Tonnoffski, secretary-treasurer of the state assembly, appealed to Powderly to rescind the debts owed by North Carolina locals, especially those that had lapsed. Tonnoffski argued that "surrounding circumstances," including theft, had contributed to the decline of several locals and that concessions might "resusticate many of them."[6]

Throughout 1888 other southern states experienced the same steady decline in membership so evident in North Carolina, a decline which continued in 1889. In Vaucluse, South Carolina, members of a textile assembly reported that the local was "holding on" against "much opposition." Members of a rural local in the small village of Clover, South Carolina, began to desert the order. In Macon, Georgia, the order also suffered a serious decline in membership. In Augusta, the once powerful textile local, decimated by defeat in the 1886 strike, had not yet been reorganized.[7] In Mississippi, the order had been seriously damaged by the defeat of the Louisiana sugar plantation strikes in the fall of 1887, which hurt the order's efforts among rural blacks, and by the failure of the loggers' strike in the Gulf Coast region in 1889.[8] Further North, the once mighty Richmond district assemblies stood on the brink of total collapse. District 84, which boasted over three thousand members in 1886, had but four hundred members early in 1889. The district was so rent by internal feuding that Leonora Barry advised Powderly that to appoint William Mullen, a founder of the Richmond order, to a lecturer's position "would be the death blow" to the district.[9] In Alabama, the order was experiencing rapid decline by late 1888. Several locals had lapsed and remained inactive despite state Master Workman Nicholas Stack's efforts to revive them. The decline had occurred primarily among locals of the Birmingham area, resulting in increased power within the state assembly for the small town and rural locals. Birmingham area members, however, managed to continue their domination of the state assembly's major offices in 1889.[10]

The Georgia order provided a graphic example of the decline of the Knights in the South's urban centers. In February 1889, Leonora Barry wrote to Powderly that the Knights of the Savannah area were at "a low ebb." Only the efforts of Victor St. Cloud, who struggled to revive lapsed locals and organize new assemblies among the blacks, kept the Savannah locals of District 139 alive.[11] By June of that year, when the state assembly convened in Roswell, Georgia's urban order had practically ceased to exist. The state assembly, dominated by representatives from the more recently formed rural and small town assemblies, elected officers who reflected the change in the order's membership. Atlanta, long the center of the Knights' activity, contributed not a single member to the slate of eight state officials elected. Macon was the largest town represented, and six of the eight came from towns or communities smaller than Macon.[12]

When Terence Powderly opened the General Assembly in Atlanta on November 12, 1889, the southern order, like the order nationally, had declined to the point that its critics regarded it with ridicule rather than fear. Defeated strikes had crippled the Knights on the Mississippi Gulf Coast; in the textile region of Alabama, Georgia, and the Carolinas; and in Birmingham and the surrounding mineral region. In Jacksonville, Lynchburg, Richmond, Raleigh-Durham, and other areas, politics had ripped the order to shreds. The Knights' cooperatives had failed; and one by one, the order's newspapers had ceased publication. Still, the true believers—for instance, Stack of Alabama, St. Cloud of Georgia, Mullen of Virginia, J. J. Holland of Florida, and Tonnoffski of North Carolina—labored to hold the crumbling structure together, to revive lapsed locals, to recruit new members, and to convice those that remained that the "just cause" they represented would yet prevail. But recruits could be found only among the poorest in the South's most economically depressed agrarian regions, and even there the order encountered difficulties. By 1889, the Southern Farmers' Alliance had become the dominant force for reform in regional politics, and it was to this banner that the more articulate and affluent rural discontented flocked. Since the Knights had failed in the cities, the landless agrarian poor—the tenants, the black day laborers, and the domestic servants—remained by default the only new group to which the order could appeal. As a failure in the urban and industrial South, the order turned to the agrarian reformers and politics, not on the Knights' own terms, but in a desperate effort to survive.[13]

While the Knights would take their first major step toward official cooperation with the Southern Alliance at the Atlanta General Assembly, the order had actually begun its flirtation with the group much earlier. At the local level, southern assemblies had sought to cooperate with the Alliance since the elections of 1888. In North Carolina, the state assembly's official paper, the *Fayetteville Messenger*, endorsed a proposal to seek Alliance support for convict labor legislation; and in legislative races, Union Labor party candidates endorsed by the Knights also sought support from the Farmers' Alliance.[14] Alabama Knights attempted to form a political coalition with the Farmers' Alliance in several areas of the state, with some small degree of success.[15] In both states, however, efforts at cooperation were based on such fairly specific issues as convict labor reform and railroad regulation.

Agrarian reform groups had contacted the leadership of the national order, including Powderly, prior to the Atlanta General Assembly. Powderly and other officers had also corresponded with agrarian organizations—including elements within the Farmers' Alliance, the Grange, and the Agricultural Wheel—in 1887 during the formation of the National Union Labor party. But at that time Powderly pulled back, refusing to commit the order to cooperation with the agrarians or to a program of political reform.[16] However, as the farmers' organizations gathered momentum and the Knights continued to decline, the temptation to join forces with the agrarians increased. Meanwhile, certain factions of the agrarian reform forces, increasingly inclined toward third party activity, sought Powderly's support. Representatives of both the Southern Farmers' Alliance and the National Agricultural Wheel contacted Powderly in June 1889 in an effort to see if he were amenable to some mutual political efforts. At the same time, Powderly was also in contact with the Grangers of the Midwest.[17]

Meanwhile, a series of events thrust the Southern Farmers' Alliance into the forefront of the national reform movement, virtually

forcing Powderly and the moribund Knights to seek an accommodation of some kind with the aroused and increasingly militant agrarians. In September 1889, the Agricultural Wheel and the Southern
Farmers' Alliance officially merged. In October, the South Dakota
Alliance switched its allegiance from the Northern Alliance to the
Southern Alliance, officially known as the National Farmers' Alliance
and Industrial Union. The Southern Alliance had already absorbed
the Louisiana Farmers' Union in addition to the Agricultural Wheel;
and in the fall of 1889, the Southern Alliance also absorbed the Northern Alliance in Kansas.[18] Thus by the time the Knights' Atlanta General Assembly was held, the Southern Alliance spanned the South and
the Midwest, was by far the most powerful "reform" organization in
the country, and was increasingly inclined toward independent political action.

At their Atlanta convention, the Knights demonstrated a considerable willingness to cooperate with the Southern Alliance and to consider independent political action. Leonidas F. Livingstone, president
of the Georgia Farmers' Alliance, and R. F. Gray, editor of the
Alliance's national journal, the *National Economist*, addressed the
delegates of the General Assembly. Both urged increased cooperation
between the Farmers' Alliance and the Knights. Henry Brown, secretary of the Georgia Alliance, also spoke to the G.A., issuing a thinly
veiled call for independent political action by a coalition of the Farmers' Alliance, the Knights, and other reform groups.[19] Responding to
these overtures and the increase in its own rural representation, the
General Assembly endorsed the single tax, adopted a strong land
reform resolution, established a committee on mortgage debtors, and
authorized Powderly to appoint three delegates to attend the December convention of the Southern Alliance in St. Louis.[20]

Acting on the General Assembly's mandate, Powderly chose Ralph
Beaumont and A. W. Wright to accompany him to the Southern Alliance convention at St. Louis. There the committee endorsed the platform adopted by the Farmers' Alliance, which featured demands for
currency, land, and railroad reform. However, Powderly refused to
consider merger or independent political action. He also expressed
the opinion that the Knights still desired reforms for the laborer in
which the farmers, themselves employers, expressed little interest.
Nevertheless, the two organizations laid plans to coordinate their con-

gressional lobbying efforts in an attempt to obtain the passage of legislation which would aid in the implementation of the programs of both groups. [21]

Powderly's reservations about full cooperation with the Farmers' Alliance reflected a number of concerns. His most pressing fear was that the Alliance, now far larger and powerful than the Knights, would swallow up the order. He also feared that the Alliance wished to use the order to test the possibilities of a third party movement without risk to the farmers. If the Knights should unsuccessfully endorse a third party, that action would destroy the order and leave the Alliance unscathed and in an even more powerful position. "The Farmers' Alliance," Powderly wrote to Hayes in April 1890, "would like to have us start the ball rolling [for a third party] and wreck us so that there would be but one industrial organization existing." [22]

Powderly was not alone in his mistrust of the Farmers' Alliance. Among the rank and file, even in the South, where the order's membership was by now overwhelmingly rural, cooperation with the Alliance aroused suspicion. Because the Alliance primarily represented landowners and employers of labor and the Knights represented agricultural laborers, especially blacks, who were employed by the farmers who made up the Alliance membership, a natural antagonism existed between the two groups even after the decline of the Knights' urban membership. This antipathy was expressed by a Knight from rural North Carolina. He complained that in 1888, the state Alliance had initiated a "nefarious scheme" to pay laborers in scrip instead of cash. The Alliance, he concluded, represented "nothing more than oppression and death to the laborer." A year earlier, a Mississippian had informed Powderly that "the farmers have an organization called the Agricultural Relief, and they imagine the Knights are antagonizing them, which retards our success." [23]

Even had their interests been more compatible, the ability of the Knights to cooperate with the Farmers' Alliance, especially in the South, had become a moot question by 1890, for the order was in no position to offer aid to anyone. In March of that year, William Mullen of Richmond informed Powderly that "our order in this city has declined until it has reached a very low ebb." He appealed to Powderly to send a speaker to the area, assuring him that as many as fifteen hundred would attend a public lecture. Powderly complied with the request, sending A. W. Wright to Richmond. Wright spoke in the city, but to an audience of less than three hundred rather than the fifteen hundred Mullen had predicted. [24] By 1891, the Birmingham area Knights had ceased to exist. In that year, for the first time since 1886, the city directory failed to list the address of a single local assembly. [25] In North Carolina, the state assembly continued to exist but was comprised almost entirely of assemblies located in the rural northeast. [26] In Mississippi and South Carolina, the order had dwindled to a few pathetic locals; and in both states the order was, as one member expressed it, "intirely over-sharved [*sic*] by the Alliance." [27] In Florida, continued feuding between locals in Jacksonville and Pensacola had depleted the Knights' ranks in that state and threatened its continued existence. [28] The southern order had become so weak by 1890 that only one delegate from the region, a doctor from Vicksburg who represented the Mississippi state assembly, attended that year's General Assembly. Not one of the South's once flourishing district assemblies reported enough members to merit even a single delegate to the assembly. [29] For all practical purposes, the southern order was dead.

As the power and prestige of the Knights declined and that of the Farmers' Alliance increased, the order was forced to move toward cooperation with the agrarians and participation in third party politics. In the South, officials in several states sought an accommodation with the Alliance. State Master Workman George Tonnoffski of North Carolina welcomed fellow Carolinian Leonidas Polk, president of the Alliance, on his return from the Alliance convention held in St. Louis in December 1889. Later, the North Carolina state assembly appointed a committee to meet with Alliance representatives to discuss mutual legislative programs. In Alabama, the Knights made overtures to the Alliance about cooperating to elect reform tickets in the 1890 elections. And in Georgia, too, the Knights' state assembly sought to strengthen its contacts with the Alliance. [30] Still, however, some members expressed doubt about a political union with the Alliance. An Alabama member attended a meeting of Knights and Farmers' Alliance members interested in joint political action. He went to see whether the Alliance and the Knights "would stand together as they have sworn to do." [31]

Meanwhile, at the national level Powderly was leading the Knights closer to participation in third party politics. He attended the convention of the Southern Alliance held at Ocala, Florida, in December 1890. There the Alliance adopted the "Ocala Platform," a set of political demands that would eventually be incorporated into the platform of the Populist party. The Knights' national leadership, including Powderly, also participated in the formation of the Populist party by reform groups meeting at St. Louis in February 1892 and in the Populists' nominating convention held in Omaha the following July. [32]

By the time of the 1892 presidential election, the Knights of Labor had few members to support Populist candidates, either in the South or in the nation at large. But the few remaining southern Knights seem to have supported Populist candidates. Knights in rural assemblies in Georgia and North Carolina expressed support for General James Weaver, the Populist presidential nominee; and Knights in Alabama supported Weaver and local Populists. [33] In his unsuccessful bid for reelection to Congress on the Populist ticket, Tom Watson appealed to Powderly for aid, especially among the laborers of Augusta. Unfortunately for Watson, the Knights had long since ceased to exert any influence among any but a few of that city's workers. [34] The *Journal of United Labor* carried several editorials supporting Watson and also attempted to influence the order's Alabama members to vote for the Populists' gubernatorial candidate, Ruben Kolb. [35] Any efforts by the Knights' national leadership on Kolb's behalf, however, were not made as a result of any commitment to his candidacy as a Populist. Rather, they were designed to encourage a large Populist turnout which could result in split ticket balloting at the presidential level and would thus throw the state's electors to the Republican presidential candidate, Benjamin Harrison. [36]

Not even the zeal of the agrarian reformers could move the South from the ranks of the Democratic party, and Weaver and such southern Populists as Watson and Kolb met with a crushing defeat. After the elections of 1892, the Knights of Labor in the South sank into obscurity. Scattered locals continued to exist, largely in the rural areas of North Carolina, Georgia, and Mississippi. In Alabama, blacks in Mobile and a few miners, along with some rural laborers, comprised the order's membership. [37] James Sovereign's defeat of Powderly for the office of Grand Master Workman in 1893 had little effect on the few small southern locals that remained. Correspondence between officers of such locals and John Hayes, who remained the order's secretary-treasurer, paints a picture of local assemblies comprised of a dispirited collection of agrarian laborers, domestics, and day laborers, many of them black, who continued to cling to a forlorn hope. Their letters are filled with the trivial minutia of what had become essentially a fraternal order—requests of charters, membership cards, and other official papers; explanations for missed per capita dues payments; and reports of lapsed assemblies and efforts to revive them, most of which resulted in failure. Ironically, even with the order in tatters, its remaining members continued to fued over the privileges of office in locals that possessed neither prestige nor power. [38]

The Knights continued to exist as a fraternal order of the region's most hopeless poor until well into the second decade of the twentieth century. A dedicated handful of "true believers" provided the order with leadership and a will to survive. They labored to reorganize the lapsed locals, find a few new recruits, and revive the old dreams. In Mobile, Alabama, M. T. Judge, one of the South's earliest organizers, struggled to keep an assembly alive. [39] In the Birmingham area, Andrew J. O'Keefe, a printer and active member since the mid-1880s, somehow managed to publish a Knights of Labor newspaper, the *Arbitrator*, during the late 1890s and early 1900s. By 1900, despite the Knights' brief flurry of activity in 1899 among miners in Walker County, the *Arbitrator* had ceased to be a labor paper. It survived on the publication of legal notices; some issues carried no labor items. Letters to the *Arbitrator* from remaining old-timers in the region revealed that the order functioned as a social club which memories prevented them from disbanding. One such correspondent in 1899, for example, reported on the activities of members of his local. His letter consisted of a description of a Sunday service, a report of a "Boogie man" seen in town, and a tale of a member's problems getting his girl friend across a swinging bridge. [40] A woman, Ellen Williams, in what must have been an incredible act of faith and will, kept the order alive in North Carolina among the black agrarian day laborers of the economically depressed eastern part of the state. [41] In Florida, a few scattered assemblies survived among the timber cutters of the Pensacola region. A brief revival of interest in the order in 1900 ended when saw mill owners broke a strike protesting wage reductions. [42]

After 1890, the Knights were a grotesque caricature of the organization that had flourished in the South's cities from 1885 to 1888. But the persistence of the order among agrarian day laborers, lumberjacks and saw mill workers, and unskilled (primarily black) urban laborers in the late 1890s and early 1900s is significant for two reasons. First, it indicates the intense commitment of some leaders, including M. T. Judge of Mobile and Ellen Williams of North Carolina, to the "cause." Undoubtedly, such persons derived some gratification from being "leaders" in spite of the small number of followers and their position on the bottom rung of the region's socioeconomic ladder. But to have endured for so long, as did Judge, despite the obvious collapse of the order after 1890, required more than ego involvement. It required a faith in the ultimate vindication of the laboring people that transcended the economic realities of the era and the region. More importantly, the Knights' tenacity demonstrated that the most exploited of the South's laborers could still respond to that faith. Perhaps they responded out of desperation, because they were on the bottom rung and to believe in nothing was to despair. Whatever their motives, their willingness to believe and to attempt to change their economic status was strong. And it was reflected in other labor organizations of the early twentieth century, including the Farmers' Union, the National Union of Textile Workers, and the Industrial Workers of the World. [43]

The fact that thousands of southern workers joined and actively participated in the programs of the Knights of Labor in an era that witnessed the creation of the image of the docile southern laborer lends yet another irony to southern history. During the rapid industrialization and urbanization of the region in the 1880s, proponents of the new economic order praised the drive and ambition of the capitalist and entrepreneur while portraying the laborer as hard working, obedient, and contented with his lot. Politicians and promoters seeking to lure northern industries southward embellished and perpetuated that image. Historians of the twentieth century gave further credence to the image by all too frequently accepting as reality the description of the labor force supplied by industrial and political figures. As a result, a consensus emerged that the industrial revolution in the South was somehow different from that in the North. White southerners, rich and poor, labored together to build an industrial base, seeking to obtain parity with a northern economy which the Civil War had proven so superior. Southerners with capital, daring, and entrepreneurial ability provided the necessary funds and leadership. Poor whites supplied an eager, willing, and contented labor force. Together, without the class conflict so evident in the North, they placed the agrarian South on the road to industrialization. The activity of the Knights of Labor contrasts sharply with this carefully cultivated image of the willing, docile, unquestioning southern laborer and clearly indicates that, with some minor exceptions, southern workers reacted to the industrial revolution much as did their northern counterparts.

The lack of attention the Knights have received is also partially a result of the interest of historians in southern agrarian groups. The agrarians captured the attention of historians because of their numbers, their ability to influence Democratic politics, their seemingly liberal racial policies, and their participation in the Populist revolt. But prior to the rise of agrarian protest groups, the Knights of Labor had begun to organize disgruntled urban and industrial workers. From early 1884 until the fall of 1886, the Knights made rapid gains among the laborers of the South's urban industries and in the mines of Alabama and Virginia. The centers of their activities in each southern state during these years were invariably urban—Richmond, Lynchburg, and Norfolk in Virginia; Raleigh-Durham in North Carolina; Atlanta, Augusta, and Savannah in Georgia; the Birmingham area in Alabama; Jacksonville in Florida; and Natchez in Mississippi. The Knights found support among all levels of the urban and industrial work force—skilled and unskilled laborers, clerks, salespeople, and small shopkeepers comprised the order's membership. The order established locals in all the major industries of the New South, including tobacco, textiles, mining, iron, and the construction trades, and among the dock workers of the seaports.

The southern laborers who joined the Knights used the order to challenge directly management's picture of a happy, docile work force and its claims of complete harmony between capital and labor. Members of the Knights voiced their objections to the abuses of labor so common in the 1880s. They complained of long hours, penurious wages, hazardous working conditions, child labor, scrip wages, convict labor, and the arbitrary power of management. Such abuses and others met with vigorous protests from Knights within each of the basic industries of the New South. Until late 1888, papers published by the Knights in several towns carried stinging criticisms of the region's new industrial order and the treatment it provided the laborer.

Nor did the southern laborer use the order merely as a vehicle for protest. Despite the lack of any significant moral or financial support from the Knights' national leadership, southern members sought to change their economic conditions through the use of the strike and boycott. While the boycott proved to be totally ineffective, the strike resulted in some minor and temporary gains for the Knights. Although many of the order's strikes were defensive, that is, initiated to prevent management from implementing policies such as wage reductions that would adversely affect members, a surprising number of strikes were offensive or designed to force management to grant desired benefits. Of the larger strikes, the Augusta textile operatives' strike of 1886 and the Louisiana sugar cane cutters' strike of 1887 were both offensive strikes designed to force management to increase wages. Miners in the Birmingham area initiated several strikes for the same reason. Strikes by lumbermen in Mississippi in 1887 forced mill owners to reduce the hours of labor, and striking construction workers in Richmond in 1886 caused contractors to grant wage increases. In each of these strikes, southern laborers demonstrated a surprising degree of solidarity against a superior adversary.

Most of the successful offensive strikes came just as the Knights' urban membership reached its peak and before management developed techniques to resist the demands of an organized labor force. Once management realized that labor was organizing and determined to resist, they used their superior financial and political power to crush the order. Management defeated the cane cutters' strike and the Newport News stevedores' strike of 1887 by convincing the governor to send in the militia. In Augusta, mill owners created a protective association and proceded, in concert, to move against the striking Knights. A less formal arrangement among Mississippi lumber mill owners defeated the Knights in that industry. In the textile, lumber, and mining industries, time and again management used its economic power to break the union. By locking out all Knights, denying them access to the company store, recruiting strikebreakers, and, if necessary, evicting members from company housing, management destroyed the order. The tactics employed by management against the Knights were later refined and expanded. In only this sense, by proving that management could destroy a labor organization or at least contribute in large measure to its destruction, can it be argued that the Knights left the southern laborer a negative legacy.

In one respect, however, the strike activity of the southern Knights did differ from that of northern workers, although not necessarily from that of northern members of the order. Southern Knights rarely engaged in violence. Only in the cane cutters' strike and the Newport News stevedores' strike did the Knights react violently. A few cane cutters exchanged gunfire with the militiamen seeking to force them into submission; the strikers' action was purely defensive. The violent behavior of the Newport News dock workers more closely resembled that engaged in by northern laborers. Frustrated by management's decision to reduce wages, the strikers vented their emotions by destroying property in the vicinity of the docks.

This lack of violence does not, however, confirm management's picture of a docile, contented work force. Docile workers do not organize and strike; and they certainly do not remain on strike for three, four, or six months, returning to work only when overwhelmed by management's superior economic power. Why, then, in a region where personal violence and racial violence was so commonplace was industrial violence a rarity?

First, it must be remembered that northern industrial violence did not become pronounced until the 1890s. The 1880s saw little actual labor violence, although the Haymarket affair caused the public to perceive laborers as violent. The violence in the East in 1877 resulted from two factors absent in the South in the 1880s. It came after years of depression, demonstrating pent-up hostility toward the major symbol of industrial power and wealth, the railroads. The depression of the 1880s was much shorter and had less of an impact upon the South than it did upon the North. In addition, the southern non-agrarian work force was a much smaller fraction of the region's total population, and it was much less concentrated in urban areas than in the North. The 1877 riots were spontaneous, the work of urban mobs numbering in the thousands. In no southern city, with the possible exception of Richmond, could such a crowd of workers be assembled.

Southern laborers were aware that they were outnumbered and that violence would be counterproductive. They also knew that management would not hesitate to use force at the slightest sign of violent resistance, as indicated by their response to strikes by the Louisiana cane cutters and the Newport News dock workers.

Two other factors discouraged violent conflicts between management and labor. The majority of southern laborers were from the farm. They shared, with others in the culture, a deep respect for property born of their ingrained respect for the land and ownership of it. While a factory was not land, it was, nevertheless, private property of an economic nature and as such received the same kind of respect. This reverence of property made it difficult for southerners to violate or destroy the property of management. To strike against an employer was one thing; to destroy his property was quite another. Finally, the attitude of the national order toward industrial conflict must be examined. The Knights' national leadership denounced violence to the extent that Powderly condemned the Anarchists for the events at Haymarket. The Knights sought to eliminate conflict between management and labor, to combine their interests, to make laborers owners of industrial property. Such a group could never tolerate class warfare. That the Knights in the South—small in numbers, members of a culture that stressed the sanctity of property, and members of an organization that condemned violence—rarely engaged in industrial violence is to be expected and should in no way be interpreted as a sign of labor's docility.

Just as the Knights sought to publicize and ameliorate the conditions endured by laborers before the agrarian revolt, the Knights also challenged the South's political leadership prior to the farmers' decision to enter politics, a decision that came in 1889, long after the decline of the order had begun. And where the order could concentrate its political forces, its challenge to the political establishment met with some success. At the municipal level, the Knights combined with other reformers to force changes in government in several southern towns, most notably in Richmond and Jacksonville. At the state level, the order forced legislative consideration of issues that related directly to the well-being of the laborer. For the first time, state legislatures seriously debated child labor, convict labor, the hours of labor, scrip wages, and factory safety laws. The few victories the Knights achieved, with the exception of the creation of the North.Carolina Bureau of Labor, in themselves proved insignificant. But the issues the Knights raised in both municipal and state politics would not die, and the progressive political forces of the early twentieth century would obtain legislation on each.

At the national level, the southern order had little political influence, securing the election of but two congressmen in 1886, both of whom were defeated in reelection bids two years later. Nor did the Knights influence national legislation as would the agrarians in the early 1890s. This poor showing resulted primarily because of the Knights' numerical weakness. Even if the entire industrial and urban labor force in the South had joined the order and focused on national reform legislation, their numbers would have been inadequate to produce significant results. In addition, the reform programs sponsored by the national order—land reform, monetary reform, and railway regulation—had little appeal to the average worker. Even the issue of trust regulation obtained the Knights' support largely as a protest of the arbitrary power of capital. On the one issue that promised immediate benefits to the laborer, the Blair Bill, southern Knights exerted all the influence they could muster to see that it received the support of their congressmen. The Knights' most significant contribution in the area of national legislation was their call for federal action to redress their economic grievances, in which they again preceded the agrarians.

Not the least of the Knights' accomplishments was the introduction of the concept of organization to the southern labor force. Because most laborers in the towns and industries of the New South came from the region's rural areas, few had any concept of a union except for members of such skilled trades as the telegraphers, typographers, cigar makers, and in some towns, carpenters and masons. To the miners, textile workers, tobacco factory hands, loggers, most construction workers, and others, the Knights offered a possibility of escape from their poor economic status through a new relationship with their fellow workers. Southern laborers responded to the concept in the same manner as did their northern counterparts. But in the South, that response resulted in devastating defeat and would hinder the further development of organized labor in the region until well into the twentieth century.

The demise of the southern Knights, like the decline of the national order, resulted from a combination of factors, some unique to the region, some shared by the order at large. The small number of urban and industrial laborers made them more vulnerable to determined managerial opposition than were northern laborers. The racial issue also hurt the southern Knights. In Richmond, Birmingham, and Augusta, racial discord helped to defeat strikes; and throughout the southern order, white Knights demonstrated an unwillingness to cooperate with black members on issues of mutual economic concern. The racial split in the order's ranks was a negative legacy, one which management would continue to use to manipulate southern workers until the present. Nevertheless, the leadership of the southern order at both the state and district levels attempted to overcome racial prejudice and unite the labor force along economic lines. Although their attempt failed, the Knights again preceded the agrarians in their efforts to form an economic coalition between the races. The evidence also indicates that the Knights' efforts were more far-reaching and, for a time, more successful. [44]

The divisiveness which plagued the southern Knights was common throughout the national order. Nevertheless, internecine fighting, together with racial prejudice and the intransigence of management, contributed most to the decline of the order. Such quarrels dissipated the order's energy, discouraged its membership, and provided grist for the mills of its critics. Few in numbers, divided by race, and dominated by a management dedicated to laissez-faire economics, the laborer could ill afford dissension within the only organization purporting to represent his interests.

The ultimate collapse of the urban order in the South, however, came because it was ineffective. In the end, the Noble Order of the Knights of Labor proved unable to provide any immediate, concrete benefits for its members. The Knights' political activity failed to aid its members directly. Management eventually moved against and defeated the more militant locals. By 1887, it was evident that cooperation was merely a dream of the national leadership, incapable of bettering the laborers' lives. Forced by events to the conclusion that the order offered little in the way of practical, immediate benefits for him, the urban laborer, especially the white urban laborer, dropped from its ranks. In offering his resignation as state master workman of Misissippi in 1892, James Jennings summed up the disappointments of many former southern Knights. He noted that many locals had lapsed and could not be revived. The national had taxed southern assemblies but provided few benefits. Since 1887, Mississippi had sent over $5000 to the national order. In return, the state had received three visits from members of the General Executive Board and expenses for four delegates who attended various General Assemblies. Altogether, Jennings complained, the order had expended less than $500 on Mississippi, a fact which "more than anything" helped disrupt the state assembly. Finally, he observed that since the state assembly had come into existence, Mississippi Knights had engaged in four strikes. Not once did the strikers receive aid from "outside"; and now most of them were unemployed, victims of the blacklist. They had suffered because they believed the Knights of Labor slogan of "an injury to one is the concern of all."[45]

As white urban and industrial laborers left the order, discouraged by its ineffectiveness, the Knights turned to rural communities for recruits. But by the time the urban order began its decline, the Farmers' Alliance had begun to organize white landowning farmers and the more affluent white tenants. By 1888, the Alliance had established ties with several black farmers' organizations, the largest of which was the Colored Farmers' National Alliance.[46] Although the relationship between the black and white Alliances was strained at best, the creation of a black Alliance limited the order's ability to recruit rural blacks. Able to join a powerful organization tailored to their economic and social needs, farmers had little incentive to join the Knights, especially those farmers who were also employers. Thus with its urban base disintegrating and with little hope of organizing the more prosperous agrarians, the order was forced to appeal to the most depressed tenants, rural day laborers, and domestics, groups comprised primarily of blacks. In so doing, the Knights further alienated their remaining white urban membership.

By 1889, the transformation of the southern order was complete. The urban assemblies were in shambles, the once vital urban district assemblies either lapsed or barely functioning. Only in North Carolina, and Mississippi, where the order had become almost totally rural and increasingly black, did the Knights exhibit any signs of expansion. The Knights had become a fraternal order for the region's economic outcasts. Its rhetoric and ritual appealed only to those whose economic and social position was so hopeless as to require a belief in the inevitable triumph of the "just principles" the order espoused. After a decade of activity in the region, "just principles" were all the order had to offer.

The 1889 Atlanta General Assembly sought to capitalize on the order's principles by voting to establish stronger ties with the agrarian reformers of the West and South. But to do that, the Knights had to acknowledge the ascendancy of the Southern Alliance and, finally, become actively involved in third party politics. The Atlanta General Assembly marked the demise of the Knights of Labor as an effective organization, both in the South and in the nation as a whole. After 1889, the national order—torn by internal strife, its treasury depleted, its leadership determined to continue their opposition to the wage system—proved no match for the more pragmatic trade union movement led by the American Federation of Labor. In the South, the order continued to exist as an association of the region's poorest class led by a few who, for whatever their reasons, refused to relinquish the hopes and dreams inspired by the Knights at their ascendancy.

Throughout the South, the Knights of Labor failed to establish an effective, enduring labor organization. But the significance of the southern Knights lies not so much in what they accomplished as in the fact that they existed and in what they attempted to do. The Knights were the first labor organization to attempt to organize southern workers on a large scale. By their very existence, local, district, and state assemblies disproved the claims of industrialists and politicians that there was no friction between capital and labor within the region. The strength of the order throughout the South from 1885 through 1887 indicates that the discontent of labor was widespread. So does the order's success in establishing locals in all the major industries of the New South and the notable strength of locals in several industries, especially textiles, mining, and lumber. The Knights were the first labor organization to voice the protest of the southern urban and industrial worker, to state through their lecturers, organizers, and newspapers that the southern worker deserved better treatment. They were the first to attempt to use the strike and boycott on a large scale to force management to redress the laborers' grievances. And though their strikes were often poorly planned and led, striking Knights nevertheless demonstrated amazing solidarity for recent recruits to the ranks of organized labor. The Knights were the first labor organization to take their fight to the ballot box, well before the farmers did so. They also attempted to implement cooperative programs to provide adequately compensated employment for members well before the cooperative efforts of the Farmers' Alliance.

Such activities are not those of a contented, docile labor force, one with no interest in the concept of organized labor. Rather, they demonstrate that southern workers found their condition within the new industrial society as deplorable as did their northern colleagues. The activities of the Knights also show that, like northerners, southern laborers were willing to attempt to organize in an effort to voice their protest and to try to change the conditions which they protested. Given the relatively small number of urban and industrial workers within the society, the political and economic power of management, and the basic reform nature of the Knights, the order's efforts were doomed to failure. By the same token, the response of southern laborers to the order, far from being negative, indicates a remarkable willingness on their part to take action against negative aspects of a new and popular industrial society. Viewed against the total backdrop of the region's economic development in the 1880s, the efforts of the Knights of Labor in the South provide convincing evidence that southern laborers responded to industrialization, just as did the northern workers, with confusion and hesitation over the methods to be employed but with a determination to change their status through united action.

Notes

INTRODUCTION

1. A complete list of just the recent works on slavery would make a much too lengthy footnote. Among the most important are: Robert Fogel and Stanley Engerman, *Time on the Cross* (Boston, 1974); Eugene Genovese, *Roll, Jordan, Roll* (New York, 1974); David B. Davis, *The Problem of Slavery in the Age of Revolution, 1770-1823* (Ithaca, 1975); and C. Duncan Rice, *The Rise and Fall of Black Slavery* (New York, 1975).

2. Broadus Mitchell and George S. Mitchell, *The Industrial Revolution in the South* (Baltimore, 1930), 215.

3. F. Ray Marshall, *Labor in the South* (Cambridge, Mass., 1967), 20-38.

4. Robert Ward and William Rogers, *Labor Revolt in Alabama: the Great Strike of 1894* (Tuscaloosa, 1965), 22-23.

5. Norman T. Ware, *The Labor Movement in the United States, 1860-1895* (New York, 1929), 68-69. Also see Frederick Meyers, "The Knights of Labor in the South," *Southern Economic Journal* 6 (April 1940), 479-87.

6. Gerald Grob, *Workers and Utopia: A Study of Ideological Conflict in the American Labor Movement* (Evanston, Ill., 1961), 50-54.

7. Marshall, *Labor in the South*, 21-24.

8. The pages of the *Manufacturer's Record* provide a continued record of this type of promotion. For an example, see Richard Spillane, "Striking Facts About Southern Cotton Mills and Cotton Mill Employees," *Manufacturer's Record* 86 (December 11, 1924), 195-96. Also see Broadus Mitchell, *The Rise of Cotton Mills in the South* (Baltimore, 1921), 176-98.

9. Nollie Hickman, *Mississippi Harvest: Lumbering in the Longleaf Pine Belt, 1840-1915* (Oxford, Miss., 1962), 252.

CHAPTER 1

1. For a discussion of the South's new economic leadership, see C. Vann Woodward, *Origins of the New South, 1877-1913* (Baton Rouge, 1971), chaps.

5 and 6; Wilbur J. Cash, *The Mind of the South* (New York, 1941), 145-85; Paul Buck, *The Road to Reunion* (Boston, 1937), chaps. 6 and 7; Melton A. McLaurin, *Paternalism and Protest, Southern Cotton Mill Workers and Organized Labor, 1875-1905* (Westport, Conn., 1971), chaps. 2 and 3.

2. Justin Fuller, "Notes and Documents: Alabama Business Leaders, 1865-1900," *Alabama Review* 16 and 17 (October 1963 and January 1964), 279-86 and 63-75; William Miller, "The Recruitment of the American Business Elite," *Quarterly Journal of Economics* 64 (May 1950), 242-53, gives a similar view of the northern economic leadership of the same period.

3. Nannie May Tilley, *The Bright-Tobacco Industry, 1860-1929* (Chapel Hill, 1948), 533-56, 577, 595-96, 610-11.

4. Ethel Armes, *The Story of Coal and Iron in Alabama* (Birmingham, 1910), 267-77, 238-42, 289-94, 308.

5. McLaurin, *Paternalism and Protest*, 4-5.

6. Ibid., 13-14.

7. Tilley, *Bright-Tobacco*, 570-76.

8. Victor S. Clark, *History of Manufacturers in the United States*, 3 vols. (New York, 1929), 1:214-15.

9. John F. Stover, *The Railroads of the South, 1865-1900* (Chapel Hill, 1955), 186-209.

10. Ibid., chap. 5.

11. Ibid., 210-29.

12. Armes, *Coal and Iron*, 279-82; Fuller, "Alabama Business Leaders," 279-86.

13. Woodward, *Origins*, 117.

14. McLaurin, *Paternalism and Protest*, 8-9; Robert S. Smith, *Mill on the Dam* (Durham, N.C., 1960), 29-30.

15. Tilley, *Bright-Tobacco*, 556-77.

16. Kirk Monroe, "Mobile, Alabama," *Harper's Weekly* 31 (July 16, 1887), 503.

17. For examples, see Robert McMath, *Populist Vanguard: A History of the Southern Farmers' Alliance* (Chapel Hill, 1975); also the classic by John D. Hicks, *The Populist Revolt* (Minneapolis, 1931).

18. Ward and Rogers, *Labor Revolt*, 20; also see Paul B. Worthman, "Working Class Mobility in Birmingham, Alabama, 1880-1914," *Anonymous Americans* (Englewood Cliffs, N.J., 1971), 172-213.

19. Compiled from Donald B. Dodd and Wynelle S. Dodd, *Historical Statistics of the South, 1790-1970* (Tuscaloosa, 1973).

20. Ibid.

21. Ibid.

22. For contemporary accounts of textile and coal-mining villages, see

Clare de Graffenried, "The Georgia Cracker in the Cotton Mill," *Century Magazine* 41 (February 1891), 495; Mrs. John Van Vorst and Marie Van Vorst, *The Woman Who Toils* (New York, 1903), 300; and Terence Powderly's series of articles on coal mining in the *Scranton Truth*, February 12, 13, and 16, 1885. Also see Nollie Hickman, *Mississippi Harvest*. 249-50.

23. North Carolina Bureau of Labor, *Report of 1887* (Raleigh, 1888), 143, hereafter cited as *N.C. Labor Report*; *Scranton Truth*, February 12, 13, and 16, 1885; *Journal of United Labor*, June 4, 1887, 2415-16, July 23, 1887, 2460, and August 20, 1887, 2476, hereafter cited as *JUL*; Hickman, *Mississippi Harvest*, 249; McLaurin, *Paternalism and Protest*, 29.

24. Tilley, *Bright-Tobacco*, 516; McLaurin, *Paternalism and Protest*, 23-24.

25. Woodward, *Origins*, 212-15; Ward and Rogers, *Labor Revolt*, 21-22; *Scranton Truth*, February 12, 1885.

26. U.S. Bureau of Labor Statistics, *History of Wages in the United States from Colonial Times to 1928* (Washington, D.C., 1934), 388.

27. McLaurin, *Paternalism and Protest*, 27.

28. Bureau of Labor, *History of Wages*, 463-64; Hickman, *Mississippi Harvest*, 234-35; *JUL*, June 11, 1887, 2423.

29. Tilley, *Bright-Tobacco*, 518-21; *JUL*, June 16, 1887, 2456, and May 7, 1887, 2379; Bureau of Labor, *History of Wages*, 569.

30. Ward and Rogers, *Labor Revolt*, 23-25.

31. Bureau of Labor, *History of Wages*, 331-32, 334.

32. *JUL*, September 10, 1887, 2488; August 27, 1887, 2480; August 20, 1887, 2476; and December 17, 1887, 2544.

33. Bureau of Labor, *History of Wages*, 242, 246, 250.

34. *JUL*, April 2, 1887, 2339; May 7, 1887, 2379; and July 16, 1887, 2456.

35. Ibid., August 13, 1887, 2472, and September 17, 1887, 2491.

36. Ibid., September 17, 1887, 2491, and July 30, 1887, 2464.

37. Bureau of Labor, *History of Wages*, 156, 163, 185.

38. *JUL*, May 7, 1887, 2379; July 9, 1887, 2452; July 16, 1887, 2456; and July 23, 1887, 2460.

39. Bureau of Labor, *History of Wages*, 226.

40. McLaurin, *Paternalism and Protests*, 24-26.

41. Tilley, *Bright-Tobacco*, 518-19.

42. *JUL*, June 11, 1887, 2423, and November 19, 1887, 2528; Hickman, *Mississippi Harvest*, 235.

43. *JUL*, August 20, 1887, 2476, October 29, 1887, 2516, and December 24, 1887, 2548; Bureau of Labor, *History of Wages*, 330.

44. Bureau of Labor, *History of Wages*, 154, 163, 197-98.

45. McLaurin, *Paternalism and Protest*, 57, 24.

46. Tilley, *Bright-Tobacco*, 517.

47. *JUL*, August 27, 1887, 2480.

48. An excellent source for laborers' views are the *Reports* of the North Carolina Bureau of Labor. Established in 1887, the bureau issued annual reports which included letters from laborers throughout the state. These reports are hereafter cited as *N.C. Labor Report*.

49. See Buck, *Road to Reunion*, 115-96; Paul Gaston, *The New South Creed: A Study in Southern Mythmaking* (New York, 1970), 167-86; Cash, *Mind of the South*, 103-88; Woodward, *Origins*, 107-75.

50. Tilley, *Bright-Tobacco*, 520; Armes, *Coal and Iron*, 242-43; Broadus Mitchell, *The Rise of the Cotton Mills in the South* (Baltimore, 1921), 132-35; Cash, *Mind of the South*, 178.

51. Cash, *Mind of the South*, 210; Tilley, *Bright-Tobacco*, 510; Hickman, *Mississippi Harvest*, 251-53; McLaurin, *Paternalism and Protest*, 45.

52. Armes, *Coal and Iron*, 335, 395.

53. Tilley, *Bright-Tobacco*, 550.

54. George T. Winston, *A Builder of the New South; Being the Story of the Life Work of Daniel A. Tompkins* (Garden City, N.Y., 1920), 237.

55. Two of the best studies of the American businessmen's efforts to apply Dawin's theories to the social and economic world are Richard Hofstadter, *Social Darwinism in American Thought*, 2d rev. ed. (Boston, 1959); and Irvin G. Wyllie, *The Self-Made Man in America: The Myth of Rags to Riches* (New Brunswick, N.J., 1954).

56. *N.C. Labor Report*, *1887*, 65-73.

57. Ibid., 68.

CHAPTER 2

1. *Report of the Committee of the Senate Upon the Relations Between Labor and Capital*, 5 vols. (Washington, D.C., 1885), 4:4, 44, 56-60, 102-103, 288, 778-79, 807-10. Also see Herbert J. Lahne, *The Cotton Mill Worker* (New York, 1944), 183-87; Hickman, *Mississippi Harvest*, 230-35; Tilley, *Bright-Tobacco*, 515-21; McLaurin, *Paternalism and Protest*, 18-20.

2. *Report on Labor and Capital*, 4:4, 306-308, 358-72, 530-39, 770-71; Tilley, *Bright-Tobacco*, 519.

3. Worthman, "Working Class Mobility," 172-213; *Report on Labor and Capital 4:289.*

4. McLaurin, *Paternalism and Protest*, 19-20.

5. South Carolina Department of Agriculture, *Cotton Mills of South Carolina* (Charleston, 1880), 1-17; *Report on Labor and Capital*, 4:539.

6. Dodd and Dodd, *Historical Statistics*, 2-3; Worthman, "Working Class Mobility," 172-213.

7. *Report on Labor and Capital*, 4:157-66, 300-308, 163, 134-35, 288-90.

8. *N.C. Labor Report* (1887), 66; Tilley, *Bright-Tobacco*, 515.

9. *N.C. Labor Report* (1887), 71, 87; *N.C. Labor Report* (1888), 171, 184-86; *Report on Labor and Capital*, 4:488, 654-56, 770-71, 807-10.

10. *Report on Labor and Capital*, 4:13-32, 102-103; *N.C. Labor Report* (1888), 178-79. Also see Hickman, *Mississippi Harvest*, 234-35.

11. For a discussion of the urban antebellum black labor force, see Richard Wade, *Slavery in the Cities: the South 1820-1860* (New York, 1964), especially chap. 2; and Robert Starobin, *Industrial Slavery in the Old South* (New York, 1970), especially chap. 2 and 4.

12. *Report on Labor and Capital*, 4:116-24, 392-402.

13. Ibid., 124, 404; *N.C. Labor Report* (1888), 187.

14. For examples, see *JUL*, April 2, 1887, 2339; *Alabama Sentinel*, May 21, 1887.

15. *N.C. Labor Report* (1887), 64.

16. Ibid., 34-35, 40, 42-43, 64.

17. See Herbert G. Gutman, *Work Culture and Society in Industrializing America* (New York, 1976), 36-39, 47-50.

18. Ibid., 36-39; McLaurin, *Paternalism and Protest*, 26, 59; *N.C. Labor Report* (1887), 67, 69, 71; Mitchell, *Cotton Mills*, 182-85; *Report on Labor and Capital*, 4:289.

19. For examples of such employee attitudes, see *Report on Labor and Capital*, 4:599-601, 315-35; McLaurin, *Paternalism and Protest*, 55-57.

20. *N.C. Labor Report* (1887), 64; *Report on Labor and Capital*, 4:10-16; Mitchell, *Cotton Mills*, 131-37.

21. *Report on Labor and Capital*, 4:285.

22. Gutman, *Work Culture*, 30, 78-117.

23. William E. Woodward, *The Gift of Life: An Autobiography* (New York, 1947), 45; *JUL*, July 23, 1887, 2460.

24. Gutman, *Work Culture*, 95-97.

25. Ibid., 30; Ben Robertson, *Red Hills and Cotton: An Upcountry Memory* (Columbia, S.C., 1960), 275-77.

26. *N.C. Labor Report* (1905), 228; *N.C. Labor Report* (1887), 69, 71-72; *N.C. Labor Report* (1888), 184, 186, 171.

27. Dodd and Dodd, *Historical Statistics*, pass.

28. *Report on Labor and Capital*, 4:358-59.

CHAPTER 3

1. Ware, *Labor Movement*, 24-31, 55-64; Terence V. Powderly, *Thirty Years of Labor, 1859-1889* (New York, 1967), 73-76, 97-105, 126-31.

2. Ware, *Labor Movement*, 80-91; Grob, *Workers and Utopia*, 39-43.

3. By far the best study of the Knights' ideology is found in Grob, *Workers and Utopia*, 34-59. Also see Ware, *Labor Movement*, 55-72, 320-33; Powderly, *30 Years*, 72-98, 230-88.

4. Meyers, "Knights of Labor in the South," 479-87; Grob, *Workers and Utopia*, 35-36; Ware, *Labor Movement*, 61-62.

5. Grob, *Workers and Utopia*, 101-18.

6. The preponderance of mixed locals in the South is clearly demonstrated by the work of Jonathan Garlock and N. C. Builder, *Knights of Labor Data Bank*, available from the Institute for Social Research, Madison, Wis.; hereafter cited as *Knights' Data*. Their study is heavily relied upon for quantitative data. Even a brief survey of reports of southern locals in the *JUL* will confirm their findings. Also see Meyers, "Knights of Labor in the South," 485; Ware, *Labor Movement*, 155-160; Grob, *Workers and Utopia*, 35-36, 119-38.

7. *JUL*, May 13, 1880, 3. The Rome local had lapsed by the end of 1880. *JUL*, December 15, 1880, 76.

8. *General Assembly Proceedings, 1879* (2nd annual), 63-64, hereafter cited as G.A. Proceedings; John Abernathy, "The Knights of Labor in Alabama" (M.A. thesis, University of Alabama, 1960), 29-30.

9. *G.A. Proceedings, 1879* (3rd annual), 111-16.

10. *G.A. Proceedings, 1880*, 209-210.

11. *G.A. Proceedings, 1881*, 333; *G.A. Proceedings, 1882*, 277; *JUL*, October 15, 1880, 59, December 15, 1880, 76, and May 15, 1881, 114-15.

12. *G.A. Proceedings, 1883*, 527-28, 540, 446-55.

13. Garlock and Builder, *Knights Data*.

14. Ware, *Labor Movement*, 128-30; *JUL*, December 1882, 367, May 1883, 470, June 1883, 498, July 1883, 524, September 1883, 560, and November 1883, 595.

15. Garlock and Builder, *Knights Data*; *JUL*, January 1884, 630, April 1884, 696, June 10, 1884, 720, July 10, 1884, 741, August 10, 1884, 765, September 10, 1884, 788, October 10, 1884, 813, November 10, 1884, 833, December 10, 1884, 864, and April 10, 1885, 959; *G.A. Proceedings, 1884*, 580, 690, 827-31.

16. Ware, *Labor Movement*, 132-35; Foster R. Dulles, *Labor in America: A History* (New York, 1966), 138-39.

17. Powderly reported on his southern tour in detail in a series of articles in the *Scranton* (Pa.) *Truth*, February 6 through March 17, 1885.

18. The best description of the Knights' rail strikes in the Southwest in 1885 and 1886 is Ruth A. Allen, *The Great Southwest Strike* (Austin, 1942); Garlock and Builder, *Knights Data*; see *JUL*, August 10, 1885, 1073, and November 10, 1885, 1123-24.

19. *JUL*, July 10, 1884, 741, April 25, 1885, 970, and July 19, 1888, 2665;

Ray to Powderly, December 21, 1885, and November 9, 1886, and Mullen to Powderly, October 30, 1884, Terence V. Powderly Papers, Archives, Catholic University, Washington, D.C..

20. Phil Hammond to Powderly, January 4, 1886, and T. J. Anderson to Powderly, March 15, 1886, Powderly Papers.

21. Ray to Powderly, December 21, 1885; W. N. Dicks to Powderly, March 10, 1886; Mullen to Powderly, March 7 and April 7, 1885; Pendleton to Powderly, May 25, 1886; W. S. Rudd to Powderly, December 7, 1885, all in Powderly Papers.

22. *JUL*, February 25, 1886, 2009; Richmond *Dispatch*, March 9, 1886.

23. *JUL*, February 10, 1886, 1192-93, and March 10, 1886, 2019-22. For examples of requests for organizers' commissions, see John Lindsey to Powderly, March 1, 1886; Robert Kruse to Powderly, February 26, 1886; L. G. Pettyjohn to Powderly, January 3, 1886; and S. C. Haviland to Powderly, August 7, 1886, all in Powderly Papers.

24. *JUL*, March 10, 1886, 2019-22, May 10, 1886, 2067-70, and June 10, 1886, 2092-95. Also see Ware, *Labor Movement*, 68.

25. *G.A. Proceedings, 1886, Special Session*, 20, 25-26; Ware, *Labor Movement*, 68; *JUL*, July 10, 1886, 2111-13, August 10, 1886, 2141-42, and September 10, 1886, 2159-60; Garlock and Builder, *Knights Data*.

26. *G.A. Proceedings, 1886, Regular Session*, 327-28; Powderly, *30 Years*, 336-37.

27. Mercer G. Evans, "The History of the Organized Labor Movement in Georgia" (unpublished Ph.D. dissertation, University of Chicago, 1929), 83.

28. Garlock and Builder, *Knights Data*; *JUL*, August 10, 1886, 2148.

29. *JUL*, July 10, 1886, 2111-13, September 10, 1886, 2159-60, and October 10, 1886, 2187-88; Garlock and Builder, *Knights Data*.

30. *G.A. Proceedings, 1886, Regular Session*, 44, 313-25.

CHAPTER 4

1. Powderly, as quoted in Nathan Fine, *Labor and Farmer Parties in the United States, 1828-1929* (New York, 1961), 121. For discussions of the Knights' complicated and continually changing strike policies, see Grob, *Workers and Utopia*, 48-52; and Ware, *Labor Movement*, 116-54.

2. *G.A. Proceedings, 1878*, 32.

3. *G.A. Proceedings, 1879*, (2nd annual), 54.

4. *G.A. Proceedings, 1880*, 169-71, 185-87, 195-96, 246.

5. *JUL*, June 10, 1886, 2090; Grob, *Workers and Utopia*, 48-52.

6. Terence V. Powderly, *The Path I Trod: An Autobiography* (New York, 1940), 105.

7. *G.A. Proceedings, 1886*, 45-46, 62; *G.A. Proceedings, 1887*, 15-66; Grob, *Workers and Utopia*, 48-52.

8. *G.A. Proceedings, 1885*, 19, 162-63.

9. Ward and Rogers, *Labor Revolt*, 24.

10. *JUL*, October 10, 1884, 809, December 10, 1884, 857, and April 25, 1885, 970-71; Abernathy, "The Knights in Alabama," 45-46.

11. Ward and Rogers, *Labor Revolt*, 25.

12. *JUL*, June 10, 1888, 2645; Nicholas B. Stack Scrapbook, Stack Collection, University of Alabama, Tuscaloosa, Alabama; Holman Head, "Organized Labor in Alabama," (Ph.D. diss. University of Alabama, 1954), 85-86; Ward and Rogers, *Labor Revolt*, 25-26.

13. *Alabama Sentinel*, May 7, June 4 and 25, and July 23, 1887; Ward and Rogers, *Labor Revolt*, 27; Abernathy, "The Knights in Alabama," 71.

14. *Alabama Sentinel*, November 10 and 26, 1887; *JUL*, December 3, 1887, 2535-36; Head, "Organized Labor," 86-87.

15. *Alabama Sentinel*, February 11, 1888.

16. Ibid., June 2 and 9, 1888; Head, "Organized Labor," 86-87.

17. *Alabama Sentinel*, June 23, 1887.

18. Ibid., July 7, 1888; Head, "Organized Labor," 87.

19. *Alabama Sentinel*, January 5, 1889.

20. Head, "Organized Labor," 88-89; Ward and Rogers, *Labor Revolt*, 28; *Alabama Sentinel*, January 26, 1889.

21. *Richmond Dispatch*, May 4, 1886; *G.A. Proceedings, 1887*, 1377; *G.A. Proceedings, 1888*, "Report of the G.E.B.," 56-57.

22. J. K. Warden to Powderly, January 19, 1889, Powderly Papers.

23. *Richmond Dispatch*, March 4, June 14, July 14, and September 2, 1886.

24. *Alabama Sentinel*, July 30 and September 3, 1887; Birmingham *Iron Age*, July 27 and 28, and August 9, 10, 25, and 28, 1887.

25. *JUL*, October 29, 1887, 2516.

26. *JUL*, July 16, 1887, 2456, and September 17, 1887, 2492.

27. Ibid., June 25, 1887, 2439, and March 14, 1889, 2804; *G.A. Proceedings, 1888*, "Report of the G.E.B.," 64; *G.A. Proceedings, 1889*, "Report of the G.E.B.," 18; John McDonald to Powderly, September 11, 1889, Powderly Papers; Donald C. Mosley, "A History of Labor Unions in Mississippi," (Ph.D. diss. University of Alabama, 1965), 39-41; Hickman, *Mississippi Harvest*, 235-37.

28. *G.A. Proceedings, 1890*, "Report of G.E.B.," 10-11.

29. *JUL*, August 6, 1887, 2468; Powderly to John Ray, December 23, 1885,

Book 12, 224, and to D. L. Kaufman, July 19 and August 16, 1887, Book 28, 38 and 169, Kaufman to Powderly, July 14, 1887, Powderly Papers; *G.A. Proceedings, 1888*, "Report of the G.E.B.," 109.

30. A. M. Cutberson to Powderly, September 7, 1887, Powderly Papers.

31. *JUL*, August 23, 1888, 2688; Tilley, *Bright-Tobacco*, 519.

32. *JUL*, February 25, 1888, 2584; Grob, *Workers and Utopia*, 114, 121; *G.A. Proceedings, 1890*, "Report of the G.E.B.," 2.

33. Grob, *Workers and Utopia*, 105, 108-109.

34. *Atlanta Constitution*, March 12 and 14, 1886; Evans, "Labor in Georgia," 54; Powderly to G. W. Andrews, May 3, 1886, Book 19, 19, Powderly Papers; *G.A. Proceedings, 1887*, 1288-89.

35. *JUL*, November 25, 1884, 848-49; *Richmond Dispatch*, February 13 and 23, March 6 and 7, July 23, and September 29, 1886.

36. *Alabama Sentinel*, May 28, 1887, and May 12, 1888.

37. *Richmond Dispatch*, March 11 and 12, and April 12, 14, and 15, 1886.

38. Ibid., January 12-15, 1887.

39. Frenise Logan, *The Negro in North Carolina, 1876-1894* (Chapel Hill, 1964), 95-96.

40. W. H. Wetmore to Powderly, April 17, 1886, Leonida Keith to Powderly, January 10, 1887, and R. W. Kruse to Powderly, December 11, 1885, all in the Powderly Papers.

41. *Alabama Sentinel*, June 29, April 13 and 20, and August 3, 1889; *G.A. Proceedings, 1889*, "Report of the G.E.B.," 23-24; Abernathy, "The Knights in Alabama," 79-82.

42. *Alabama Sentinel*, November 1, 1887; John Andrews to Powderly, November 3, 1887, and Powderly to Andrews, November 9, 1887, Book 30, 70, Powderly Papers; *G.A. Proceedings, 1888*, "Report of the G.E.B.," 65.

43. Evans, "Labor in Georgia," 83.

44. The following account of the Knights in the textile industry is taken from McLaurin, *Paternalism and Protest*, chap. 4, unless otherwise noted. References to primary material are contained in the following notes, however. Also see Merle Reed, "The Augusta Textile Mills and the Strike of 1886," *Labor History* 14 (spring 1973), 228-46.

45. Henry Hammett to Dexter Converse, March 30, 1886, Piedmont Letter Book 1, 252, University of South Carolina, Caroliniana Library, Columbia, S.C., hereafter cited as PLB; Hammett to Ellison Smyth, April 23, 1886, PLB 1, 289; *Augusta Chronicle*, April 25, 1886; W. A. Fogleman to Powderly, October 18, 1886, and Powderly to Fogleman, November 10, 1886, Book 23, 87, Powderly Papers; W. J. Benning and R. M. Sasser to Powderly, August 12, 1886, W. J. Benning to Powderly, October 9, 1886, and Powderly to Sasser,

August 16, 1886, Book 21, 108, all in Powderly Papers; *Alabama Sentinel*, July 2, 1887.

46. *Augusta Chronicle*, July 8-13, 1886; *Charleston News and Courier*, July 8-14, 1886; Powderly to Mullen, July 12, 1886, Book 19, 235, Powderly Papers.

47. McLaurin, *Paternalism and Protest*, 100-102; *Augusta Chronicle*, August 8-12, 1886.

48. Meynardie to Powderly, August 10, 1886, and Mullen to Powderly, August 14, 1886, Powderly Papers.

49. Hammett to W. E. McCoy, August 14, 1886, PLB 1, 493-95; Hammett to McCoy, August 19, 1886, PLB 2, 5-6; Hammett to McCoy, September 2, 1886, PLB 2, 39; Hammett to McCoy, September 16, 1886, PLB 2, 49.

50. Meynardie to Powderly, August 30, 1886, Powderly Papers; *G.A. Proceedings, 1886*, 102-103; *G.A. Proceedings, 1887*, 1566; *Augusta Chronicle*, September 15-October 1, 1886.

51. Discussed in Chap. 7.

52. *Augusta Chronicle*, October 1-12, 1886.

53. Ibid., October 12-26, 1886; *G.A. Proceedings, 1886*, 45-56; *G.A. Proceedings, 1886*, 1566; Powderly to Meynardie, December 23, 1886, Book 24, 21, Powderly Papers.

54. *Augusta Chronicle*, October 27-November 8, 1886.

55. David D. Wallace, "One Hundred Years of Gregg and Graniteville" (Graniteville, South Carolina: William Gregg Foundation, 1954), 224; Hammett to James F. Iler, October 12, 1886, PLB 2, 118; Hammett to James A. Brice, October 14, 1886, PLB 2, 120; Hammett to Dexter Converse, November 18, 1886, PLB 2, 214; Hammett to Francis J. Pelzer, October 16, 1886, PLB 3, 126; T. L. Bowers to Powderly, October 18, 1886, Powderly Papers; *JUL*, November 10, 1886, 2200.

56. Meynardie to Powderly, December 12, 1886, Powderly to Meynardie, December 23, 1886, Book 24, 21; M. M. Connor to Powderly, January 27 and February 4, 1887, Powderly to Connor, February 19, 1887, Mullen to Powderly, January 22 and 29, and February 18, 1887, Powderly to Mullen, January 18, 1887, Book 27, 3; and January 26, 1887, Book 27, 63, all in the Powderly Papers.

57. Evans, "Labor in Georgia," 410-412, McLaurin, *Paternalism and Protest*, 112.

58. Andrew W. Pierpont, "Development of the Textile Industry in Alamance County, North Carolina," (Ph.D. diss., University of North Carolina, 1953), 136-56.

59. *JUL*. October 15, 1887, 2508; *Carolina Spartan*, September 14, 19, and 20, 1887; *Fayetteville Messenger*, November 18 and December 2, 1887.

60. *G.A. Proceedings, 1888,* 50; George S. Mitchell, *Textile Unionism in the South* (Chapel Hill, 1931), 25.
61. Mitchell, *Textile Unionism,* 25.
62. *Alabama Sentinel,* January 21, February 11, May 12 and 19, and October 6, 1888.
63. Richard Street, "Black Militancy of 1887: The Louisiana Sugar Plantation Strike," unpublished manuscript in the possession of the author, Madison, Wisconsin.
64. Mitchell Beasley to John Hayes, January 22, 1889, Hayes Papers, Box 18, John Hayes Collection, Catholic University, Washington, D.C.
65. John Andrews to Powderly, November 3, 1887, Powderly Papers.
66. *Report on Labor and Capital,* 4:300-306, 309.

CHAPTER 5

1. Powderly, *Thirty Years,* 52-55, 146; Grob, *Workers and Utopia.*
2. *G.A. Proceedings, 1888,* "Report of the General Secretary," 1-16.
3. *G.A. Proceedings, 1882,* 277; *G.A. Proceedings, 1886, Special Session,* 40-42; Powderly, *Path I Trod,* 385-86; Grob, *Workers and Utopia,* 79-98; Wright, "Historical Sketch of the Knights," 157-59.
4. Pendleton to Powderly, May 25 and September 26, 1886, Powderly Papers.
5. *G.A. Proceedings, 1886, Regular Session,* 313-325; Pendleton to Powderly, September 26, 1886, Powderly Papers.
6. *News and Observer,* April 16, 1886; Josephus Daniels, *Tar Heel Editor* (Chapel Hill, 1939), 332-37.
7. *News and Observer,* June 23, and September 10, 1886; *State Chronicle,* September 30, 1886; *Messenger,* July 13, 1888; *Biographical Directory of the American Congress, 1774-1961* (Washington, D.C., 1961), 1388.
8. *News and Observer,* August 7, 15, 1886; *State Chronicle,* July 22, 1886.
9. John Nichols, *For Congress, Fourth District, John Nichols of Wake County: Address to the Voters of the Fourth District,* pamphlet in the North Carolina Collection. University of North Carolina at Chapel Hill, n.p., 1886; *News and Observer,* September 12, 18, 1886; Nichols to Powderly, November 26, 1886, Powderly Papers.
10. Set the *News and Observer,* September-October, 1886. For specific speeches by Graham see the *Observer,* September 11, 18 and October 21. 1886; *State Chronicle,* September 23, 1886; W. T. H. Woodward to Powderly,

August 15, 1886, Powderly Papers.

11. *News and Observer*, September 10, 19, and October 9, 12, 19, 20, 1886; *State Chronicle*, September 23, and October 7, 1886; for other examples of press reaction to the Richmond incident see "Knights of Labor and the Color Line," *Public Opinion* 2 (October 16, 1886), 1.

12. United States Department of the Interior, Census Office, *Compendium of the Eleventh Census, 1890*, Part 1, *Population* (Washington, D.C., 1892), 499-501; Daniels, *Tar Heel Editor*, 332-37; *News and Observer*, November 4, 1886; *State Chronicle*, November 4, 1886.

13. *Virginian*, September 30, October 1-3, 1886; *Richmond Dispatch*, September 30-October 5, 1886.

14. *Richmond Dispatch*, October 26, 1886; *Virginian*, October 9, 23, 26, 1886.

15. *Virginian*, October 29 and November 3-5, 1886.

16. *Richmond Dispatch*, September 1-6, 1886.

17. Ibid., September 11, 1886.

18. Ibid., September 16 and 25 and October 3, 1886.

19. For details of the Baughman boycott, see chapter 3.

20. For a complete discussion of the Richmond racial incident, see chapter 6.

21. *Richmond Dispatch*, September 29 and October 6-31, 1886.

22. Ibid., October 30 through November 3, 1886.

23. Ibid., February 21, 1886.

24. Ibid., February 23 and March 3, 1886.

25. Ibid., March 9, 1886.

26. Ibid., May 2, March 4 and 12, and April 14 and 15, 1886.

27. Ibid., May 18-20, 1886.

28. Ibid., May 17-27, 1886.

29. Ibid., May 28 through June 1, 1886.

30. Ibid., June 25, July 2, and August 10, 1886; Allen W. Moger, "Industrial and Urban Progress in Virginia, 1880 to 1900," *Virginia Magazine of History and Biography* 46 (July 1958), 324-25.

31. *Richmond Dispatch*, May 28, 1886.

32. *G.A. Proceedings, 1888*, "Report of the G.E.B.," 37; John Crawford to Powderly, September 23, 1887, Powderly Papers.

33. *Times Union* (Jacksonville), March 31 through April 5, 1887; Frederick Davis, *History of Jacksonville, Florida, and Vicinity, 1513 to 1924* (Gainesville, Fla., 1964), 176, 298-300. Also see Edward Akin, "When a Minority Becomes the Majority, Blacks in Jacksonville Politics, 1887-1907," *Florida Historical Quarterly* 53 (October 1974), 123-39.

34. *Times Union*, November 9, 1887; *News Herald*, June 12, 1887.

35. *Times Union*, April 5 and May 3, 1887.

36. Ibid., November 26 through December 5, 1887; *News Herald*, November 26 through December 5, 1887.

37. *Times Union*, December 5-8, 1887; *News Herald*, same dates.

38. *Times Union* and *News Herald*, December 9 and 10, 1887.

39. *Times Union* and *News Herald*, December 10-14, 1887; Akin, "When a Minority," 123-39.

40. *Times Union*, December 15, 1887, through January 4, 1888, and March 27-29, 1888.

41. Ibid., January 18, 1888; *Minutes of the Jacksonville, Florida, City Council*, 1888, Book A; Akin, "When a Minority," 133-34.

42. J. J. Holland to Powderly, August 14, 1888, Powderly to Holland, August 27, 1888, Book 36, 183, and Thomas J. Mott to Powderly, September 27, 1888, all in Powderly Papers; *JUL*, October 11, 1888, 2714; *Times Union*, October 16, 1888.

43. Davis, *Jacksonville*, 184, 299, 300; Akin, "When a Minority," 133-39; Mott to Powderly, September 23, 1888, Powderly Papers.

44. Davis, *Jacksonville*, 184; Akin, "When a Minority," 133-39.

45. *Minutes of the Jacksonville City Council*, June 4, 1889, Book A, 468-73; *Times Union*, June 5, 1889.

46. *Alabama Sentinel*, February 9 and March 10, 1888, and May 11, 1889.

47. Melton McLaurin, "The Knights of Labor in North Carolina Politics," *North Carolina Historical Review* 49 (summer 1972), 307-308.

48. *Alabama Sentinel*, February 9 and March 10, 1888, and May 11, 1889.

49. W. P. Russell to Powderly, November 17, 1886, A. C. Franklin to Powderly, January 29, 1887, Powderly to Franklin, February 1, 1887, Book 27, 108, all in Powderly Papers.

50. *JUL*, April 7, 1888, 2608.

51. "Minute Book of Raleigh Local Assembly 3606, Knights of Labor, 1886-1890," North Carolina Department of Archives and History, Raleigh, N.C., December 27, 1886, 67; *News and Observer*, January 28, 1887; *JUL*, April 2, 1887, 2339.

52. *State Chronicle*, January 27, 1887; *News and Observer*, January 27, 1887.

53. *News and Observer*, January 29 through March 4, 1887; also see *JUL*, March 26, 1887, 2337; Harley E. Jolley, "The Labor Movement in North Carolina: 1880-1922," *North Carolina Historical Review* 30 (July 1953). 360.

54. For details of the stevedores' strike, see chapter 3.

55. Frenise A. Logan, *The Negro in North Carolina, 1876-1894* (Chapel Hill, 1964), 95-96.

56. *News and Observer*, January 29 through March 4, 1887.

57. John Nichols to Powderly, March 8, 1887, Powderly Papers.

58. *News and Observer*, January 29 through March 4, 1887; Daniels, *Tar Heel Editor*, 338-43.

59. *Messenger*, June 15, July 6 and 13, August 17, September 14, October 19 and 26, and November 4, 1888; *JUL*, August 2, 1888, 2676.

60. *Constitution*, March 14, 1886.

61. Evans, "Labor in Georgia," 410.

62. *Constitution* (Atlanta) September 25, 1886; Victor St. Cloud to Powderly, November 21, 1886, and Powderly to St. Cloud, November 26, 1886, Powderly Papers.

63. Evans, "Labor in Georgia," 411-12.

64. Ibid., 411-15, 446-51; *Constitution*, September 22, 1889.

65. *Richmond Dispatch*, September 19, 1885; Mullen to Powderly, August 24, 1885, Powderly Papers.

66. *JUL*, August 20, 1887, 2476, September 3, 1887, 2484.

67. *Alabama Sentinel*, July 23, 1887.

68. Ibid., August 20 and September 3, 17, and 24, 1887.

69. Ibid., January 21 and 28, 1888.

70. Ibid., March 24 and 31, 1888.

71. Abernathy, "The Knights in Alabama," 73-74, Head, "Organized Labor," 71-72; *Alabama Sentinel*, April 7 and 14, June 9 and 30, July 14, and December 8, 1888.

72. *Alabama Sentinel*, August 11 and 25, 1888.

73. McLaurin, "Knights in N.C. Politics," 312-14.

74. *Virginian*, November 1-8, 1888.

75. *Alabama Sentinel*, November 3, 1888; *Messenger*, August 31, October 12, 19, and 26, and November 9, 1888.

76. *Alabama Sentinel*, July 23, 1887; *Messenger*, February 3, 1888.

77. *G.A. Proceedings, 1887*, 1460-61.

78. Powderly to Nichols, March 14, 1887, Book 29, 58-59, Powderly to Holland, February 6, 1888, Book 32, 183, A. C. Franklin to Powderly, January 29, 1887, and Powderly to Franklin, February 1, 1887, Book 27, 108, all in Powderly Papers.

79. Woodward, *Origins*, 105.

80. Lawrence Goodwyn, *Democratic Promise: The Populist Movement in America* (New York, 1976), 308-309.

81. Grob, *Workers and Utopia*, 84-89, For other views of the order's political activity, see Marshall, *Labor in the South*, 23-24; Philip Foner, *History of the Labor Movement in the United States*, 3 vols. (New York, 1947-64), 2:115-31.

82. Broughton to Powderly, December 16, 1886, Powderly Papers.

83. McLaurin, "Knights in N.C. Politics," 310; *G.A. Proceedings, 1887*, 1364.

84. *Messenger*, November 9, 1888; *Alabama Sentinel*, December 8, 1888.

CHAPTER 6

1. For example, see Henry Hammett to Dexter Converse, March 30, 1886, and to Ellison Smyth, April 23, 1886, Piedmont Letter Book 1, 252, 259, University of South Carolina, Caroliniana Library, Columbia, S.C.; *JUL*, December 3, 1887, 2536, and November 12, 1887, 2524; Sidney Kessler, "The Organization of Negroes in the Knights of Labor," *Journal of Negro History* 37 (July 1952), 264-68.

2. *JUL*, August 25, 1885, 1067, April 25, 1885, 970-71, and June 16, 1888, 2648; Power to Powderly, December 11, 1885, and December 16, 1887, J. A. Belton to Powderly, November 15, 1886, James McHugh to Powderly, August 19, 1888, all in Powderly Papers.

3. For example, see N. B. Stack to Powderly, August 17, 1887, Powderly Papers.

4. O'Riley to Powderly, March 4, 1887; *JUL*, May 7, 1887, 2380, September 13, 1888, 2697, September 27, 1888, 2705, October 4, 1888, 2712, and November 22, 1888, 2740.

5. *G.A. Proceedings, 1889*, "Report of the G.E.B.," 1-4.

6. Ibid.; O'Riley to Powderly, March 4, 1887, Powderly Papers; *Alabama Sentinel*, March 16 and 23, 1889; *Scranton Truth*, February 6, 7, and 12, 1885; "Minute Book of the Raleigh Knights of Labor, Local Assembly 3606," 8-9, North Carolina State Department of Archives and History, Raleigh, N.C. (hereafter cited as "Raleigh Knights Minutes").

7. J. B. Smith to Powderly, October 6, 1888, Powderly Papers.

8. Ray to Powderly, November 9, 1886, James Haywood to Powderly, October 14, 1886, Stack to Powderly, October 14, 1888, and Power to Powderly, August 29, 1887, all in Powderly Papers; *Alabama Sentinel*, June 23, 1888, and January 26, 1889.

9. "Raleigh Knights Minutes," 8-9, 98-99, 17, 146, 76, 177.

10. Ibid., 27, 28, 65-66; John B. Loughrain to Powderly, March 16, 1887, Powderly Papers.

11. Letters from southerners are particularly numerous after mid-1886.

12. *JUL*, April 9, 1887, 2351, May 7, 1887, 2381, May 21, 1887, 2397, and March 3, 1888, 2588; T. C. Green to Powderly, February 1, 1887, and G. K. Woodward to Powderly, June 10, 1888, Powderly Papers.

13. *Alabama Sentinel*, April 2, 1887.

14. *Messenger*, January 20 and February 10 and 24, 1888.

15. *Sentinel* is in the Alabama Collection of the University of Alabama, in terrible condition, and needs to be microfilmed. The originals of the *Messen-*

ger are at the North Carolina State Department of Archives and History, Raleigh, N.C.; and the paper has been microfilmed. See the *Sentinel*, February 4 and August 11 and 25, 1888.

16. For examples, see the *Sentinel*, December 29, 1887, January 7, 1888, and May 28 and September 24, 1887; *Messenger*, December 9, 1887, and January 6 and August 10, 1888.

17. For examples, see the *Messenger*, November 16, 17, and 25, 1887, and January 13 and March 9, 1888.

18. See the *Sentinel*, September 17 and 24 and November 26, 1887.

19. *Sentinel*, April 9 and December 10, 1887; *Messenger*, November 25 and December 2, 1887.

20. *Messenger*, October 14 and 21, November 18 and 25, and December 23, 1887, March 9 and October 28, 1888; *Sentinel*, April 2 and 23, June 25, July 2 and December 10, 1887.

21. For examples, see the *'Messenger*, January 30, 1888, and November 11, 1887. Advertising varied little in either paper throughout their existence.

22. *G.A. Proceedings, 1880*, 170-71; *JUL*, May 25, 1884, 706.

23. For a thorough discussion of the Knights' cooperative program, see Grob, *Workers and Utopia*, 43-47; Ware, *Labor Movement*. 320-33; Powderly, *Thirty Years*, 230-39.

24. *Messenger*, January 13, February 17, March 2, June 29, and October 5, 1888.

25. *Sentinel*, May 14 and June 11 and 25, 1887.

26. Broughton to Powderly, November 28, 1887.

27. *JUL*, August 10, 1886, 2139.

28. "Report of Directors and Officers of the Stockholders of the National Knights of Labor Co-Operative Tobacco Company," Raleigh, N.C., June 15, 1886, pamphlet in the Powderly Papers, Box 184.

29. *G.A. Proceedings, 1887*, "Report of the Cooperative Board," 1589-90, 1611, 12, and "Report of the G.E.B.," 1417-18.

30. *Proceedings of the State Assembly of North Carolina Knights of Labor, Tarboro, N.C., Jan. 28 and 29, 1890* (Raleigh, 1890), back cover, in the Southern Historical Collection, University of North Carolina, Chapel Hill, N.C.

31. *JUL*, May 28, 1887, 2402; Abernathy, "The Knights in Alabama," 65-66; Head, "Organized Labor," 74-75.

32. *JUL*, November 5, 1887, 2520; *Sentinel*, April 30, September 3, and November 5, 1887, and February 4, 1888; Abernathy, "The Knights in Alabama," 65-66, 68.

33. *JUL*, May 28, 1887, 2402; Abernathy, "The Knights in Alabama," 68.

34. *Sentinel*, April 23, 1887, and March 3 and November 10, 1888; Head, "Organized Labor," 75.

35. *JUL*, August 25, 1886, 2150; *G.A. Proceedings, 1887*, "Report of the G.E.B.," 1393-95.

36. Circular from Ben H. Doster, recording secretary of D.A. 105, Atlanta, to its members, October 16, 1886, Powderly Papers.

37. George Schall to Powderly, October 19, 1886, Powderly to Schall, November 9, 1886, Book 23, 84, and Doster to Powderly, December 30, 1886, all in Powderly Papers.

38. For examples, see *JUL*, December 17, 1887, 2544, December 31, 1887, 2582, January 28, 1888, 2567, February 11, 1888, 2576, February 25, 1888, 2584, and April 28, 1888, 2619.

39. McMath, *Populist Vanguard*, 48-58, gives a good account of the Alliance cooperative efforts.

40. *JUL*, November 26, 1887, 2532, and October 1, 1887, 2500; W. H. Haines to Powderly, September 25, 1887, Powderly Papers.

41. *JUL*, December 31, 1887, 2552.

42. Alex Anthony to Powderly, April 7, 1888, Powderly Papers.

CHAPTER 7

1. C. Vann Woodward, *The Strange Career of Jim Crow* (New York, 1966), chap. 2 and 3 contain the most thorough case for the late development of segregation. This argument is countered most effectively by Joel Williamson, *After Slavery: The Negro in South Carolina During Reconstruction, 1861-1877* (Chapel Hill, 1965), chap. 10.

2. The best work on the Knights' racial policies is Sidney H. Kessler, "The Organization of Negroes in the Knights of Labor," *Journal of Negro History* 37 (July 1952), 248-76. Kessler presents the Knights' racial policies in a very favorable light and credits the order with more success in this area than they deserve. He is writing about the entire order, however, and not just the order in the South.

3. Kessler, "Negroes in the Knights," 250; Ware, *Labor Movement*, 26-27.

4. Stephens to M. F. Moran, February 2, 1879, Powderly Papers. Book B, 516.

5. A brief survey of Powderly's racial views can be found in Kessler, "Negroes in the Knights," 248-50. Further information is provided in Sister William Marie Turnbach, "The Attitudes of Terence V. Powderly Toward Minority Groups, 1879-1893" (M.A. thesis, Catholic University, 1956).

6. Powderly, *Path I Trod*, 11.

7. Powderly, *Thirty Years*, 32.

8. *G.A. Proceedings, 1880*, 257.

9. Powderly, *Thirty Years*, 347-53.

10. Powderly to J. O. Parsons, July 19, 1887, Powderly Papers; Turnbach, "Powderly," 56.

11. Powderly to Broughton, June 12, 1885, Book 11, 66, Powderly Papers.

12. Taylor to Powderly, November 17, 1889, and Yarboro to Powderly, November 18, 1889, Powderly Papers.

13. Powderly, *Thirty Years*, 352-53.

14. *Alabama Sentinel*, February 9, 1888; *Birmingham Iron Age*, July 27 through August 28, 1887.

15. *Fayetteville Messenger*, October 21, 1887, and March 30, 1888.

16. Bodenhamer to Powderly, April 15, 1889, Powderly Papers.

17. For examples, see *JUL*, October 1, 1887, 2500, December 10, 1887, 2540, and July 16, 1887, 2456. Also see George Vogel to Powderly, June 8, 1886, Powderly Papers; Harris Brown to John Hayes, May 5, 1891, Box 11, John Hayes Papers, Catholic University, Washington, D.C.; Kessler, "Negroes in the Knights," 256-57.

18. *G.A. Proceedings, 1885*, 204.

19. *JUL*, November 10, 1886, 2000-2001. Also see Kessler, "Negroes in the Knights," 258. He incorrectly implies that the black Portsmouth locals sought to form a separate district. M. W. Gunn, master workman of District Assembly 123, wrote that the locals were invited to "help form the district" (that is, District 123) but declined. Instead, they determined to join "the colored district," meaning District Assembly 92.

20. *G.A. Proceedings, 1888*, "Report of the General Executive Board," 107-108; R. W. Kruse to Powderly, April 28, 1886, Powderly Papers.

21. A good example of the integrated district can be found in T. M. Barry's description of District Assembly 193, Lynchburg, Virginia, in *G.A. Proceedings, 1888*, "Report of the General Executive Board," 37.

22. *Alabama Sentinel*, February 11, 1888; John Ray to Powderly, February 10, 1887, Powderly Papers.

23. *Richmond Dispatch*, October 6, 1886.

24. *JUL*, August 10, 1885, 1067; Powderly to John Ray, March 20, 1885, Book 10, 347, Powderly Papers.

25. Kessler, "Negroes in the Knights," 263-69; Mullen to Powderly, March 7, 1885, Powderly Papers.

26. *G.A. Proceedings, 1885*, 100.

27. For examples, see W. S. Rudd to Powderly, December 7, 1885, H. C. Cogwell to Powderly, December 6, 1886, and E. L. Lafoulaine to Powderly, January 13, 1886, all in the Powderly Papers.

28. John Ray to Powderly, February 10, 1887, Powderly Papers.

29. E. L. Lafoulaine to Powderly, January 13, 1886, C. V. Menstern to Powderly, January 17, 1887, J. M. Broughton to Powderly, February 8, 1887, John

Ray to Powderly, February 10, 1887, A. J. Loveless to Powderly, April 1, 1887, Alexander Walker to Powderly, April 6, 1887, S. F. Sweet to Powderly, March 4, 1887, and R. W. Kruse to Powderly, August 3, 1886, all in the Powderly Papers.

30. Ambrose Harrison to Powderly, June 2, 1886, Powderly Papers; Alex O'Donnell to John Hayes, May 11, 1889, Hayes Papers; Frank Johnson to Powderly, February 14, 1887, and Alexander Walker to Powderly, April 6, 1887, Powderly Papers.

31. John Ray to Powderly, February 14, 1887, Powderly Papers.

32. W. S. Rudd to Powderly, December 7, 1885, Powderly Papers.

33. S. F. Sweet to Powderly, March 4, 1887, Powderly Papers.

34. A. J. Loveless to Powderly, April 1, 1887, and Rudd to Powderly, December 7, 1885, Powderly Papers.

35. *JUL*, September 10, 1886, 2162. Also see Kessler, "Negroes in the Knights," 256.

36. A survey of letters in the *JUL* from southern locals after 1888 will confirm this trend; see *JUL*, March 17, 1888, 2596, April 7, 1888, 2608, and June 9, 1888, 2644; clipping from the *Scranton Truth*, February 7, 1885, Scrapbook 17, Powderly Papers.

37. *JUL*, August 13, 1887, 2472, and December 10, 1887, 2540; Kessler, "Negroes in the Knights," 273-74.

38. C. R. Alexander to Powderly, October 14, 1886, Powderly Papers; *JUL*, June 9, 1888, 2644.

39. McMath, *Populist Vanguard*, 44-46, 53.

40. *G.A. Proceedings, 1886*, 44; *JUL*, July 23, 1887, 2460; Tom O'Riley to Powderly, March 4, 1887, Powderly Papers.

41. William W. Rogers, "Negro Knights of Labor in Arkansas: A Case Study of the 'Miscellaneous' Strike," *Labor History* 10 (summer 1969), 498-504.

42. Kessler, "Negroes in the Knights," 268-70.

43. Richard S. Street, "Black Militancy, 1887: The Louisiana Sugar Plantation Strike," unpublished M.S. in the possession of the author. Street is a graduate student at the University of Wisconsin.

44. Mitchell Beasley to Hayes, January 22, 1889, Box 18, Hayes Papers.

45. *JUL*, June 9, 1888, 2644, October 8, 1887, 2504, July 11, 1887, 2460, August 27, 1887, 2480, November 12, 1887, 2524, January 28, 1888, 2567, and February 18, 1888, 2580.

46. *JUL*, August 2, 1888, 2676; Mildred Murray to Hayes, March 20, 1889, Box 19, Hayes Papers; *JUL*, November 12, 1887, 2524.

47. J. A. Bodenhamer to Powderly, April 15, 1889; Powderly Papers; *JUL*, June 11, 1887, 2422-23; St. Cloud to Powderly, June 16, 1889, Powderly Papers.

48. Miller to Powderly, December 20, 1884, Box 11, Hayes Papers.

49. Powderly, *Thirty Years*, 347-49.

50. All of these quotes were taken from *Public Opinion* 2 (October 16, 1886), 1-5.

51. *JUL*, June 11, 1887, 2422, August 6, 1887, 2468, and February 18, 1888, 2579-80; Hillard McNair to Powderly, March 2, 1888, Powderly Papers; *Fayetteville Messenger*, March 16 and April 20, 1888; *News and Observer* (Raleigh), July 15, 1886; Kessler, "Negroes in the Knights," 267-68.

52. R. W. Kruse to Powderly, September 23, 1886, W. L. Ellis to Powderly, August 17, 1886, and George Walsh to Powderly, July 6, 1887, all in Powderly Papers.

53. I. J. Ellis to Hayes, September, 1891, Box 22, Hayes Papers; John Ray to Powderly, January 19, 1885, Box 12, Hayes Papers.

54. Joseph Starr to Powderly, June 12, 1887, Powderly Papers; *JUL*, July 16, 1887, 2456.

55. Such stories are contained in several issues; for example, see *Alabama Sentinel*, June 18, 1887.

56. Samuel Wilson to Powderly, October 6, 1886, Powderly Papers.

57. Alexander Walker to Powderly, May 18, 1886, and John Devlin to Powderly, November 2, 1890 (contains similar material), both in Powderly Papers.

58. William Mullen to Powderly, April 7, 1885, Powderly Papers.

59. Allen W. Moger, "Industrial and Urban Progress in Virginia From 1880 to 1900," *Virginia Magazine of History and Biography* 46 (July 1958), 324-25.

60. *Fayetteville Messenger*, November 2, 1888.

61. McLaurin, *Paternalism and Protest*, 107; *Savannah Tribune*, February 26, 1887.

62. Birmingham *Iron Age*, July 27 through August 28, 1887.

63. *Savannah Tribune*, October 23, 1886, and February 19 and 26, and March 5, 1887.

64. For contrasting views, see Kessler, "Negroes in the Knights," 274-76; Frederick Meyers, "The Knights of Labor in the South," *Southern Economic Journal* 6 (April 1940), 486; F. Ray Marshall, *Labor in the South* (Cambridge, Mass., 1967), 22-23.

65. McLaurin, *Paternalism and Protest*, 65.

66. Belton to Powderly, November 15, 1886, Powderly Papers.

CHAPTER 8

1. For a discussion of the national order's internal problems, see Grob, *Workers and Utopia*, 43-59; and Ware, *Labor Movement*, 103-16.

2. R. J. Steel to Powderly, February 17, 1886, and R. P. Nicholas to Powderly, January 13, 1886, Powderly Papers.

3. J. T. Blackwood to Powderly, July 23, 1886, Powderly Papers.

4. Power to Powderly, December 11, 1885, and February 13, 1888, Powderly Papers.

5. McLaurin, "Knights in North Carolina Politics," 298-315; *G.A. Proceedings, 1886*, 313-25; Pendleton to Powderly, September 26, 1886, Powderly Papers; *Richmond Dispatch*, September 24 through October 31, 1886; Lynchburg *Virginian*, October 4 through November 5, 1886. Also see chapter 4.

6. Jacksonville *Times-Union*, November 26 through December 10, 1887. Also see chapter 4.

7. *JUL*, July 19, 1888, 2665; Power to Powderly, December 11, 1885, and Broughton to Powderly, November 28, 1887, Powderly Papers; *G.A. Proceedings, 1887*, 1595, 1611-12.

8. Ray to Powderly, November 9, 1886, Powderly Papers; McLaurin, *Paternalism and Protest*, 94-110.

9. Stack to Powderly, October 14, 1888, Powderly Papers.

10. T. T. Allen to Stack, April 22, 1886, Nicholas Stack Collection, University of Alabama, Tuscaloosa, Ala.; *JUL*, July 19, 1888, 2665.

11. Jacksonville *Times-Union*, November 26 through 30, 1887; *Birmingham City Directory, 1887*, 122; *Raleigh City Directory, 1888*, 26.

12. *G.A. Proceedings, 1887*, 1831-34.

13. *JUL*, June 16, 1888, 2645; Birmingham *News*, July 29, 1931; Stack to his son, February 10, 1914, Stack Collection.

14. *JUL*, July 19, 1888, 2665.

15. *JUL*, December 27, 1888, 2760.

16. William Mullen to Powderly, October 30, 1884, Powderly Papers.

17. Badger Terrill to Powderly, April 11, 1888, and Alex Anthony to Powderly, April 9, 1888, Powderly Papers.

18. *JUL*, November 19, 1887, 2528, May 26, 1888, 2636, September 20, 1888, 2304, April 25, 1889, 2828, and June 27, 1889, 2864.

19. For example, see M. E. Stone to Powderly, December 14, 1885, George Schall to Powderly, October 19, 1886, Ben Doster to Powderly, December 30, 1886, and T. P. Towns to Powderly, August 29, 1887, all in Powderly Papers.

20. Ray to Powderly, November 9, 1886, Backenstoe to Powderly, August 14, 1891, W. B. Maston to Powderly, August 16, 1891, Learing to Powderly, July 22, 1891, L. T. Perry to Powderly, January 7, 1887 and W. H. Gunn to Powderly, December 20, 1886, all in Powderly Papers.

21. Henry Smith to Powderly, May 8, 1886, Invison Goodwin to Powderly, July 7, 1886, Gibbs Gardiner to Charles Litchman, February 16, 1887, Louis

Du Brok to Powderly, May 10, 1887, Powderly to George Schall, November 9, 1886, Book 23, all in Powderly Papers.

22. Victor St. Cloud to Powderly, December 19, 1886, Powderly Papers.

23. M. E. Stone to Powderly, December 14, 1885, and C. H. Bowling to Powderly, August 3, 1886, Powderly Papers.

24. *G.A. Proceedings, 1887*, 1364, 1375, 1439.

25. *G.A. Proceedings, 1887*, 1340, and *1888*, 58; George Schall to Powderly, October 19, 1886, Ben Doster to Powderly, December 20, 1886, James McGuin to Powderly, January 22, 1887, A. C. Franklin to Powderly, January 29, 1887, and Victor St. Cloud to Powderly, April 10, 1887, all in Powderly Papers.

26. John Crawford to Powderly, March 20, 1888, and Powderly to Crawford, March 26, 1888, Book 39, Powderly Papers.

27. St. Cloud to Powderly, April 10, 1887, Powderly Papers.

28. *G.A. Proceedings, 1888*, 24.

29. T. W. White to Powderly, August 1, 1889, Powderly Papers.

30. H. N. Moore to Powderly, April 15, 1888, Powderly Papers.

31. R. W. Kruse to Powderly, April 28, 1886, Powderly Papers.

32. *G.A. Proceedings, 1888*, 24, 107; Powderly to S. D. Brown, February 23, 1888, Book 32, J. L. Sanges to Powderly, July 16, 1888, and Richard Bowen to Powderly, March 21, 1887, all in Powderly Papers.

33. Correspondence on this issue is abundant. See Powderly to A. W. Fletcher, January 5, 1892, Book 60, S. G. Learing to Powderly, September 10, 1891, and John Devlin to Powderly, January 21, 1891, all in Powderly Papers.

34. W. P. Russell to Powderly, November 17, 1886, Powderly Papers; *Fayetteville Messenger* November 9, 1888.

35. John O'Brien to Powderly, November 21, 1886, Powderly to J. L. McGinn, March 28, 1887, Book 29, and J. W. White to Powderly, November 6, 1890, all in Powderly Papers.

36. *JUL*, November 10, 1886, 2000-2001; *G.A. Proceedings, 1888*, "Report of the General Executive Board," 107-108; R. W. Kruse to Powderly, April 28, 1886, Powderly Papers.

37. Alexander Walker to Powderly, May 18, 1886, Samuel Wilson to Powderly, October 6, 1886, John Devlin to Powderly, November 2, 1890, and William Mullen to Powderly, April 7, 1885, all in Powderly Papers.

38. *G.A. Proceedings, 1887*, 1364, 1582, 1439; John O'Brien to Powderly, March 12, 1887, Powderly Papers.

39. *G.A. Proceedings, 1888*, "Report of the General Executive Board," 37, 50-53, 107-108.

40. *G.A. Proceedings, 1889*, "Report of the General Executive Board," 23-24; Devlin to Powderly, January 21, 1891, Powderly Papers.

41. Powderly to John Crawford, March 26, 1888, Book 39, Powderly Papers.

42. See, for example, John Andrews to Powderly, November 3, 1887, and Powderly to Andrews, November 9, 1887, Book 30, Powderly Papers.

43. Mullen to Powderly, January 22, 1887, and Powderly to Mullen, January 26, 1887, Book 27, Powderly Papers.

44. McDonald to Powderly, September 11, 1889, and F. P. Singletary to Powderly, September 23, 1888, Powderly Papers.

45. *JUL*, September 13, 1888, 2697, September 27, 1888, 2705, October 4, 1888, 2712, and November 22, 1888, 2740.

46. *G.A. Proceedings, 1888*, 50, 52, 90.

47. *G.A. Proceedings, 1889*, 3-4.

48. *Alabama Sentinel*, December 15, 1888.

49. Powderly, *Thirty Years*, 298-30; Ware, *Labor Movement*, 115.

50. Powderly to Mrs. Barry, February 7, 1889, Powderly Papers.

51. St. Cloud to Powderly, February 24, 1889, and Powderly to St. Cloud, February 27, 1889, Powderly Papers.

52. St. Cloud to Powderly, March 19, April 7 and 16, August 26, July 16, September 8 and October 1, 1889, and Powderly to St. Cloud, March 26, April 20, and September 3, 1889, Powderly Papers.

53. William Kates to Powderly, September 22, 1889, St. Cloud to Powderly, September 20 and 23, 1889, Frank Barber to Powderly, September 30, 1889, and Powderly to Barber, October 15, 1889, all in Powderly Papers; Powderly to Hayes, September 16, and December 17, 1889, Hayes Papers.

54. St. Cloud to Powderly, October 18, 1889, and Barker to Powderly, November 7, 1889, Powderly Papers.

55. St. Cloud to Powderly, December 22, 1889, and January 26, 1890, Powderly Papers.

56. Powderly to St. Cloud, December 19, 1889, and January 5, 1890, and St. Cloud to Powderly, December 14, 27, 1889, Powderly Papers.

57. St. Cloud to Powderly, April 21 and June 6, 1890, Powderly Papers.

58. *G.A. Proceedings, 1887*, "Report of the G.E.B.," 1808-1809; Grob, *Workers and Utopia*, 49-52; Ware, *Labor Movement*, 134-54.

59. *N.C. State Assembly Proceedings, 1890*, 22-23.

60. *JUL*, September 3, 1887, 2484, September 17, 1887, 2491, October 29, 1887, 2516, November 12, 1887, 2524, and January 28, 1888, 2568.

61. *JUL*, April 14, 1888, 2612, May 12, 1888, 2628, and June 23, 1888, 2652; M. D. Walsh to Powderly, August 16, 1888, Box 9, Hayes Papers.

62. George Tonnoffski to Powderly, December 18, 1888, Powderly Papers; Lexitia Smith to Hayes, May 29, 1888, Box 5, Hayes Papers.

63. G. F. Fulton to Powderly, August 19, 1887, Powderly Papers; Grob,

Workers and Utopia, 51-52.

64. *JUL*, September 10, 1886, 2179-80, November 10, 1886, 2194, and April 16, 1887, 2357; *G.A. Proceedings, 1888*, "Report of the G.E.B.," 52-53; Stack to Powderly, October 14, 1888, and John McDonald to Powderly, September 11, 1889, Powderly Papers.

65. For example, see H. F. Hoover to Powderly, May 22, 1886, Powderly Papers.

CHAPTER 9

1. Garlock and Builder, *Knights Data*.

2. *G.A. Proceedings, 1888*, "Report of the Secretary-Treasurer," 2-5.

3. T. P. Toms to Powderly, August 29, 1887, Powderly Papers.

4. F. M. McCaffy to John Hayes, August 24, 1887, Box 26, Hayes Papers.

5. John Crawford to Powderly, September 23, 1887, Powderly Papers.

6. *JUL*, April 14, 1888, 2612, and June 9, 1888, 2644; Eddie Thurston to Hayes, July 12, 1889, Box 23, Hayes Papers; Tonnoffski to Powderly, December 18, 1888, Powderly Papers.

7. *JUL*, May 12, 1888, 2628, May 26, 1888, 2636, September 27, 1888, 2708, and April 21, 1888, 2616.

8. John Power to Powderly, December 16, 1887, and John McDonald to Powderly, September 1889, Powderly Papers.

9. Barry to Powderly, February 6, 1889, Box 3, Hayes Papers.

10. Stack to Powderly, October 14, 1888, Powderly Papers; Abernathy, "The Knights in Alabama," 81-83; *Alabama Sentinel*, January 19, 1889.

11. *JUL*, February 21, 1889, 2790; St. Cloud to Powderly, December 22, 1889, Powderly Papers.

12. *JUL*, June 20, 1889, 2860.

13. For examples of the rural assemblies formed by the Knights after late 1887, see *JUL*, August 27, 1887, 2480, February 11, 1888, 2576, February 18, 1888, 2580, March 24, 1888, 2600, and April 7, 1888, 2608.

14. See the *Messenger*, August 24 and September 14, 1888. See also chapter 3.

15. Head, "Organized Labor," 70-71; Abernathy, "The Knights in Alabama," 73-74; see also chapter 3.

16. Ware, *Labor Movement*, 363.

17. R. F. Gray to Powderly, June 10, 1889, and Isaac McCraken to Powderly, June 24, 1889, Powderly Papers; Ware, *Labor Movement*, 366-68.

18. For details of the growth of the Southern Alliance, see McMath, *Populist Vanguard*, especially 58-60 and 83-84.

19. *G.A. Proceedings, 1889*, 88-96; *Atlanta Constitution*, November 13 through 16, 1889.

20. Grob, *Workers and Utopia*, 91-92; Ware, *Labor Movement*, 366-68; *G.A. Proceedings, 1889*, 4, 8, 33, 73-76, 87-93.

21. Hicks, *Populist Revolt*, 113-27, McMath, *Populist Vanguard*, 87-89; *JUL*, January 16, 1890.

22. Powderly to Hayes, April 20, 1890, Box 36, Hayes Papers.

23. *JUL*, August 2, 1888, 2676; John Henderson to Powderly, August 26, 1887, Powderly Papers. Even historians who minimize the differences between the Knights and the Alliance note their existence. In his excellent study of Populism, for example, Lawrence Goodwyn argues that Alliance members were willing to work with the Knights. Yet he admits that the 1886 Southwest railroad strike caused a bad rift in the Alliance between those who favored supporting the striking Knights and those who opposed such support. This division poses an interesting dilemma. Since the railroads were the Alliance's favorite enemy and since the strike did not directly threaten the economic interests of farmers, why did the issue of supporting the Knights cause such a furor in the Alliance camp? See Goodwyn, *Democratic Promise*, 58-65.

24. Mullen to Powderly, March 3 and 10, 1890, Powderly Papers.

25. The 1890 directory had listed two locals; see *Birmingham City Directory, 1890*, 27.

26. *N.C. State Assembly Proceedings, 1890*.

27. Enoch M. Smith to Hayes, June 15, 1891, Box 9, Hayes Papers.

28. For evidence of the problems of the Florida order, see John Devlin to Powderly, January 21, 1891, Powderly Papers.

29. *G.A. Proceedings, 1890*, 1-2, 74-75.

30. *JUL*, January 2, 1890, January 16 and 17, 1890, and October 16, 1890.

31. Ibid., July 10, 1890.

32. For details on the Knights' participation in the birth of the Populist party, see Hicks, *Populist Revolt*, 205-37; McMath, *Populist Vanguard*, 130-31; Ware, *Labor Movement*, 367-70.

33. C. L. Ellis to John Hayes, July 12, 1892, Box 22, and James Foster to Hayes, August 14, 1892, Hayes Papers; *JUL*, September 8, 1892.

34. Watson to Powderly, October 8, 1892, and H. E. Taubeneck to Powderly, October 11, 1892, Powderly Papers.

35. *JUL*, August 1 and September 11, 1892.

36. Tom O'Riley, one of Powderly's closest lieutenants, was most involved in the plot to deliver Alabama to Harrison by supporting Kolb. See O'Riley to Powderly, September 23 and 30, 1892, Powderly Papers.

37. *G.A. Proceedings, 1892*, 30-31; Abernathy, "The Knights in Alabama," 84-85.

38. For examples of continued feuding within the order see Pete Bulloch to Hayes, May ?, 1893, Box 15, A. T. Racine to Hayes, August 31, 1896, Box 23, Julia Armstrong to Hayes, July 12, 1909, and August 4, 1912, Box 4, all in

Hayes Papers. Also, for details on the Knights in Alabama after 1892, see Abernathy, "The Knights in Alabama," 84-93.

39. *JUL*, February 7, 1896, and August 1900, 5.

40. The *Arbitrator*, August 7, 1899. Issues after late 1899 carry little labor news. By July 1900, the regular "Knights of Labor" column had been discontinued. The May 15, 1901, issue did not carry a single labor item.

41. *JUL*, April 8, 1897, February 14, 1896, and January 20, 1898.

42. Ibid., September 1900, 3.

43. Marshall, *Labor in the South*, 90-100; McLaurin, *Paternalism and Protest*, 121-95.

44. Among the best discussions of the racial policies of the Populists are Jack Abramowitz, "The Negro in the Agrarian Revolt," *Agricultural History* 24 (April 1950), 89-93; and Robert M. Saunders, "Southern Populism and the Negro, 1893-1905," *Journal of Negro History* 54 (July 1969), 240-57. Also see Woodward, *Strange Career of Jim Crow*, 60-65.

45. James Jennings to Powderly, October 27, 1892, Powderly Papers.

46. McMath, *Populist Vanguard*, 44-46.

Bibliography

PRIVATE PAPERS

Hayes, John W. Private Papers, 1854-1942. 56 boxes. Department of Archives and Manuscripts, Catholic University, Washington, D.C.

Piedmont Manufacturing Company. Letter Books, 1886-1899. Caroliniana Library, University of South Carolina, Columbia, S.C.

Powderly, Terence Vincent. Private Papers, 1871-1924. 193 boxes, 50 letter-press copy books, and additional miscellaneous items. Department of Archives and Manuscripts, Catholic University, Washington, D.C.

Stack, Nicholas B. Private Papers. Scrapbook, letters, flyers, and other printed matter. Alabama Collection, University of Alabama, Tusca-loosa, Ala.

PROCEEDINGS AND MINUTES

Knights of Labor. *Records of the Proceedings of the General Assembly, 1878-1896.*

"Minute Book of Raleigh Local Assembly 3606, Knights of Labor, 1886-1890." North Carolina Department of Archives and History, Raleigh, N.C.

Nichols, John. *For Congress, Fourth District, John Nichols of Wake County: Address to the Voters of the Fourth District.* A pamphlet in the North Carolina Collection, University of North Carolina at Chapel Hill, n.p., n.p., 1886.

North Carolina State Assembly of the Knights of Labor. *Proceedings of the Assembly, 1890.* In the Southern Historical Collection, University of North Carolina at Chapel Hill.

NEWSPAPERS

Alabama Sentinel (Birmingham), 1887-1889.

Arbitrator (Birmingham), 1899-1901.
Atlanta Constitution, 1882-1896.
Augusta (Ga.) *Chronicle*, 1885-1888.
Birmingham *Iron Age*, 1887-1890.
Birmingham *News*, 1931.
Carolina Spartan (Spartanburg, S.C.), 1885-1888.
Charleston (S.C.) *News and Courier*, 1885-1889.
Fayetteville (N.C.) *Messenger*, 1887-1888.
Journal of United Labor, 1880-1906.
Lynchburg *Virginian*, 1885-1888.
News and Observer (Raleigh, N.C.), 1885-1896.
News Herald (Jacksonville, Fla.), 1884-1888.
Richmond Dispatch, 1884-1890.
Savannah (Ga.) *Tribune*, 1886-1888.
Scranton (Pa.) *Truth*, 1884-1888.
State Chronicle (Raleigh, N.C.), 1885-1888.
Times-Union (Jacksonville, Fla.), 1884-1888.

GOVERNMENT DOCUMENTS

Biographical Directory of the American Congress, 1774-1961. Washington, D.C.: Government Printing Office, 1961.
Birmingham City Directory, 1890. Birmingham, 1890.
Minutes of the Jacksonville, Florida, City Council, 1885-1889.
North Carolina Bureau of Labor. *Annual Reports, 1887-1892.* Raleigh: State Printer, 1887-1892.
Raleigh City Directory, 1888. Raleigh, 1888.
South Carolina Department of Agriculture. *Cotton Mills of South Carolina, Their Names, Location, Capacity, and History.* Charleston, S.C.: News and Courier Book Presses, 1880.
United States Bureau of Labor. *Annual Reports of the Commissioner of Labor, 1888-1905.* Washington, D.C.: Government Printing Office, 1888-1905.
United States Bureau of Labor Statistics. *History of Wages in the United States from Colonial Times to 1928.* Washington, D.C.: Government Printing Office, 1934.
United States Congress. Senate. *Report of the Committee of the Senate Upon the Relations Between Labor and Capital.* 5 vols. Washington, D.C.: Government Printing Office, 1885.
United States Department of the Interior. Census Office. *Compendium of the Eleventh Census, 1890.* P. 1, *Population.* Washington, D.C.: Government Printing Office, 1892.

BOOKS

Allen, Ruth A. *The Great Southwest Strike*. Austin: University of Texas Press, 1942.

Armes, Ethel. *The Story of Coal and Iron in Alabama*. Birmingham: Birmingham Chamber of Commerce, 1910.

Buck, Paul. *The Road to Reunion*. Boston: Little, Brown, and Co., 1937.

Cash, Wilbur J. *The Mind of the South*. New York: Alfred Knopf, 1941.

Clark, Victor S. *History of Manufacturers in the United States*. 3 vols. New York: McGraw-Hill, 1929.

Daniels, Josephus. *Tar Heel Editor*. Chapel Hill: University of North Carolina Press, 1939.

Davis, David B. *The Problem of Slavery in the Age of Revolution, 1770-1823*. Ithaca: Cornell University Press, 1975.

Davis, Frederick. *History of Jacksonville, Florida, and Vicinity, 1513 to 1924*. Gainesville: University of Florida Press, 1964.

Dodd, Donald B., and Dodd, Wynelle S. *Historical Statistics of the South, 1790-1970*. Tuscaloosa: University of Alabama Press, 1973.

Dulles, Foster R. *Labor in America: A History*. New York: Thomas Crowell, 1966.

Fine, Nathan. *Labor and Farmer Parties in the United States, 1828-1928*. New York: Russell and Russell, 1961.

Fogel, Robert, and Engerman, Stanley. *Time on the Cross*. 2 vols. Boston: Little, Brown, 1974.

Foner, Philip. *History of the Labor Movement in the United States*. 3 vols. New York: International Publishers, 1947-64.

Garlock, Jonathan, and Builder, N. C. *Knights of Labor Data Bank*. Computer printout. Madison, Wis.: Institute for Social Research, 1975.

Gaston, Paul. *The New South Creed: A Study in Southern Mythmaking*. New York: Alfred Knopf, 1970.

Genovese, Eugene. *Roll, Jordan Roll*. New York: Pantheon, 1974.

Goodwyn, Lawrence. *Democratic Promise: The Populist Movement in America*. New York: Oxford University Press, 1976.

Grob, Gerald. *Workers and Utopia: A Study of Ideological Conflict in the American Labor Movement*. Evanston, Ill.: Northwestern University Press, 1961.

Gutman, Herbert G. *Work Culture and Society in Industrializing America*. New York: Alfred Knopf, 1976.

Hickman, Nollie. *Mississippi Harvest: Lumbering in the Longleaf Pine Belt, 1840-1915*. Oxford Miss.: University of Mississippi Press, 1962.

Hicks, John D. *The Populist Revolt*. Minneapolis: University of Minnesota Press, 1931.

Hofstadter, Richard. *Social Darwinism in American Thought.* 2n rev. ed. Boston: Beacon Press, 1959.

Lahne, Herbert J. *The Cotton Mill Worker.* New York: Farrar and Rinehart, 1944.

Logan, Frenise. *The Negro in North Carolina, 1876-1894.* Chapel Hill: University of North Carolina Press, 1964.

McLaurin, Melton A. *Paternalism and Protest, Southern Cotton Mill Workers and Organized Labor, 1875-1905.* Westport, Conn.: Greenwood Press, 1971.

McMath, Robert. *Populist Vanguard: A History of the Southern Farmers' Alliance.* Chapel Hill: University of North Carolina Press, 1975.

Marshall, F. Ray. *Labor in the South.* Cambridge, Mass.: Harvard University Press, 1967.

Mitchell, Broadus. *The Rise of Cotton Mills in the South.* Baltimore: Johns Hopkins University Press, 1921.

Mitchell, Broadus, and Mitchell, George S. *The Industrial Revolution in the South.* Baltimore: Johns Hopkins University Press, 1930.

Mitchell, George S. *Textile Unionism in the South.* Chapel Hill: University of North Carolina Press, 1931.

Powderly, Terence V. *The Path I Trod: An Autobiography.* New York: Columbia University Press, 1940.

———. *Thirty Years of Labor, 1859-1889.* Reprint. New York: August M. Kelley, 1967.

Rice, C. Duncan. *The Rise and Fall of Black Slavery.* New York: Harper and Row, 1975.

Robertson, Ben. *Red Hills and Cotton: An Upcountry Memory.* Columbia, S.C.: University of South Carolina Press, 1960.

Smith, Robert S. *Mill on the Dan.* Durham, N.C.: Duke University Press, 1960.

Starobin, Robert. *Industrial Slavery in the Old South.* New York: Oxford University Press, 1970.

Stover, John F. *The Railroads of the South, 1865-1900.* Chapel Hill: University of North Carolina Press, 1955.

Tilley, Nannie May. *The Bright-Tobacco Industry, 1860-1929.* Chapel Hill: University of North Carolina Press, 1948.

Van Vorst, Mrs. John, and Van Vorst, Marie. *The Woman Who Toils: Being the Experience of Two Ladies as Factory Girls.* New York: Doubleday, Page and Company, 1903.

Wade, Richard. *Slavery in the Cities: The South 1820-1860.* New York: Oxford University Press, 1964.

Ward, Robert, and Rogers, William. *Labor Revolt in Alabama: The Great Strike of 1894.* Tuscaloosa: University of Alabama Press, 1965.

Ware, Norman T. *The Labor Movement in the United States, 1860-1895*. New York: Alfred Knopf, 1929.

Williamson, Joel. *After Slavery: The Negro in South Carolina During Reconstruction*. Chapel Hill: University of North Carolina Press, 1965.

Winston, George T. *A Builder of the New South; Being the Story of the Life Work of Daniel A. Tompkins*. Garden City, N.Y.: Doubleday, Page, and Co., 1920.

Woodward, C. Vann. *Origins of the New South, 1877-1913*. Baton Rouge: Louisiana State University Press, 1971.

―――. *The Strange Career of Jim Crow*. New York: Oxford University Press, 1966.

Woodward, William E. *The Gift of Life: An Autobiography*. New York: E. P. Dulton, 1947.

Worthman, Paul B. "Working Class Mobility in Birmingham, Alabama, 1880-1914." In *Anonymous Americans*, ed. Tamara K. Harever. Englewood Cliffs, N.J.: Prentice Hall, 1971.

Wyllie, Irwin G. *The Self-Made Man in America: The Myth of Rags to Riches*. New Brunswick, N.J.: Rutgers University Press, 1954.

ARTICLES

Abramowitz, Jack. "The Negro in the Agrarian Revolt." *Agricultural History* 24 (1950), 89-95.

Akin, Edward. "When a Minority Becomes the Majority, Blacks in Jacksonville Politics, 1887-1907." *Florida Historical Quarterly* 53 (October 1974), 123-39.

Black, Paul V. "The Knights of Labor and the South: 1876-1893." *Southern Quarterly* 1 (1963), 201-12.

de Graffenried, Clare. "The Georgia Cracker in the Cotton Mill." *Century Magazine* 41 (February 1891), 484-98.

Fuller, Justin. "Notes and Documents: Alabama Business Leaders, 1865-1900." *Alabama Review* 16 and 17 (October 1963 and January 1964), 279-86 and 63-75.

Jolley, Harley E. "The Labor Movement in North Carolina: 1880-1922." *North Carolina Historical Review* 30 (July 1953), 354-75.

Kessler, Sidney H. "The Organization of Negroes in the Knights of Labor." *Journal of Negro History* 37 (July 1952), 228-76.

"Knights of Labor and the Color Line." *Public Opinion* 2 (October 16, 1886), 1.

McLaurin, Melton A. "The Knights of Labor in North Carolina Politics." *North Carolina Historical Review* 49 (summer 1972), 298-315.

Marcus, Irwin M. "The Southern Negro and the Knights of Labor." *Negro History Bulletin* 30 (March 1967), 5-7.

Meyers, Frederick. "The Knights of Labor in the South." *Southern Economic Journal* 6 (April 1940), 479-87.

Miller, William. "The Recruitment of the American Business Elite." *Quarterly Journal of Economics* 64 (May 1950), 242-53.

Moger, Allen W. "Industrial and Urban Progress in Virginia From 1880 to 1900." *Virginia Magazine of History and Biography* 46 (July 1958), 307-36.

Monroe, Kirk. "Mobile, Alabama." *Harper's Weekly* 31 (July 16, 1887), 503.

Reed, Merle. "The Augusta Textile Mills and the Strike of 1886." *Labor History* 14 (spring 1973), 228-46.

Rogers, William W. "The Negro Alliance in Alabama." *Journal of Negro History* 45 (1950), 38-44.

―――. "Negro Knights in Arkansas: A Case Study of the Miscellaneous Strike." *Labor History* 10 (summer 1969), 498-504.

Saunders, Robert M. "Southern Populism and the Negro, 1893-1905." *Journal of Negro History* 54 (July 1969), 240-57.

Spillane, Richard. "Striking Facts About Southern Cotton Mills and Cotton Mill Employees." *Manufacturer's Record* 86 (December 11, 1924), 195-96.

Wright, Carrol D. "A Historical Sketch of the Knights of Labor." *Quarterly Journal of Economics* 1 (January 1887), 137-67.

UNPUBLISHED MATERIAL

Abernathy, John. "The Knights of Labor in Alabama." Master's thesis, University of Alabama, 1960.

Douty, Harry M. "The North Carolina Industrial Worker, 1880-1930." Ph.D. dissertation, University of North Carolina, 1936.

Evans, Mercer G. "The History of the Organized Labor Movement in Georgia." Ph.D. dissertation, University of Chicago, 1929.

Head, Holman. "Organized Labor in Alabama." Ph.D. dissertation, University of Alabama, 1954.

Mosley, Donald C. "A History of Labor Unions in Mississippi." Ph.D. dissertation, University of Alabama, 1965.

Pierpont, Andrew W. "Development of the Textile Industry in Alamance County, North Carolina," Ph.D. dissertation, University of North Carolina, 1953.

Street, Richard. "Black Militancy of 1887: The Louisiana Sugar Plantation

Strike." Manuscript in the possession of the author, Madison, Wisconsin.

Turnback, Sister William Marie. "The Attitudes of Terence V. Powderly Toward Minority Groups, 1879-1893." Master's thesis, Catholic University, 1956.

Wallace, David D. "One Hundred Years of Gregg and Graniteville." Graniteville, S.C. William Gregg Foundation, 1954.

Index

ABOUT THE AUTHOR

Melton Alonza McLaurin is Professor of History at the University of North Carolina, Wilmington. Among his books and articles are *Mobile, An American River City* and *Paternalism and Protest: Southern Cotton Mill Worker and Organized Labor 1875-1905* (Greenwood Press, 1971).